THE GATE OF GLORY

By the same author:

THE ARCHBISHOP SPEAKS
I BELIEVE
THE GREAT ACQUITTAL
THE CHURCH IN THE MARKET PLACE
GETTING THE MESSAGE
THE GREAT GOD ROBBERY
THE MESSAGE OF THE BIBLE
GOD INCARNATE
THE MEETING OF THE WATERS

THE GATE OF GLORY

GEORGE CAREY

Hodder & Stoughton
LONDON SYDNEY AUCKLAND

British Library Cataloguing in Publication Data

Carey, Most Rev. George
 The Gate of Glory – 2nd ed.
 I. Title
 232.963

 ISBN 0-340-57637-5

Published by Hodder and Stoughton,
a division of Hodder and Stoughton Ltd,
Mill Road, Dunton Green, Sevenoaks, Kent TN13 2YA
Editorial Office: 47 Bedford Square, London WC1B 3DP

Typeset by Phoenix Typesetting, Burley-in-Wharfedale, West Yorkshire

Printed in Great Britain by Clays Ltd, St Ives plc

CONTENTS

Preface to the Second Edition

I was initially very hesitant to agree to the re-publication of *The Gate of Glory* because it seemed to me that it belonged to a particular period of my past and there seemed little point in revisiting a doctrine which has already received so much attention over the centuries. But further reflection made me change my mind. The first reason has to do with my reflection on the western Church. I have become alarmed by the growth of what I call a religious pluralism in First World Churches. I mean by this a shift of focus from a Trinitarian faith anchored in the centrality of Christ to a vague, amorphous belief in God in which Christ is not the definitive focus, but only one of many foci of faith. Such a shift will, I firmly believe, result not only in stunted Christians, but also in a pitiful, reductionist Church life that will compel little enthusiasm and make few disciples. Such anaemic faith needs the blood transfusion that can only come through an unapologetic and firm, historic faith.

Secondly, a fresh re-reading of this book makes me confident that it makes a positive contribution to what we are calling the Decade of Evangelism. It is my firm conviction that our preaching and teaching will only have relevance as the cross is preached, taught and lived by the Church today. I hope that this book will be a stimulus, an aid and a teaching tool that will equip the intelligent layperson. I am aware that it will require thorough study, but I trust that it is accessible to those who, though lacking a formal theological education, are sufficiently motivated to use this as a stepping stone towards a deeper understanding of the cross of our Lord.

There is a third reason and it is one which I submit with some hesitation. It is my reluctant admission that we have failed the cross again and again by our inability to preach it with conviction and life. I have failed – and you, too. And yet the themes of the cross are as compelling and as exciting as they were to the first Christians on the day of Pentecost. This book is based on the confidence that such is the contemporaneity of the Atonement of Christ, and such are the rich metaphors it induces, that there exist all around us themes and ideas that we can quarry to make alive in fresh ways this wonderful doctrine which has power to give life.

Such is my desire. And to you, the reader of this book, comes my prayer that the Risen Christ will be so real to you through his cross and resurrection that you, too, will take up your cross and follow him, wherever he leads you.

George Cantuar
Lambeth Palace
January 1992

Father of all, we give you thanks and praise, that when we were still far off you met us in your Son and brought us home. Dying and living, he declared your love, gave us grace, and opened

the gate of glory.

May we who share Christ's body live his risen life; we who drink his cup bring life to others; we whom the Spirit lights give light to the world. Keep us firm in the hope you have set before us, so we and all your children shall be free, and the whole earth live to praise your Name; through Christ our Lord. Amen.

ASB Holy Communion
Service 1980

Introduction

When asked why he wanted to climb Mt Everest Mallory apparently replied, 'Because it is there'. It may be in the nature of humanity to climb what appears to be impossible or to explain what seems to be inexplicable. Certainly, anyone who attempts to write about the cross of Christ finds himself with an equivalent task. The cross is the heart of the Christian faith – but it is also its compelling and majestic peak which towers over all our attempts to master it by our intellect or to bring it within the scope of our tidy theological systems. It is because 'It is there' that I want to write about it – not because I believe that I have the last word to pronounce on the subject. Indeed, one of the most irritating features of theologians is their assumption that God has not clearly spoken until their book appeared!

But two more pressing reasons have encouraged me to write this book. First, I have become alarmed by the way modern Christians appear to brush the cross aside. We may pay lip service to it, but it does not loom as significantly in our preaching and teaching as it once did. The impression given is that the resurrection, the Spirit, and the Church are much more relevant subjects. Important as such topics are, it seems to me highly dangerous when the cross is obscured. However, it is difficult to be sure what has caused this shift in the Church's teaching. Perhaps it is because the cross is so very mysterious and its categories – sin, sacrifice, holiness, suffering and death – somewhat old-fashioned, that we no longer think that the 'climb' is worthwhile. But as I shall contend later, lose the cross and you lose everything; shift it from the centre to the circumference and everything becomes out of focus.

My second reason is ecumenical. While all the churches regard the cross as the centre of faith, our interpretations separate us from one another. Catholics, Protestants, liberals and evangelicals all have different emphases which appear to be treated in an exclusive fashion. We therefore take different routes up the mountain, and all but our own route is declared 'out of bounds'. My viewpoint will be seen as evangelical in the main, but I do so hope that it will not duck the issues which other Christians raise, or deny the genuine biblical insights they offer to us. In short, I hope that this will be a book which all Christians, who embrace Christ to their hearts, will be able to use with profit, even if they cannot agree with all they read.

But let me describe the companion with whom I wish to climb. It is not the academic theologian. He or she will find my pace too slow. Let him go ahead: there are many other guides he can go with. I want to travel with the kind of folk who don't climb theological mountains all that often. I have in mind the average intelligent Christian; church leaders who wish to deepen their understanding of the faith; theological and Bible college students who want a comprehensive guide; pastors, priests and clergy who want to be reminded of previous climbs – in fact, I hope any concerned Christian might find this treatment of help.

The book is divided into four sections. In Part One we shall look at some of the problems that appear when we consider the cross and we shall examine some of the Old Testament themes which bear on our theme. In Part Two, we shall look at Jesus in the New Testament and see how the apostolic writers viewed his death. Then in Part Three we shall study some of the explanations of the cross that have been worked out by Christians. Our final section, Part Four, attempts to relate the cross to our life today. Technical jargon will be kept to a minimum but a glossary is provided for the theological words which stray into the text!

So let's prepare to climb. The peak invites us to step out with enthusiasm and joy. It is rumoured that climbers who have penetrated beyond the foothills have sometimes met Another who is the only one to have reached the top. If this book helps to bring him into sight and to bring home to us the glory of his climb, then the labour of this book will not have been in vain.

PART ONE

BACKGROUND TO THE CROSS

I

The Offence of the Cross

THE OFFENCE IN THE EARLY CHURCH

In a way Christianity got off to a very unpromising start with its emphasis upon the cross. The first Christians did not need a promotional survey to tell them that this would be a major switch-off for their contemporaries. It seemed to be a certain way of killing a new faith stone-dead. Paul admits as much in his first letter to the church at Corinth, 'we preach Christ crucified; a stumbling-block to Jews and foolishness to Gentiles' (1 Cor. 1:23). Paul, of course, does not apologise for this, but rather sees it as evidence of the way God works. He delights in overthrowing human wisdom and might, and reveals his power in human weakness.

But Paul would have been the first to admit that this paradox would not have been seen as anything remotely like wisdom by the non-Christians of his day. The Greek world, with its accumulated treasure of human genius in art, science and rhetoric, was totally at odds with the tiny Christian body which proclaimed a crucified and risen Saviour. It scarcely merited serious attention. If that were not sufficient opposition, Christianity's parent body, Judaism, was only too keen to reject this illegitimate and deformed offspring. The crucified Messiah was a horrifying blasphemy to Jewish ears. How could God's Chosen One end his life in such a degraded way? Jesus deserved to die for the way he set himself up above the law and even claimed to fulfil it. His failure to come down from the cross was proof enough that God had rejected him. His death, then, was a judicial act which effectively dealt with an impostor and heretic.

As the Church grew, so controversy mounted around the cross. In the ancient world people could accept new religions and new teachers quite easily and, let's be in no doubt about it, the character of Jesus and his teaching as set forth in the gospels and the Church were very attractive to many. But the cross was an enormous barrier to the acceptance of Christianity and the first Christians knew it. The problem was threefold.

The death of the Messiah seemed so obviously nonsense

Justin Martyr, a second-century Christian writer and philosopher, acknowledged quite candidly the difficulty which many found in the cross of Jesus. 'They proclaim our madness to consist in this, that we give to a crucified man a place second to the unchangeable and eternal God, creator of all.'[1] There is a clue in this sentence about the nature of the problem for educated people of the second century. They had such a high doctrine of God as transcendent and unchangeable that it was almost impossible for them to accept that a man, let alone a crucified man, shared God's nature and dignity.

The most formidable critic and opponent of the Christian faith in the early period was Celsus, a prolific writer and defender of the old traditions. It is clear from his attacks on the Christian faith that he was worried by the success of this strange religion. But for him it was the most contemptible of faiths and the account of the death of its Saviour its most pitiful expression. He mocked the Christian notions of the 'tree of life' and 'resurrection of the dead' as complete fables. 'What drunken old women, telling stories to lull a small child to sleep, would not be ashamed of muttering such preposterous things?'[2] For Celsus and many of his sophisticated contemporaries, the idea that the pre-existent Son of God, the mediator of creation, had appeared in recent times in Galilee, an outpost of the Roman Empire, as a member of the obscure and despised Jewish people and, even worse, had died the death of a common criminal on a wooden cross – this could only be the height of folly and stupidity of the most shameful and perverse kind. So Celsus appeals to his readers, 'And you, do you not believe that the Son of God sent to the Jews is the most ridiculous makeshift of all?'[3]

Vivid expressions of contempt for the Christian faith are captured in murals and inscriptions which come from the early period. One which was found in the excavation of the Palatine in Rome, the residence of the emperors for many years, shows a Christian pageboy kneeling in worship before a cross. But the figure he is worshipping on the cross has a human body with an ass's head. The inscription mocks, 'Alexamenos worships a god!' Whoever Alexamenos was, he could not have found it easy being a Christian in the home of Caesar and one admires his courage in nailing his colours to the mast. Another caricature, a fourth-century 'cartoon' found in present-day Hungary, shows a picture of Christ staggering under the weight of the cross. His body is deformed and made grotesque and his tongue is the length of his body. Pictures like these say more effectively than words what many people felt about the cross. The growing band of Christians, with their unashamed proclamation of Jesus crucified and risen, offended the sensitivities of their society and the reaction was that of fury and contempt.

Only criminals died on crosses

The cross was offensive because crucifixion was a penalty levied out to only the most evil and wretched of men. In origin crucifixion probably began among the Persians, who used it as an effective way of subjugating stubborn and independent tribes. It gradually spread to other nations and was eventually adopted by Roman and Greek peoples. In Roman law it was considered the most awful of punishments, followed in descending order by burning, decapitation and being thrown to wild beasts. The form of crucifixion varied greatly, although what was common to the various forms was the aim to subject the victim to as much indignity as possible. Crucifixion was popular not only because it was an efficient deterrent but it was also easy to implement and inexpensive – given a tree, a victim could be crucified anywhere. It was, furthermore, a punishment in which the sadism and caprice of the executioners could be given full and malicious expression.

No wonder that civilised people spoke of crucifixion with such tones of hushed horror: 'The accursed tree', 'the barren tree', 'the terror of the cross'. Cicero, the famous Roman statesman, argued that a true citizen would not lower himself to allow this barbaric form of execution even to enter his mind: 'The very word "cross" should be far removed not only from the person of a Roman citizen but also from his thought, his eyes and his ears.'[4] It was, in fact, extremely rare for this punishment to be applied to a Roman citizen. In the main it was inflicted upon the lower classes, whereas the more privileged groups in society could reckon on more dignified treatment – whatever crime they had committed.

It was not surprising, then, that there was such a reaction to the idea of a saviour dying in so dreadful a way. It was a horrifying concept. So offensive was the punishment itself that the cultured literary world wanted to have nothing to do with it and tried to shut it out, in spite of its prevalence in their society. Its associations with evil, with degraded and vicious men, made almost contemptible the link between salvation and a crucified Saviour.

The cross clashed with assumed notions about the character of God

As in any time or culture, the message of Christianity challenged accepted notions about God in the early period of the Church. The gods of the Greeks and the Romans could at least be distinguished from mortals by the very fact that they were immortal. While in popular mythology they might disport themselves on earth in heroic deeds, however close they might come in likeness to human emotions and form, there was still an essential 'otherness' about them. The story of Christianity broke with normal conventions about the ways of divine beings with men. The birth of the Saviour in a stable, his growth in knowledge and experience until the start of his ministry among a backward people, and the ending of his life in an ignominious death – this faith bore little resemblance to the human–divine world of the intelligentsia of the day. Gods simply did not do things like that! As they saw it, there was nothing heroic or inspiring about dying on a cross. So Celsus argued that there had been a way out of the dilemma which faced Jesus – he could have proved his divinity by being transported by God away from the cross, either at the point of his capture or just before he was crucified: 'But if he were really so great, he ought, in order to display his divinity, to have disappeared from the cross.'[5] At the very least, the opponents of Christianity questioned, why did not God devise a more 'honourable' death for Jesus?[6]

The power of the cross

So the most devastating criticisms were levelled at this new and tiny sect, and the condemnation and abuse threatened its survival. We must make no mistake about it, the abuse and mockery was so intense that it is a wonder that the faith survived. But in spite of the fierce opposition which came through satire, contempt, abuse and scorn – and eventually physical persecution – the Church grew. It grew from the cross. The cross became its proud symbol; the sign of the cross the early Christians' secret identification signal; the way of the cross the only life the followers of Jesus wanted to live. They were happy to go with him to death – and sometimes to a crucifixion, too. Ironically, within three hundred years of the carpenter's death, Christianity became the religion of the Empire. When Constantine embraced Christianity and advanced on the capital, it was a vision of the cross he claimed to have seen shortly before his decisive battle at Milvium Bridge, signalling: 'In This Sign, Conquer.'

THE OFFENCE TODAY

Perhaps offence is too strong a word because Christians and non-Christians alike are so used to the cross and its essential link with Christianity that it does not surprise or horrify us in the way it would have done someone who lived in the earliest period of Christian history. This does not mean that the cross is acceptable to all and that everyone understands its meaning fully and agrees with it. Christianity faces more subtle reactions today than those the first Christians encountered, and these are just as difficult to combat. On the one hand there is indifference and apathy, which simply brush the cross aside as a great yawn and an irrelevant tale and, on the other hand, there is disdain because it is assumed to belong to an outmoded world-view. Colin Wilson spoke for many when he explained why he wrote *The Outsider*: 'It was my failure to see any need for Christ. The need for God I could accept and the need for religion . . . but ultimately I could not accept the need for redemption by a Saviour.'[7]

In four different ways modern people find the cross of Jesus a very strange and disconcerting idea.

The cross is too personal

We acknowledge freely that the cosmology of the ancient world differed profoundly from our own. Their three-decker universe, with heaven above and hell below, was an environment filled with the divine. God was close at hand. In fact, there were so many divinities to choose from that it was almost a consumer's market. But our cosmology is of a significantly different kind. We dispensed with the three-decker model long ago. We know that we live in a universe which exceeds our wildest ideas of space and time. We gasp in awe as we try to take in the fact that two million light years separate our galaxy from our nearest neighbouring galaxy, Andromeda. Yet, we are reliably informed, there are untold numbers of galaxies in the universe, each with countless moons, planets and stars. Surely, the modern man or woman finds himself or herself thinking, if there is a God who created all things, he cannot possibly be interested in our tiny third-rate planet circling a rather ordinary sun? If the idea of a personal God then becomes hard to swallow, the claim of Christians that God became a man and actually went to the cross to save humanity seems, at least to many of our contemporaries, too incredible for words.

However, if we follow this train of thought we are in danger of emulating Celsus and other early critics of Christianity who dismissed the Christian faith because it did not fit in with their assumptions about God and his ways. For Celsus, just because God had deigned to send his Son to Palestine and not to Rome, and to a cross and not to a throne, the story lacked credibility. So we, in turn, look through our telescopes, listen to the radio signals coming from the far reaches of space, and send our spaceships to interview the stars and we say: 'God, if there is one, cannot be interested in us.' But what we are tacitly doing is reducing God to our image. The size of the universe has no bearing upon the character of God. If God created this universe – as Christians confidently claim – he is obviously capable of caring for individual elements in it and is able to enter intimately into a personal relationship with his creatures. It is irrational, therefore, to conclude that the size of the universe removes God from intimate contact with us.

Furthermore, if it is not unintelligible to think of the creator taking an interest in his workmanship, it is certainly not beyond the bounds of credibility to believe that he is able to show the full extent of his love by coming to us in Christ and going to that lonely cross. We have to admit, however, that to someone who is not yet a believer the concept of the cross does strain one's credulity. It seems to make God too parochial; it seems impossible for God to stoop that low or that we are worth that much. But is not this argument also, at heart, unreasonable? If God can pay us the attention of his love and care, then he can give us individual attention also. Indeed, he can pay us the most staggering compliment of all by personally coming to us and by uniting himself to us by a cross.

The cross has become unintelligible to us

Although it is not impossible for God to be personally involved in saving humanity through a cross, modern people find it a strange way to choose because our conceptual framework of living is quite different from the world in which

Christianity appeared. For all its supposed inadequacies to non-Christians in the ancient world, the point of the cross was meaningful to some degree because notions of sacrifice, ransom, and sin offerings were all part and parcel of societies which believed in this form of redemption. The Jews lived in a world in which relationship with God depended upon faithful observation of the sacrificial system. Ordered lives and an ordered society were intimately connected with religious duties and obedience to ceremonial law. God's covenant with men and women required that the law should be kept and the rhythm of the festivals hallowed. The Gentiles, also, were very familiar with similar concepts and practices; pagan gods were placated through sacrifice when offences were committed; notions of ransom were meaningful through the manumission of slaves in the temples.

The early preaching of the cross, therefore, drew upon familiar concepts and practices which made the meaning of the cross instantly recognisable. But that's a long way from today. The sacrificial system and ritual observances are totally alien to our culture. Whereas for them life itself was essentially religious – indeed, impoverished if life was separated from God – life for us is almost totally secular. For them sacrifice was the best they could give God – gladly and cheerfully; for us it is an act we should avoid at all costs and becomes a heroic deed if the act is costly. Thus, the very elements which made a theology of the cross highly charged with meaning to people of an earlier period are absent from our culture. Naturally, therefore, people ask about the cross: 'What does it mean? Was it necessary for God to go to such lengths? Couldn't God simply just forgive us?'

We have lost the sense of sin

In Christian teaching sin and the cross are opposites. Lose a sense of sin and the meaning of the cross is lost. I am not suggesting, of course, that our contemporaries are immoral or lacking values. Indeed not: the majority believe in the importance of a moral code based upon concepts of right and wrong. But when this is examined carefully we can see that at the heart of contemporary morality the sense of obligation to God is missing. Instead, our sense of right and wrong is based upon the values inherent in our society. Thus, morality runs the risk of becoming a hand-maid, serving the interests of our society. We can see that this is clearly the case in personal morality. Unlike previous generations, the mood of our day is that if personal morality, especially in the sexual sphere, does not affect, influence or harm others, it should be left to the individual conscience to decide whether it is right or wrong. At the very basest of levels, then, 'Thou shalt not be found out' is the unspoken value judgment of some who look at morality in terms of what serves to further my personal self-interest.

Now, this way of looking at moral values will obviously affect our view of the cross. If sin – in its personal and public expressions – is mysterious to us, the death of Jesus will be inexplicable also. This is because the meaning of both stems from the breakdown of a relationship between God and humanity. Sin is much more than a bad act which is given a religious name, or even a series of wrong choices – it describes a broken relationship between men and women and their maker. Just as divorce represents the final state of estrangement between two people whose marriage has collapsed, so sinfulness represents the state of estrangement between God and humanity with its consequent rebellion and penetration into every corner of human life. Indeed, one might say, the triumph of sin is complete when we deny its existence, so completely one with us does it become. V. A. Demant once observed that the word 'sinner' is a label of responsibility denoting that a person is not a weed or a puppet but a responsible being who is able to make moral choices. While it is fashionable for secular thinkers to criticise Christianity for introducing so-called morbid terminology like 'miserable sinners' in western culture, the fact remains that the issue of sinfulness goes to the very heart of what it is to be human. We *know* that we fall short of the ideals we feel are possible. We sometimes find ourselves asking what power makes it impossible for us to be perfect. Why is it that we cannot resist the most trivial of temptations? Why is it that so many make shipwrecks of their lives because of some moral indiscretion, and then spend the rest of their lives cursing their mistake? Why was it that, when I was a prison chaplain in a remand centre, hundreds of young men vowed that this would be their last time 'in the nick' and I would never see them again – only to see their faces nine months later after yet another failure to keep out of trouble?

Just as a round-the-world yachtsman measures the success of his voyage by the storms and perils he has successfully circumnavigated, so the cross can only be properly assessed by its power to release people from their bondage and by the peace and power it gives them.

The morality of the cross

The cross also offends us by its unspoken testimony that it alone saves us and reconciles us to God. It is an affront to our pride to be told that we have nothing to contribute to our salvation except our repentance. In Christian history there have been two forms of this offence which have been linked with the names of fierce critics of the cross.

The first was Pelagius, a British monk in the fifth century who was angered by St Augustine's teaching that we cannot save ourselves. Augustine emphasised God's grace which flowed from the cross: men and women are so helpless in their sin that they can offer nothing to God to please him. Pelagius was deeply troubled by this teaching, believing that it would lead to moral laxity, and argued that perfection is possible in this life. Adam's sin, he asserted, only affected himself and has no bearing upon us. Sin is always personal. Having cut our sins off from Adam, Pelagius proceeded to do the same with the cross. Christ's death was an example of suffering and obedience which we must emulate. Pelagianism was duly and properly condemned by the Church because it was recognised that such a teaching made Christianity just a moral code and Christ merely a great teacher and an inspiring example.

It is surprising how deeply embedded in the human heart is Pelagianism, even if we have never heard of the monk who gave the heresy its name. None of us likes the idea of being described as 'dead and buried in our sins'. That kind of description offends our pride and sense of rightness. We don't need someone else to show us the way – we can handle our own problems. However, the cross contradicts this assumption emphatically, because there is no room for human pride in its shadow. We either come to God on his terms, or not at all.

The second great opponent of the cross was Faustus Socinus who lived in the sixteenth century. Socinus' quarrel with the Christian faith has a peculiarly modern ring about it. He objected to the notion that Christ's death was vicarious, that is, Christ died *for us*. 'Merit, guilt and punishment cannot be transferable,' he protested. He went on to argue that such values are not like debts of money which may be borne by others instead of us. A moral debt cannot be carried by another. God could forgive sins without the necessity of Jesus' atonement. Moral wrongdoing is not atoned for until the guilty person atones for it himself.

We must resist the temptation to deal with this issue here. It is true to say that Socinus' objection and others similar to it are with us today, and they will be considered later in this book. The cross certainly raises the question of justice: in what meaningful way is it possible for God's Son to die for our sins? Can he carry the burden when he was not guilty? Are moral misdemeanours transferable?

Well, then, we can see that the task of explaining the cross is formidable. It attracts violent opposition as well as devotion. For some, it is still the 'barren tree' which people attack and ridicule. For others it is the tree of 'glory' because it has become for them the way to God and to life. We must address ourselves to discovering why the cross attracts such opposition on the one hand and why, on the other, it is for many the centre of faith.

2

The Enemy Within

It is customary, when people write about the cross, to begin with sin. This is completely understandable because the cross is God's way of dealing with the sin and evil in us. However, the problem with beginning here is two-fold. First of all, by starting with sin we are in danger of distorting the character of the relationship between God and people. It suggests that the character of God is that of a wrathful, unloving, implacable deity whose main delight lies in attributing as much blame as possible to humanity, whose only misfortune consists in being his creatures. It has to be said that certain forms of Christianity in the past have exaggerated this idea, with the result that a sin- and guilt-ridden faith has developed.

Serious as sin is, the Bible does not begin there. 'Sin never comes first,' declared the theologian Emil Brunner, 'it pre-supposes a relationship.' That is, the first thing we are told about the God–humanity relationship is that we are called to a special relationship of love with him. This is the starting point of the cross: it commences in God's commitment to his creation, especially to that being who is made 'in his image' (Gen. 1:26). If we start anywhere else we do less than justice to the character of God himself. He is not primarily a vindictive God who hates sinners; his nature is to love and to reconcile. What we have to grasp is that God loves humanity with an overwhelming desire for fellowship which exceeds anything we have ever experienced in human life. His intention from the beginning has never been to accuse humanity, or to sentence us to eternal damnation, or to call us to a life of morbid introspection and legalism. Indeed not: his longing and delight is for us to find life and hope in him. What we must note is that starting with God's tender love for us all does not minimise the sadness and awfulness of sin, but puts it in its proper context. Human morality would have little respect for God if his concern was solely upon ethical standards and divine dignity. But it bows before a God whose essential nature is to love and to show it in his beloved Son.

The second wrong assumption that people commonly make about sin is that it is often treated as something which is *external* to us. We think of sin as something we *do*; something like a sack of coal, grimy and black, which we carry around with us, accumulating extra loads of the stuff until a merciful Christ relieves us of the burden. It is a strange but clear fact when one looks at our society that although we are obsessed with improving our education, our amenities, our way of life – we are not concerned about improving ourselves morally! How strange it is that little or no attention is given to developing our inner lives, our moral lives, our spiritual selves. Growing up and growing old, sadly, rarely means growing as people, conquering ourselves as well as our environment. Rightly did Winston Churchill once observe: 'Man's control has extended over practically every sphere – except over himself.'

At this point, then, we need to look more closely at the nature of sin. If it is not something external to us, what is it? How does it affect me personally? What can be done about it?

Deformed humanity

Whether we like it or not, most of us have grown up with a view of humankind's origins which seems to exclude the idea of a blessed state of perfection, from which we have been evicted because of our sin. Our understanding of an evolving, ever-developing and adapting universe appears incompatible with the somewhat mythological account in Genesis. It is not my intention in this book to deal at length with this issue. I have written about this elsewhere and the literature on the subject is endless.[1] But as a thinking, intelligent and modern human being I do not regard contemporary views as totally at odds with the Genesis account of creation. I offer two reflections to anyone who is troubled by this problem.

First, if we look carefully at the story in Genesis we shall find that it does not suggest that humanity was in a fixed state of blessedness in a garden shared with almighty God. The passage is obviously describing a real and tragic breakdown in relationship in a pictorial form. The allegoric nature of the story is expressed not only in the structure of a narrative in which God walks in a garden, but also in the terms used which indicate a mythic portrayal of a deeper reality – Adam (man), Eve (mother of living things), and the serpent as denoting evil. To assume, as some people still do today, that the story is stating an actual account of the break between God and humankind is to misinterpret Scripture. The account in Genesis does not tell us how sin entered the world, but it does tell us that it is here and that, because of its reality, we live in an estranged relationship with God.

In other words, the early part of Genesis posits a real breakdown between God and humanity, and expresses it in a parabolic form. But we must also beware of trivialising the story. To treat the passage as a very primitive legend or aetiological tale to explain to primitive people how sin entered the world is again to misunderstand the depth and richness of the passage. Genesis 1–3 is among the deepest sections of Scripture. Its emphases upon humanity's relationship with God, of being made in his image and likeness, and the centrality of humankind in the story of creation suggest that the writer was seeking to express truths which could only be portrayed in a visual and parabolic form.

We are therefore forced to be reverently 'agnostic' about the state of human beings prior to their rejection of God. The Bible reveals very little. It says little about the state of humanity in the 'garden' and does not explain how one person's sin can affect others. This is because, I repeat, the Bible's main concentration is to describe *why* things are as they are, and not to explain exhaustively *how* we came to be in this state.

This leads into my second reflection. If the Bible's main task is to show us our real situation, we can scarcely deny its accuracy. The notion that people are essentially sinful and unable to perfect themselves is known as the doctrine of 'original sin'. It is not a very complimentary doctrine and it is scarcely surprising that it has been unpopular with very many. The verdict of Scripture that 'all have sinned and fall short of the glory of God' and Paul's agonised exclamation that 'what I do is not the good I want to do' (Rom. 3:23; 7:19) go against the grain and are too close for comfort. But we have to ask, even if we cannot deny its offence to people who want to do things their way, is it not a fact that it accords with human nature? G. K. Chesterton used to refer to the doctrine of original sin as 'the one directly ascertainable doctrine of Christianity'. A more recent writer remarked: 'Our grandfathers in their simplicity found it hard, if not impossible, to believe in Original Sin; it is not so with us; perhaps among the traditional dogmas this one alone can now be accepted as almost self-evident.'[2]

It is, frankly, very difficult to deny this concrete fact. Human nature is in a real sense 'fallen'. We are aware of our bias to evil; of sharing in a universal, endemic sickness from which we all feel a need to be healed. But does it not also accord with human experience? We don't have to look much further than our newspapers to be aware of the experience of sinfulness. Consider the words our daily and TV news use to describe acts of evil – rape, stealing, muggings, strikes, murder, anger, drunkenness and so on. Regrettably, such words can mask the sin and evil behind the acts of violence. By differentiating them as we do to denote different forms of evil, we can so easily overlook their common ancestry.

But does it not also accord with personal experience? We do not have to look far into our own souls to discover the rottenness within. As a pastor of some years' standing, I ceased years ago to be staggered when people of repute and apparent uprightness fell from their positions of moral integrity. When we really know ourselves we are not at all dumbfounded, because each one of us has to say: 'There, but for the grace of God, go I.' Anyone who knows the weakness of his or her own heart will know that there are few sins we could not commit in certain circumstances. But they don't have to be the spectacular, the colourful sins – the sins which make page three of the Sunday newspapers. The problem I am really getting at is the sin which diminishes us as people; the enemy within which stops me becoming the kind of person I would be pleased to live with, the cancer within my own soul which stunts my growth as a person open to all the possibilities of the truly human life, as it was meant to be.

The quest for wholeness

But sin is much more than deformation from an original ideal. It troubles me when I hear preachers treating personal evil as if it is that impersonal 'sack of coal' which Christ takes away from us when we trust in him. The problem with this approach is that it is a 'sin-grid' type of mentality; it has to do more with offences against a holy God than the sadness of a broken relationship which has resulted in a deformed humanity. What I am getting at may be expressed in the familiarity of social relationships today. Take Bill, a young prisoner at a remand centre where I used to work as a part-time chaplain. Bill was a regular visitor to the prison for the offences he committed. He was clearly to blame, as he freely admitted. 'But I can't help myself,' he used to say. 'Every time I leave this place I say, "That's the last time you'll see me," but then I do something wrong again – I don't know what gets into me.' He was clearly to blame – but not totally to blame, as we all knew. His father was in and out of jail, his mother was on the bottle, he had eight brothers and three sisters, most of whom had been inside, he was poorly educated in an area where unemployment was high – now where do we allot blame? What Bill serves to illustrate is the importance of environment. What he had inherited had shaped and conditioned him – not that it had taken away his responsibility, but it had made it very difficult for him to have freedom to grow to the maturity and moral responsibility that many of us enjoy. He was robbed of *wholeness* by the environment which had imprisoned him.

I see the story of Bill as an expression of the effect of sin in our lives. Far more serious than our moral bankruptcy, and failure to live up to God's high standards, is our failure to arrive at God's ideal for each one of us. I think that this is where God's pitying glance must be. He is not a 'sin-grid' God, giving prizes to those who get more than 90 per cent in the Holiness Exam: his concern is that his people never reach the wholeness offered to all who walk with him.

Now wholeness means different things to different people. We must put some flesh on it. Wholeness is basically entering a new environment where, in partnership with our Lord, we may grow to that maturity which is his will. If human environment affects us so much as to shape us for better or for worse, why should this not be the same for the divine–human relationship? But of course it is. Humankind bereft of God's warmth, love and guidance is left to develop alone, with the sorry results that we see all around us. Sin, therefore, brings punishment from within itself in terms of disintegration and alienation. Instead of being the integrated, Christ-centred people God wants us to be – people developing in love and maturity as we reach out to others – we are cut off from our full potential and from the wholeness God intended us to possess. But to find wholeness involves us in committing ourselves to a new relationship of love through the surrender of ourselves.

So we can see that to put sin in the context of what God originally intended for his people helps us to set it against the backcloth of God's tender love, instead of his wrathful judgment. We can see it as deviation from the essential destiny given to us by God. It is, according to the theologian John Oman, 'the attempt to get out of life what God has not put into it'. Again, I can look at life and find many examples that assist me in discovering the truth of this. For example, the all too familiar stories we read in our newspapers of youngsters who die from a drug overdose, who want to live life to the full and scoff at all those in authority who warn them of the perils of drug addiction – they serve as reminders that those who try to improve on the creator's plan for us, never do.

The universality of guilt

Although I have been attacking the sin-grid approach to the broken relationship between God and humanity, it is impossible to ignore this strand totally. And we would not wish to do so as it is an important element in the problem, because if we want to get to the heart of the Bible's teaching about human nature we must realise that our essential condition before almighty God is that of guilt. Moral guilt is not the invention of the Bible or a few narrow-minded theologians of the past – it is the universal condition of my soul and yours. No amount of protest can deny this fact.

However, in talking about guilt we must observe that normal guilt and not neurotic guilt is in mind. Sigmund Freud considered guilt to be the most important problem in the evolution of humanity and declared that it must be the intention of psychiatry to eradicate it. Because he rejected the concept of God there was no place for moral guilt. Guilt was a feeling which had no place in his closed system, where the health of the person was paramount. Interestingly enough, although Freud dismissed the Christian idea of the fall, he replaced it with his own anthropological theory of the transmission of guilt based upon the myth of a violent and jealous father who keeps all the females for himself and drives away his sons. The angry sons kill and devour their father, but instead of this incident resolving the situation it drives them to remorse and to feel guilt for the deed they committed. Even though, then, Freud comes close to the Christian perspective that 'all have sinned and fall short of the glory of God', the ideal from which we have fallen, in his opinion, is our well-being as people.[3]

Other psychiatrists have not followed Freud's teaching that guilt is essentially neurotic. Rollo May, for example, saw guilt feelings in normal life as a positive and constructive emotion. It is the perception of the difference between what *is* and what *ought* to be. It is inseparably connected with my freedom as a moral person. But May develops guilt beyond moral guilt to what we might call universal guilt. He delineates three forms of 'ontological' guilt. The first – *Eigenwelt*, my world – is the guilt which arises from forfeiting the possibilities of human growth; when I lock them up in myself. In Christian terms we would call this selfishness: the universe revolves around me and my way of looking at life. A second form of guilt May calls *Mitwelt*, that is, the failure to see others as people too. We look at our fellows from a biased point of view. We cannot know them as they are but only in terms of how they appear to us. Thus in our social relationships we find the seeds of social breakdown in the way we limit, mistreat and despise others. The third form of guilt, according to May, is *Umwelt* – guilt which separates us from the cosmos. We are aware of ourselves as being 'in' nature yet different from it; belonging to it but over against it and out of sorts with it. We must note that in Rollo May's treatment guilt is not always bad – ideally, guilt should lead to a sharpened sensitivity towards ourselves, others and the world.[4]

May's understanding of guilt comes quite close to the Christian interpretation of this mysterious element in human life. We often hear it said that modern people no longer feel guilt about wrongdoing, that the widening chasm between the Christian ethic and secular life has led to a rejection of this way of looking at life. It is said that modern people echo Robbie Burns' poem 'The Song of the Jolly Beggars':

> A fig for those by law protected,
> Liberty's a glorious feast.
> Courts for cowards were erected,
> Churches built to please the priests.

But my experience of life – and, I must add, the experience of many friends in the medical and social professions, as well as those involved in extensive counselling – is that this is simply not vindicated in normal life; people today are no more liberated from the bonds of their past, from the burden of sins, imagined and real, than people of previous generations. Augustine speaks for our day as well as for his own when he writes about the power and effect of sins in these poignant words: 'Many sins are committed through pride but not at all proudly . . . they happen so often by ignorance, by human weakness; many are committed by men weeping and groaning in their distress.'

Yet in this word 'guilt' we stumble upon what it is to be human. If guilt is to have any reality at all, it must involve responsibility for moral failure and lapses from the goals I set myself. Edward Stein remarks: 'Guilt is the peg on which the meaning of "man" hangs. It is also the peg on which man too often hangs himself.' This is well put. Guilt which I cannot handle, guilt from which I cannot free myself, can so easily lead to despair. I well recall speaking with Yvonne, a lady in prison convicted of manslaughter. She knew her guilt and yet her punishment did not appear to her to fit the crime: 'I want to be punished,' she exclaimed. 'I am guilty because I have killed someone.' It is ironic that in our 'enlightened' days our concepts of punishment avoid talking about rights and wrongs on the one hand and retribution on the other, with the result that we do not touch the real heart of the human predicament which is that we are beings with a moral sense and that it belongs to our nature to know guilt. Instead, more often than not we treat the offender as someone who has infringed social morality so that a period of imprisonment is required to assuage society's displeasure. Our society's confusion about sin and wrongdoing is most vividly expressed in contemporary penology: there is no clear policy, we have abandoned retribution, quite rightly, and, yet, we have lost all hope of reforming offenders.

Against this confusion the Bible speaks refreshingly and hopefully of humanity as sinful and guilty before Almighty God. This is essentially a hopeful doctrine because we are seen as creatures made in God's image and therefore capable of making moral choices. Our basic predicament is estrangement from God, which causes us to be alienated from our inner being and from our fellow-beings. Guilt, therefore, from a Christian point of view, is both negative and positive. It is bad news in that it describes the state of condemnation under which we lie. 'Guilty, vile and helpless we' goes Bliss's famous hymn. That is first a statement of fact. I am, you are, guilty whether we feel it or not. In God's sight I am in need of his mercy and grace, and this is a fact which is not dependent upon moods or guilt feelings. It is an objective reality, as tangible as the guilt of the offender before the judgment of human law. But it is also often a subjective experience, too. 'We are all failures – at least, the best of us are,' remarked the writer J. M. Barrie half-seriously. That is, we are not always conscious of the sense of falling short of our ideals and the sense of unworthiness and guilt which may result. When we first come to God a sense of guilt may not be the first thing we are aware of, but it is normal for the Spirit of God to bring to our consciousness how much we need God's grace and help. And as we go on in the Christian life, the more aware we become of the hopefulness of God, as well as the weakness of human nature to cope with the power of sin. But guilt is also positive. A sense of unworthiness may bring us to God. A recognition of humanity's guilt – of our involvement in it and contribution towards it – is the beginning of realism concerning the way things truly are. It may therefore drive us towards healing and wholeness.

Light and darkness

It was customary in Christianity of a bygone era to paint such a dark picture of human wickedness that not only was the character of God so distorted that he ended up as a capricious despot, who delighted in sending as many people to hell as possible, but also sin itself began to be expressed in technicolour. The more colourful the better, the greater the sin the greater the grace. 'One reason that sin flourishes,' preached the evangelist Billy Sunday fiercely, 'is that it is treated like a cream-puff instead of a rattle snake.' While this is certainly true, a great deal of delight went into describing the snake-bites, with the result that the 'ordinariness' of sin was lost. The ordinary man or woman, not aware of any great or spectacular acts of wrongdoing, could understand why it was that the thief, the scoundrel, the prostitute and so on needed redemption, but was perplexed by the insinuation that they too needed forgiveness.

In C. S. Lewis' masterpiece *The Screwtape Letters* the experienced devil writing to a novice devil speaks of the importance of small sins. 'Do remember,' he writes, 'the only thing that matters is the extent to which you separate the man from the Enemy. It does not matter how small the sins are provided that their cumulative effect is to edge the man away from the Light and out into the Nothing . . . the safest road to Hell is the gradual one – the gentle slope, soft underfoot, without sudden turnings, without milestones, without signposts.'[5] Without any question at all, this is the way the Bible views sin too.

Spectacular as the fall is, the history of humankind is the gradual slope away from God and away from life. In the Old Testament there is no special word for the notion of sin, although there are three words in particular which are important for the notion. There is first of all the word *hattat*, which means to 'miss the mark' or 'to go astray', and describes the sinner as one who strays from the right pathway and is lost. We can appreciate that this word-picture would have been most vivid for a rural community: 'We all, like sheep, have gone astray' (Isa. 53:6). A second word, *awon*, meaning to 'leave the right path', suggests that the offender does so deliberately, quite aware that the choice goes against his conscience. A third term, which is most popular with the prophets, is *pesha*, often translated 'rebellion'. This rich and descriptive word should not be understood in a political sense but rather as the breakdown of relationships between a loving parent and child. This is how the great prophets viewed the nature of sin. It was a rejection of the love which Yahweh, their God, desired to shower upon his people. Hosea pictures God as a lover waiting for his beloved to return home; yet he pleads in vain because Israel will not heed the call of love. Amos and Micah echo the same idea. The rebellion of the people of God had affected the whole life of the community so that an insular, selfish spirit dominated the way people lived.

Thus, long before a full doctrine of sin developed, we find in the teaching that there is no such thing as private sin. Sin is contagious, it affects others and may even influence the character of the community. Little wonder, then, that from God's point of view sin is also seen as 'foolishness' which can only lead to disaster. So Jeremiah speaks for God in the tones of a deserted husband yearning for his former bride: 'Why then, my people, do you turn away from me without ever turning back? You cling to your idols and refuse to return to me . . . Not one of you has been sorry for his wickedness; not one of you has asked, "What have I done wrong?" . . . Even storks know when it is time to return . . . But, my people, you do not know the laws by which I rule you. How can you say that you are wise?' (Jer. 8:5–9, GNB)

The main thing to keep in mind when we read the Bible's account of human wrongdoing is that its main preoccupation is not with great sins which anger God and offend his moral laws, but the *state* of sin which leads us to rebel against his right to rule. Small and great sinners are at one in their state of rebellion which will not allow the light of God's love and justice to penetrate the darkness of their selfish wills.

It is against this background that the New Testament treats sin. Jesus in the gospels never speculated about the origin of sin or explained what he understood by it, but he accepted the reality of its power; he treated people as lost and in need of God's love and forgiveness. He spoke with a clear, though compassionate, understanding of the inner nature of humanity, teaching that evil has its root in the heart of each individual. That humanity is lost, enslaved and in desperate need of a saviour is at the heart of the incarnation, and Christianity becomes inexplicable if we lose sight of this centre in the gospels.

But it was Paul's distinctive contribution to give us the fullest theology of sin in the New Testament. The word for sin occurs over sixty times in his letters and was therefore a dominating idea in his teaching. For him sin is universal, something locked into every heart and soul from which only Christ can release us. It is a power which has us in its grip. We are 'under sin' in the same way that a child is under its parents. It 'lords it over us' as a despot ill-treats a slave; it 'takes us captive' as a victorious army captures a defeated people. But sin is not merely external to us in Paul's thought, it enters every fibre of our being and we cannot escape its power. It is a tyrant and we are a subject people in the dominion of darkness.

Redeeming love

But this chapter must not end on the note of human sin, tragic though that is. Sin never comes first or even last because it is preceded and followed by God's redeeming love. It is not followed by anger which threatens to engulf the sinner in the flames of righteous indignation and holy justice. It is pursued, rather, by God's tender love which wants the sinner to be a sinner no longer but to be a ransomed and redeemed child of God. This does not minimise the seriousness of sin but puts it against the proper backcloth of God's nature to love. It was such a God who decided to do something about the enemy within.

3

Holy Fire

FORGIVENESS AND SACRIFICE

As we have seen, sin reveals as much about God as about our need for him. It just shows him to be a God who longs for us to return to him and find his forgiveness. But very sadly for our modern world, forgiveness has become a mysterious, puzzling idea. We are well acquainted with the problem of wrongdoing but we hardly ever associate forgiveness with it. The criminal is rarely confronted with the need to be forgiven, and the innocent who are wronged do not think in these terms. What happens is that the offender is sentenced and punished, either by the payment of a fine, or the payment of his or her time at Her Majesty's pleasure. But whatever form the sentence takes, it is extremely unlikely that the offender will think: 'I have hurt another human being and I need to be reconciled to that person.' The same applies to less serious offences. In ordinary life we seldom speak of forgiveness. Our faults are our failures to live up to our ideals and if we offend others, then that's just too bad. 'This is the way I intend to live – hard luck if people don't agree,' we sometimes hear people say. Many, then, would approve of Bernard Shaw's dictum: 'Forgiveness is a beggar's refuge: we must pay our debts.'

This has serious consequences for modern life. A society which finds the idea of forgiveness strange to understand will become a hard, unforgiving society which is long of memory but short of love. Guilt is thus trivialised and, as a result, buried deep in the lives of many. Forbidden expression, it may poison relationships and deepen personal anxiety. Take the story of John, a typical secular and successful man. He threw himself into his career. His business prospered while his family relationships declined. He spent less and less time at home. His wife grew increasingly bitter and they only held on to their marriage for the sake of their children. The poisoned atmosphere at home drove John to find comfort in his secretary and he consequently saw even less of his children. A stranger at home, discovering that his wife and three teenagers needed him less and less, and a stranger to himself and the ideals he once held dear, he could not help wishing that things could be as they once were. But as he saw very clearly, not only was reconciliation needed, but a change of life was also required. That was a price he was not prepared to pay.

If, then, forgiveness is at the centre of what it is to be human – the need to forgive ourselves as well as to forgive others – how does this apply to the most basic of relationships, that between God and human beings? What has God done to show that he forgives us and what form does reconciliation take?

One of the most universal and basic of ritual activities is that of sacrifice. It is central to most faiths and was crucial to Israel's relationship with God. The notion of sacrifice, in its literal sense of the blood-stained altar, the cries of the victim and the activities of the priests, is completely outside modern experience and to a large degree completely revolting to us. We cannot understand why this was considered necessary or what kind of God would be pleased with this behaviour. It is important to suspend judgment on this at the moment and try to understand the rationale behind the Old Testament's emphasis upon the sacrificial system. Where better to start, indeed, than where we are today, because whether we are talking about worship two thousand years ago or in London in 1992, a worshipping community engages in certain formal or symbolic acts. The actions – prayers, music, sermons, sacraments, etc. – are much more than just human activities; they are thought of as conveying something from humankind to God and from God to humankind.

Symbolic they may be in the main, but we regard them as effective symbols, nonetheless.

It was largely from this perspective that the Old Testament worshipper approached sacrifice. The focus of attention was not upon the victim given over in death as such, but rather upon it as a means of establishing contact with the holy and righteous God. The sacrificial system provided him with a way to obtain God's forgiveness. But how comprehensive was the system and how effective was it as an agency of forgiveness?

Atonement and sacrifice

Old Testament scholars are not in agreement concerning the nature and point of sacrifice in the Hebrew Scriptures. But even though modern scholarship has made us aware of the complexity of some of the issues surrounding the matter, there is no hesitation concerning the fact that sacrifices were integral to the way the ancient Hebrews saw their relationship with God, and the form in which forgiveness was sought and given.

One of the earliest types of sacrifice was the peace offering. The Hebrew word is *shelem*, to which the word *shalom* (peace) is related. The purpose of *shelem* seemed to be that of maintaining a harmonious relationship with God. The significance of the peace offering lay in the fact that it was a meal and conveyed the idea of communion with God, with thanksgiving and praise as central ideas.

A completely different concept meets us when we contemplate burnt offerings. Perhaps the most popular and important of all Hebrew sacrifices, the burnt offering, may have been taken over from the Canaanites who inhabited the land before the Israelites came (Jer. 7:21). The burnt offering, as the name indicates, denoted a sacrifice burnt by fire. The term *olah* can be translated as 'that which goes up', and possibly goes back to the primitive idea of the satisfying smell of the sacrifice ascending to the appreciative nostrils of a divine being!

What distinguished the burnt offering or, as it is sometimes called, the 'holocaust' offering, was that it was wholly consumed by fire on the altar. Whereas only part of the peace offering was burnt, whilst the rest was consumed by the people, the burnt offering was wholly given to God as a sacrificial offering.

Was there any significance in the totality of the sacrifice offered? There must have been. It must surely have related to the conviction that the worshipper offered to God the very best with a free and generous heart. The burnt offering was therefore an act of homage, a giving that was total in its commitment.

As the most frequent of all sacrifices, it is not surprising that it was used for a variety of purposes. Daily worship in the temple commenced with the 'holocaust' of the lamb (Num. 28:4,6). Burnt offerings often served as special sacrifices for feast days (Num. 28:1–29) and they were often used to express joy, gladness and the recognition of Yahweh's greatness (1 Sam. 15:22). A burnt offering could also be used by an individual as an act of homage (Ezek. 44:11).

The variety of use reveals the richness and the complexity of the burnt offering in Israel's faith. It was very special. As such, only the best was good enough to offer to their God. It was expected of the wealthier offerer that he would bring an unblemished male from his flock or herd. In the case of the poor, a healthy turtle dove or pigeon would suffice. In the early stages of Israel's faith the best sacrifice one could offer led to its instant acceptability to God. It was a 'sweet savour unto the Lord' (Lev. 1:9, AV). The anthropomorphic sense of such phrases, which appear frequently in Leviticus (see Lev. 1:13, 17), suggests that the deity was actually soothed or placated by the appetising smell of the offering. It did not take the Israelites long to realise that they could not prevail upon God automatically. God could accept or reject the sacrifice if he so chose. It was up to his sovereign grace and dependent upon the disposition of the worshipper. God could not be bought. If there were no genuine repentance, there was no forgiveness (Isa. 1:11–17). The eighth-century prophets such as Amos, and later prophets such as Jeremiah, were particularly critical of the use of the sacrificial system, which operated on the assumption that God could be manipulated according to the richness

of the offering and the order of the ceremonial associated
with it. They thundered at a corrupt society which tried to
placate God with external religious observances. 'Your burnt
offerings are not acceptable' (Jer. 6:20).

> I hate, I despise your religious feasts . . .
> Even though you bring me burnt offerings
>   and grain offerings,
>   I will not accept them . . .
> But let justice roll on like a river,
>   righteousness like a never-failing stream!
>
> (Amos 5:21–4)

So it appears that the burnt offering reveals the fundamental paradox of any religion which commences from us –
that is, from a human end. We may offer the best of all
our crops, herds and flocks, yet all is vain if it does not
start with the gift of ourselves.

But maintaining a relationship is one thing. What happened
when the relationship was broken – how did the ancient
Hebrew handle sin and guilt?

Sin and guilt offerings

Sin and guilt offerings developed quite late in Israel's history
and it is extremely difficult to distinguish between the two.
As a rough 'rule of thumb' it might be found useful to
think of sin offerings as a way of making atonement to
God for offences against his holiness (Lev. 4:1–2), and guilt
offerings as reparation for dues withheld from God (Lev.
5:16) or from man (Lev. 6:1–7).

But two very important qualifications should be kept in
mind concerning the terms 'sin' and 'guilt' offerings. The
first is that Israel had a highly ritualistic and social understanding of sin. We think of sin as personal, moral and
usually spiritual offences before God. The concept of sin
behind the sacrificial system is that of sin as a contagious
disease which contaminated the whole of society if allowed

to spread. So we can see why Achan and his family were dealt with so brutally after Achan had disobeyed God and stolen things from the city of Jericho which had previously been devoted to the Lord (Josh. 7:1). Our western sensitivities are appalled by such a drastic punishment which swallowed up the innocent in its wrath. But this is all of a piece with the Hebrew approach to life. Achan's family were involved in Achan's guilt because they were of his flesh. The sin had to be dealt with, and everything associated with Achan's name had to be destroyed (Josh. 7:24–6). The revealing aspect of the Achan incident is that it is taken for granted that forgiveness is not possible for such an act of disobedience. There is nothing in Israel's sacrificial system (such as it was at that period) which could give hope to the likes of Achan.

But this leads into the second observation. The sacrificial system was not set up to deal with deliberate sin. The book of Leviticus makes it clear that sin and guilt offerings were only for sins committed in ignorance (4:2, 13, 22, 27; 5:15, 17, 18). In a community which had a highly material idea of offences against God and which expressed this in a sharp differentiation between 'clean' and 'unclean' objects (Lev. 5:2–6), it was all too easy to sin in 'ignorance'. The prescriptions of the sacrificial system offered a way for those who had offended innocently to be cleared of their offences. Sins, however, committed with a 'high hand', that is deliberate sins, could not find atonement because they placed the person outside the covenant people of God.

THE MAKING OF ATONEMENT

There were two outstanding features in the ritual of sin and guilt offerings which we must consider. The victim was presented in the usual way and then, in the case of the sin offering only, the penitent laid his hands on the victim and slaughtered the animal himself. This 'laying on of hands' is quite obviously an identification with the victim and shows a certain connection between the worshipper and his offering. The Catholic scholar Robert Daly argues that this is not 'penal substitution', but whether it is penal or not it is difficult to avoid the conclusion that some form of substituting is going on.[1] The victim is 'standing in for' the worshipper, even if the passages in Leviticus do not give us clues as to what the connection is.

The second outstanding feature is the blood ritual. The blood was important in all types of sacrifice but in the case of sin and guilt offerings takes on a deeper significance. If the sacrifice was a burnt offering, the priest took the blood and sprinkled it against the sides of the altar (Lev. 1:5). But more elaborate procedures took place when the offering was for sin. If the offender was a priest, or the whole congregation of Israel, the blood was sprinkled seven times in front of the curtain which marked off the holy of holies. Then the blood was smeared on the horns of the altar of incense which stood before the curtain, and the rest was poured at the base of the altar (Lev. 4:3–7). In the case of individual members of the people, the ritual was the same except for the sprinkling before the curtain (Lev. 4:27–30).

The classic expression of atonement ritual is to be found, of course, in the Day of Atonement ceremonial, Yom Kippur (Lev. 16). Perhaps the most important day in Israel's ecclesiastical calendar, it is considered by most scholars to mark the latest stages in Israel's development of sacrifice, although it is very probable that the heart of the ritual goes back to much earlier times, especially the 'scapegoat' section. The verb *kippur* (atonement) literally means 'to cover' and conveys the idea of the covering of sin from God's eyes. But this should not be misconstrued as suggesting that the Hebrews tried to placate an angry deity. It is essential to observe that atonement in the Old Testament is never divorced from the activity of God. Although atonement is made to remove sin from God's sight, God himself is directly involved in the removal of evil. In P. T. Forsyth's words, even in the Old Testament atonement was 'the sacrament of God's grace'.[2]

The Day of Atonement was not a feast but a fast. On this most solemn day the people of God remembered the holiness of God, his transcendence and power. After special sacrifices had been offered for the high priest, two goats were presented before the Lord. Having drawn lots over the goats, 'one lot for the Lord and the other for the scape-goat' (Lev. 16:8), the one chosen for the Lord was sacrificed and the blood taken into the holy of holies and sprinkled before the mercy seat. The blood is thus brought 'within the veil' (v. 15, RSV) as an atonement for the holy place for the sins of the people (v. 16).

A great deal of mystery surrounds the second goat. Aaron, representing the people of God, lays his hands upon the head of the victim and confesses all the iniquities of the people, putting them 'on the goat's head' (v. 21). Thus transferred, the goat bears the sins away into the wilderness 'for Azazel' or 'scapegoat' (compare verses 8, 10, 26 in the RSV and NIV). There is some dispute about the meaning of this mysterious phrase. Some scholars believe that the name is intended to refer to Satan, so that the meaning is that the evil is sent back to where it belongs. The dominant and most likely view is that Azazel was a wilderness demon of popular imagination and that here in this story we are touching extremely primitive Hebrew elements. But, whatever the meaning of the name, it is clear that on the Day of Atonement the people saw their sins to be no more. The sins were transferred to the goat and taken away from the community. The way was open to God.

COVENANT AND WRATH

Strictly speaking, a discussion of covenant should precede an examination of sacrifice instead of following it, but the reason we are taking it up here is so that we may see the true purpose of the sacrificial system and observe that God's holiness and love are not in competition.

The Corn Market in Bristol is world famous for four bronze pillars or 'nails' on which corn merchants used to show corn samples and complete their transactions. Hence, it is said, came the saying 'to pay on the nail', meaning to pay promptly or to keep your word. This rather old-fashioned business agreement was in essence a *covenant*. There are many examples of non-religious covenants in the Old Testament which are agreements between individuals and communities. A covenant may be between leaders (Gen. 21:27), between husband and wife (Mal. 2:14), between tribes (1 Sam. 11:1), between king and people (2 Kings 11:4). The sealing of the covenant varies as well, and the following are different ways of 'signing on the dotted line': by the offering of gifts (Gen. 21:27), by a handshake (Ezek. 17:18), by a kiss (1 Sam. 10:1), by a common meal (Gen. 26:27–31), by eating salt (Ezra 4:14, RSV) and by a sacrificial meal (Gen. 31:44–6).

But of greater interest to us are the covenants between God and his people. There are three in the Old Testament which merit our attention. The first, with Noah (Gen. 9:9–11), was a covenant established by God promising that never again would such fierce judgment fall upon the earth. No mention is made in the passage of any ceremony but the rainbow was a 'sacramental' sign, we might say, of the covenant (v. 13). The second, with Abraham (Gen. 15:5–7), is of greater importance to the Christian because it dominates the New Testament. God promises to give innumerable descendants to Abraham and to make of them a people. Abraham's part in this covenant is to bring his faith and trust in the word of Yahweh: 'Abram believed the Lord, and he credited it to him as righteousness' (v. 6).

The third covenant, with Moses (Exod. 24), marks the start of Israel's consciousness as the people of the Lord. Its origin lies in an enslaved and persecuted people in the land of Egypt who see their liberation in two mighty acts of God – the Passover and the Red Sea victory. God is consequently and rightly hailed as Israel's Saviour, and Moses sings following the Red Sea battle:

> The Lord is my strength and my song;
>   he has become my salvation.
> He is my God, and I will praise him . . .
> The Lord is a warrior,
>   the Lord is his name.

> (Exod. 15:2–3)

Here then is a characteristic which never leaves the rest of the biblical record, that God is a Saviour who ransoms and redeems his people. He reveals himself in his saving activity.

The victory, of course, has a very serious consequence for Israel in that it is interpreted as binding Israel to God in a precious relationship of love. The character of this was succinctly stated by Jeremiah as he looked back on the Sinai covenant: 'Obey me, and I will be your God and you will be my people' (Jer. 7:23). The two sides of the bargain are clearly discerned in that verse. God had already shown his commitment to Israel in delivering the nation from slavery. He loved her with an abiding love. He desired a permanent and exclusive relationship which would make Israel a witness to the ends of the earth. Through his salvation he had already disclosed his eternal name, Yahweh, and drawn near to a bedraggled and unprepossessing people. Love and obedience were all he required. Israel's part in the bargain was to keep God's commandments as a sign of her loyalty to her Lord. This aspect is a striking feature of the covenant in Exodus. We are told that Moses read all the words of the Lord and all the people answered, 'Everything the Lord has said we will do' (Exod. 24:3,7).

We should note that this insistence upon obedience is not a sterile form of legalism or salvation by works. It is certainly true that the Pharisees in the time of Jesus had made of the law (Torah) a burden too great for men to bear (Matt. 23:4) but this was not the Old Testament concept of Torah. Torah denotes guidance or instruction which comes from God and which is the whole content of God's revelation of his nature and purpose. As such, it made clear to the people of Israel their responsibilities before God and those things which required obedience. Torah, then, was a moral and spiritual framework for Israel's walk with God. It was meant to protect her from evil, to keep her close to her Lord and to make her a light to the nations. 'Now if you obey me fully and keep my covenant, then out of all nations you will be my treasured possession . . . you will be for me a kingdom of priests and a holy nation' (Exod. 19:5–6).

That Israel did not keep the covenant is mournfully recorded throughout the remainder of the Scriptures. The psalmist declares:

> . . . they did not keep God's covenant
> and refused to live by his law.

> (Ps. 78:10, see also vv. 32, 37)

Isaiah complains:

> . . . they have disobeyed the laws,
> violated the statutes
> and broken the everlasting covenant.

> (Isa. 24:5)

Jeremiah and Ezekiel add to the testimony of the prophets that the people of the Lord have 'broken the covenant' (Jer. 11:10; Ezek. 16:59). In spite of the sacrificial system, which bolstered up the covenant and which was at the heart of the worshipping life of Israel, the old covenant manifestly failed from humanity's side of the bargain. Again and again the covenant was violated and the relationship which God desired was treated as a thing of nought.

It is against this background that we should consider the *wrath of God*. There are two extremes we must avoid if we wish to understand the biblical meaning of wrath. The first tendency is that which avoids applying it to God at all. 'God is love,' we hear it said, 'it does not belong to his nature to be angry with his people. Anger is a primitive emotion and it is wrong to ascribe such a violent response to a loving Heavenly Father.' The well-known scholar C. H. Dodd gave credence to this view with his interpretation that the 'wrath of God' is not God's personal response to sin and evil but part of an inevitable 'cause and effect' in a moral universe. Dodd argued that 'in speaking of wrath and judgment the prophets and the psalmists have their minds mainly on events, actual or expected, conceived as the inevitable results of sin; and when they speak of mercy they are thinking mainly of the personal relation between God and His people. Wrath is the effect of human sin: mercy is not the effect of human goodness, but is inherent in the character of God.'[3]

But this will not do. One can understand Dodd's desire to get away from a pre-Christian understanding of God, but wrath as an impersonal and inevitable process of judgment against sin finds no support in Scripture. Furthermore, his differentiation between mercy, which is integral to God's nature, and wrath, which is not, owes more, I suspect, to a theological motive than to the evidence of the text.

But there is a second tendency we should also bypass, the one Dodd so clearly wanted to avoid, namely a naive fundamentalism that attributes to God an anger which is out of character with his nature of love. What we have to remember is that God's revelation in Scripture is not all of one piece. There is a progressive development of revelation, an unfolding of his will to the minds of men which winds its way from its shadowy portrayal to the patriarchs and to an oppressed people in Egypt, on to clearer understanding in the minds of the prophets and to its final and unambiguous expression in Christ. It is not surprising, then, to discover in some parts of the Old Testament disclosures of God which seem to be a long way from the New Testament picture of a holy and loving God. Such expressions and pictures of harshness will not worry any sensible Christian who recognises that, as the drama of redemption unfolds in the Bible and a clearer picture of God's nature is revealed, the nearer we get to the heart of the Christian story, God's full definitive and final revelation in Christ. We must assess all that precedes the coming of Christ in the light of that.

We are thus warned to avoid the extreme which denies that God is personally angry with sin and that which attributes to him baser emotions than we would give to ourselves. What we cannot avoid is that the wrath of God is a concept frequently encountered in the Bible. There are more than 580 references to God's wrath in the Old Testament alone and we can scarcely say that it is an incidental subject. If we had 580 references to the Holy Spirit in the Old Testament we would reckon to possess a rich theological deposit indeed. Instead, there are a mere handful of references. Such then is the emphasis upon this aspect of God's character. But what does it mean? What we must dismiss at once is the commonly met view that it is the irrational, irresponsible action of a God whose moral standards are somewhat old-fashioned and prudish. What lends support to this view is that it is hard for us to imagine 'wrath' which is entirely free from spite, revenge and personal malice. Not so God. His wrath is never isolated from his covenantal love. The Bible is not the story of God's steady anger against sin – but it is the story of his steady anger against all those who reject his love and persist in their wrongdoing, disobedience and sin. 'His wrath', wrote Stephen Neill long ago, 'is no more than the *clear shining of His light*, which must go forth implacably to the destruction of all darkness . . . It is only the doctrine of the wrath of God, of His irreconcilable hostility to all evil, which makes life tolerable in such a world as ours.'[4] And yet, is it not more than that? Do we not observe that wrath is also, in a mysterious way, the *clear shining of his love*? Because God *cares* he punishes so as to bring us closer to him. His wrath is not vindictive but flows from a heart which is in pain from the wounds inflicted by a disobedient and gainsaying people. Yet, some might argue, is there not something terribly fundamentalistic and primitive in the idea of the creator of the universe paying us the dubious honour of punishing us for sins against his laws?

But this is no more extraordinary than God giving us individual attention in love and mercy. If he can show us love he can also show his displeasure with sin. Love and wrath are not incompatible opposites but twin aspects of God's attitude to those created in his image and called into a covenant relationship with him. Though he is strong and firm in his stand against sin and evil which undermine his righteousness, he is constant and firm in his love. It is not his will that any should perish but rather that they should turn to him and live. God never sends anyone to hell. We send ourselves by our refusal to accept his love and forgiveness.

PUNISHMENT AND RESTORATION

We have seen that the Old Testament is a reservoir of ideas and concepts which forms the rich and fertile background to the coming of Christ. It presents humanity's situation before God as guilty, lost and helpless. It portrays Israel as reaching out to God with the pleading arms of sacrifice, only to fall again and again. Part of the problem, indeed, lay in the character of the sacrifices themselves. Their inadequacies were plain to all. The writer to the Hebrews succinctly expresses the impersonal nature of Old Testament ritualism, 'it is impossible for the blood of bulls and goats to take away sins' (Heb. 10:4). But as that same writer fully recognised, this does not mean that the sacrificial system was wrong. Far from it; it was God-given. Nevertheless it was *provisional* and *symbolic* because it pointed ahead to its fulfilment in One who would come not as a helpless animal who could not identify with human nature, but as our representative and God's own Son.

However, the concepts of the Old Testament point to an equally deep reality; namely, the nature of sin which demands exclusion from the presence of God and warrants his punishment. It is common to western thought – and, sadly, it really is a serious deficiency in our understanding of human nature – to think of sinfulness and punishment as external to us. But not so the Scriptures. The sinfulness of sin lies in the way it corrupts everything and sets in motion moral decay. The Old Testament idea of corporate solidarity reveals an awareness of inter-personal relationships which we, now surfacing from years of subjective individualism, are only beginning to understand. 'No man is an island' sums up the Old Testament view of human life and it grasps that sin is essentially social, and seriously tragic, because it separates us from our true centre and being in God himself.

It is against this backcloth that the biblical idea of punishment must be understood. It is true, as we shall see later, that punishment has a retributive element in it. Wickedness and wrongdoing deserve punishment. But the biblical view of punishment is not solely nor entirely retributive. Punishment is given not to 'pay humanity back' but in order to restore us to God. We need only cite Israel's relationship with God to show the worth of this statement. Frequently Israel was punished by God – through plagues, illnesses and defeats – in order to bring her back home.

We are now at the heart of the dilemma concerning atonement. Atonement is not a game to God; neither is it merely an interesting theological idea. What its subsequent development in the New Testament tells us is that humanity's situation was so desperately tragic and disastrous that it required all of God to rescue us.

PART TWO

THE CROSS
EXPLORED

4

Jesus and His Cross

One could say that the moon has never been quite the same since 20 July 1969. On that historic day man invaded earth's satellite and took his first tiny but important step to conquer space. That small ball in the sky, so favoured by travellers and lovers, now symbolised the birth of a new age, one in which earthlings began to reach out to the stars.

In a much more important sense, we could say that the world has never been the same since Jesus Christ lived among us. His impact upon humanity has been quite enormous, as even the most anti-Christian spokesman would grudgingly acknowledge. It is a remarkable fact that within a few years of his death people were calling him 'Lord Jesus Christ'. These three words are very significant in describing how his followers saw him.

The human name *Jesus* takes us to a precise and specific historical and geographical location. It means 'Yahweh saves' and makes contact with the rich story of the Jewish people as it is recorded in the Old Testament. The name reminds us that we separate Jesus from his nation at our peril. The whole sweep of Old Testament history is dominated by a God who 'saves', who longs for his people to know him and take him to others. The choice of name, therefore, was far from accidental. It represents Jesus' life-work. He came to save others. But the human name reminds us that we are not talking about an alien being, like Superman, who only 'appears' to be human,

but one who is human in the fullest sense. The Jesus who
meets us in the gospels is one who shares our humanity in
its weakness. He grew from childhood to maturity, he knew
hunger and thirst, he experienced suffering – and he died. That
there were very important differences we readily acknowledge
and will return to these 'signs' of Jesus' otherness later. But
for the moment we must observe the emphasis in the gospels
upon his humanity. When he commenced his ministry his
neighbours were astonished, saying, ' "Where did this man
get these things? . . . Isn't this the carpenter? Isn't this Mary's
son . . . ?" And they took offence at him' (Mark 6:3). His
family were equally perplexed and embarrassed about the
bad publicity they were all getting (Mark 3:21).

But the application of the term *Christ* to Jesus was a second
important step, which took him from being just another
trouble-maker to a person of religious and political significance because *Christ* was a technical term meaning 'Messiah'
– the 'anointed one of God'. When ascribed to Jesus, the word
retains this meaning. So, for example, Peter preaching on the
day of Pentecost asserts that, 'God has made this Jesus . . .
both Lord and Christ' (Acts 2:36). It is not long before Christ,
when applied to Jesus, almost has the force of a surname, as in
Acts 3:6: 'In the name of Jesus Christ of Nazareth, walk.'

Did Jesus see himself as the Christ? There are scholars who
doubt this, arguing that it was the later Church who applied
this to Jesus. They point out Jesus' reticence concerning
himself (Mark 3:12; 5:43) and his preference for the enigmatic
term 'Son of Man' (Mark 8:38). It is certainly true that Jesus
displayed a remarkable coyness when it came to revealing his
person. However, this is hardly surprising when one considers
the problems associated with the term 'Christ'. The devout
Jews of Jesus' day longed for the coming of the Messiah who
would overthrow the Roman oppressors and restore Israel to
them again. Christ, consequently, was for them a political
figure and Jesus' avoidance of the term in public now becomes
understandable. However, when used by his followers Jesus
accepted the term but still urged caution (Mark 8:30).

It is very probable then that this appropriation of the term
'Son of Man' was a brilliant innovative idea. Although more

scholarly ink has been spilt over this than perhaps any other topic in recent research, most scholars believe that Jesus drew upon Daniel 7:13 for his inspiration. In that mysterious passage Daniel records that after a great number of kingdoms passed before the prophet: 'I looked, and there before me was one like a son of man, coming with the clouds of heaven. He approached the Ancient of Days and was led into his presence. He was given authority, glory and sovereign power; all peoples, nations and men of every language worshipped him. His dominion is an everlasting dominion that will not pass away.'

The prophet's concentration was not upon an individual who is the 'son of man' but upon the nation. It is a collective term, in other words. Written at a time when the people of God were facing persecution and discouragement, the prophecy looked ahead to when the humiliation of God's people would be followed by glory.

Jesus adopts this collective term and uses it in connection with humiliation and glory: 'He began to teach them that the Son of Man must suffer many things' (Mark 8:31); 'If anyone is ashamed of me and my words . . . the Son of Man will be ashamed of him when he comes in his father's glory' (Mark 8:38).

Jesus, therefore, did not deny that he was the Messiah but he approached it by a different route. He was aware that he was God's chosen one, but to come out with it just like that was not appropriate for the conditions. It is ironic that following Jesus' resurrection the Church preferred to use such terms as 'Christ', 'Son', 'Son of God' and 'Lord' instead of 'Son of Man', which fell into disuse because it was not explicit enough to proclaim Jesus' status.

The third term, *Lord*, is even more startling in its application to the man, Jesus. We must not think that the ancient world was totally incredulous in its approach to things. Neither the Jews with their fierce monotheism, nor the Greeks with their love of knowledge, went around divinising every interesting messianic figure. There was probably as much scepticism as today – indeed, the deep interest in all things religious was combined with a healthy examination of beliefs (Acts 17:16–34). The application of 'Lord', then, to this obscure

Galilean carpenter who was crucified just like another criminal, was the most extraordinary thing of all – because 'Lord' was tantamount to saying 'Jesus is *God*'. 'Lord' is Peter's favourite word for Jesus and he knew what he was doing by applying this to the crucified Jesus. He was saying that the claims of Jesus Christ took precedence over everything else. He alone was worthy of worship; he alone was to be followed and obeyed; he alone was the way to God the Father. His resurrection had shown clearly that he was God's Saviour and vindicated his ministry. 'Let all Israel be assured of this: God has made this Jesus, whom you crucified, both Lord and Christ,' preached Peter (Acts 2:36). Paul's confession was no less sweeping: 'for us there is but one God, the Father, from whom all things came and for whom we live; and there is but one Lord, Jesus Christ, through whom all things came and through whom we live' (1 Cor. 8:6). The attribution of the mediation of the whole creation to Jesus just a mere twenty years or so after his crucifixion is quite staggering. It was a stupendous claim which took the early Church into a collision course with the secular authorities.

So with the description 'Lord Jesus Christ', which was the first-century confession, we see the transition from regarding Jesus as a man to seeing him as God's chosen one, who through his life, ministry, death and resurrection is the only hope of humanity's existence and salvation. But why, we must ask? Why is this mysterious man from Galilee chosen to be the recipient of such exalted titles? And why do people regard him even today as the 'way, the truth and the life' and are willing to go to their own deaths for his sake?[1]

The answer to these questions lies in the meaning of his death. There can be little doubt that the first Christians would not have proclaimed Jesus as Lord unless he was first their Saviour. These were not men and women interested in theological speculation, which they kept removed from the rest of life – of course not. Meeting Jesus changed their whole existence. Some of them had been healed by him, others had embraced his teaching – but all of them regarded him as 'Saviour'. He had given them faith, hope and meaning. We must now trace the steps that led them to call him Saviour.

TEACHING ABOUT THE KINGDOM

The central thrust of Jesus' teaching was the kingdom of God. There was nothing new about this. The Old Testament prophets expected the coming of God's kingdom. Some saw it in terms of blessing, like Obadiah; others, like Amos, viewed it in terms of judgment. What was common to Jewish expectation was an identification of God's kingdom with the earthly house of David. Jesus introduced a number of novel concepts into his teaching about the kingdom. First, it transcends earthly ideas. It was God's kingdom which Jesus proclaimed, not humanity's. Furthermore, it was a universal kingdom and was not merely limited to the Jews. It was open to all and was dependent upon God's initiative and grace.

Secondly, the character of Jesus' teaching about the kingdom ran directly against the teaching of his day, which was strongly legalistic. Jesus proclaimed a loving heavenly Father who cared for the lowly, the needy and the oppressed. Middleton Murray once remarked, aptly, 'The secret of the Kingdom of God was that there was no King – only a Father.'[2] This paradox contains a real truth. The king proclaimed by Jesus was a Father who wanted all people everywhere to return to him. The fatherhood of God is seen in its most profound and amazing form in the way Jesus addressed his heavenly Father. He called him 'Abba'. Research has shown Jesus' unprecedented usage here. 'Abba' and 'Imma' are the Jewish equivalents of our 'daddy' and 'mummy' and no person before Jesus ever addressed the creator of the universe in this fashion.[3] Surely this is testimony to his sense of divine Sonship.

But let us not fall into the common mistake of thinking that Jesus went around teaching that all people may lay claim to a natural sonship. The German theologian Adolf von Harnack made the fatherhood of God and the brotherhood of man the two central tenets of this theology. But it finds no support in Jesus' teaching. It is true that we may in a guarded sense claim God as Father because he has created us and called us into existence (Eph. 3:15) but no one has an inalienable right to call God his Father except through Jesus.

So Jesus states: 'No-one knows the Father except the Son and those to whom the Son chooses to reveal him' (Matt. 11:27). Thus, drawing deeply upon the Old Testament Scriptures and illuminating his teaching with arresting pictures from nature, as well as from life, he spoke of a God who longs for men to find and know him. The cluster of parables in Matthew 13 describes in various ways the wonder of the kingdom and how worthwhile the search is.

Thirdly, the key to the kingdom is Jesus. This took Jesus to his cross. The blasphemy to the Jews was not Jesus' miracles or his revolutionary teaching. It was not even the irritating digs he made about the blindness of the scribes and Pharisees. The blasphemy of Jesus consisted in his arrogance, as they saw it, in making himself the key to the kingdom. The signs of the kingdom were already there in his miracles. When John the Baptist asked for proofs that Jesus was the chosen one, Jesus sent back the message: 'The blind receive sight, the lame walk, those who have leprosy are cured, the deaf hear, the dead are raised, and the good news is preached to the poor' (Matt. 11:5). These are signs which people neglect at their peril. The refusal of the Pharisees to recognise that God was at work in Jesus met with the stern words: 'If I drive out demons by the finger of God, then the kingdom of God has come to you' (Luke 11:20). Jesus, then, manifests the kingdom in his ministry, teaching that to know him is to know the king.

THE KINGDOM AND WORKS

It is sometimes asked, Why is it that there is such a discrepancy between the teaching of Paul and Jesus? Paul scarcely mentions the kingdom and for him salvation consists in faith, whereas Jesus preached the kingdom, at the heart of which was not faith but works.

At first sight there does appear to be a great difference of approach. 'Not everyone who says to me, "Lord, Lord", will enter the kingdom of heaven, but only he who does the will of my Father who is in heaven' (Matt. 7:21, see v. 26). He also spoke of 'rewards and punishment' (Matt.

19:23ff) which seem a far cry from the emphasis later in the
New Testament that we can do nothing to inherit salvation
– but that all proceeds from grace (Eph. 2:8).

But the difference is more apparent than real. Jesus did
not preach good deeds as much as obedience: 'Everyone who
hears these words of mine and puts them into practice is like
a wise man . . . ' (Matt. 7:24) and faith is inextricably linked
with obedience. To listen to this man from Galilee and treat
his words as if they were the words of God was the way of
faith. To leave everything behind, even your family and your
unburied father (Matt. 8:18–22), is not simply obedience but
the obedience of faith. And Jesus rewards the faith which
sees him as Lord. So to the believing centurion, who is
content to rely on the word of Jesus alone, Jesus responds,
'I tell you the truth, I have not found anyone in Israel
with such great faith.' And this faith is also the basis of
the healing of the servant. 'Go! It will be done just as you
believed it would' (Matt. 8:10,13).

But linked with faith is the character of 'repentance'. Jesus
bids men enter the kingdom, but before they do so a condition
must be fulfilled – they must repent of their sins and their
past ways of living. John the Baptist preached the gospel
of repentance before Jesus began his ministry and it forms
the backcloth to the preaching of the kingdom. In many
ways 'repentance' is a very poor translation of a very rich
word. Repentance smacks of 'doing penance' and saying
sorry for our misdeeds. But the Greek word *metanoia* really
means 'to think again' or to 'have second thoughts' and it
implies a complete change of mind and outlook. When Jesus
preached, 'Repent, for the kingdom of heaven is near,' he was
demanding of people a complete turnaround – not just a moral
change but a revolution whereby they should become wholly
other than what they were. Unlike the Pharisees of his day,
who concentrated upon externals in moral behaviour, Jesus
interiorised the demands of God. 'You have heard that it
was said . . . "Do not murder" . . . But I tell you that anyone
who is angry with his brother will be subject to judgment . . .
You have heard that it was said, "Do not commit adultery."
But I tell you that anyone who looks at a woman lustfully

has already committed adultery with her in his heart' (Matt.
5:21–2, 27–8). In these and many other sayings Jesus rammed
home the point that sin and evil well up from the very heart
of each human being and that salvation must begin within.

THE KINGDOM AND THE CROSS

At what point was Jesus consciously aware of the inevitability
of the cross? This is far from being an academic question
because the meaning of the cross swings on this issue. For
example, if we treat the cross as a tragedy which took Jesus
by surprise and crushed a promising social and political
movement, we shall not have an atonement doctrine. We
shall treat the New Testament's teaching about the cross as
a Christian cover-up – as an attempt to justify the ministry of
Jesus. This, in fact, is the consequence of Albert Schweitzer's
theory of Christ's death. Jesus, according to Schweitzer, had
proclaimed the kingdom of God. He knew that its coming
must be preceded by messianic affliction; and so, to force
its coming and to spare his followers, he went to Jerusalem
and deliberately engineered his own death. He succeeded in
bringing to pass his own death but failed to bring in the
kingdom. 'The wheel rolls onward and the mangled body
of the one immeasurably great Man, who was strong enough
to think of himself as the spiritual ruler of mankind and to
bend history to his purpose, is hanging upon it still. That
is His victory and His reign.'[4]

But such an interpretation of history is no more than a
clever theologising of the ministry of Jesus, and only achieves
plausibility by virtually ignoring the testimony of the gospels.

From one point of view, we could say that the shadow
of the cross was there from the start of his life. 'You are
to give him the name Jesus [saviour], because he will save
his people from their sins' were the words of the angel in
Matthew 1:21. True, there is no mention of a cross here,
but then again the angel is not giving to Jesus the role of
teacher or social worker or guru, but of delivering people
from bondage. In that sense the shadow is there. So P. T.
Forsyth states: 'The Cross was not simply a fate awaiting

Christ in the future; it pervaded subliminally His holy Person. He was born for the Cross. It was His genius, His destiny.'[5] But in his 'incarnation' (God becoming a person) we may trace the cross-shaped pattern of his ministry. We have to confess that evangelical theology is generally weak on the subject of Jesus' life. We generally emphasise the last week of Jesus' ministry so much that his teaching, his miracles, his way of life and the movement to the cross become just an introduction to an atoning death. Surely this is a mistake. His life and death are one and the incarnation, if it is anything at all, is Jesus' deliberate choosing to live out the cross in his life and to take the sin, the sickness, the injustice and all the hurt of humanity and to nail them to the tree.

But we must tackle the issue more directly. Is it possible that Jesus never intended the cross to happen and that the references to his death for others are *vaticinia ex eventu*, that is, statements read back into the story of Jesus? We have to say, 'Yes, it is possible – but it is highly unlikely,' for the following reasons. First, it is assuming that some theological geniuses in the very early Church decided that a highly successful religion could be concocted if the death of their leader were dressed up as an atoning sacrifice. As we saw in the opening chapter, this would not have dawned on any religious entrepreneur as the best way of going about things! No, this is most improbable. Secondly, and most importantly, the references to the cross and his impending sacrifice are too numerous for us to sweep them aside in a cavalier fashion. Let us glance at a number of them.

Teaching about the kingdom is replaced by the cross

From Caesarea Philippi onwards Jesus started to preach the cross. It is not a question of Jesus changing direction, we must note, or the kingdom being ignored. Rather the cross became the burning focus of the kingdom, its splendid and terrible centre. Caesarea Philippi was a turning point in the disciples' understanding of Jesus' ministry. We cannot be sure when Jesus himself became consciously sure of the necessity of the cross, although it is likely that he saw it coming quite early on in his ministry. But at Caesarea Philippi Jesus disclosed something to his disciples that was disturbing and wholly new in their understanding of him. It is probable that most of them regarded him as God's chosen one but it was not consciously brought out into the open until Jesus asked: 'Who do people say I am?' After receiving some answers, Jesus asked them, 'But what about you? . . . Who do you say I am?' Peter's reply may have surprised himself: 'You are the Christ' (Mark 8:29).

This great confession is followed in Mark's gospel by no less than five explicit references to his impending suffering and fate (8:31; 9:12, 31; 10:33–4; 10:45). Jesus in Mark does not say that he has to suffer, as if it were simply there in the future, but that he 'must' suffer – that is, there was a pressing necessity. Suffering and death came with the job of saving others. Here in these verses, and especially in 10:45, we hear the echo of the suffering servant in Isaiah 53.

'For even the Son of Man did not come to be served, but to serve and to give his life as a ransom for many' Mark 10:45.

'He poured out his soul unto death, and was numbered with the transgressors. For he bore the sin of many . . . ' Isa. 53:12.

However, Professor Morna Hooker disagrees. She does not believe that Jesus consciously thought of himself as the suffering servant and considers that the verse may be understood without reference to the suffering of the mysterious figure in Isaiah 53.[6] However, a number of facts make Professor Hooker's thesis unconvincing. First, the writers of the gospels allude to Isaiah 53 elsewhere. Matthew 8:17 quotes Isaiah 53:4, 'He took up our infirmities and carried our diseases', as being fulfilled in the ministry of Jesus. Luke 22:37 applies Isaiah 53:12, 'he was numbered with the transgressors', to the coming fate of Jesus. Such verses suggest that the gospel writers found it natural to relate the incredibly apt passage in Isaiah to Jesus. Secondly, 1 Peter 2:21ff shows the author

writing to persecuted Christians in Asia Minor drawing exten-
sively upon Isaiah 53 as a commentary upon the suffering
and death of Jesus. Thirdly, is it likely that such writers
saw the extraordinary relevance of the passage in Isaiah
before Jesus did? It hardly seems likely, and I for one am
convinced that Jesus, aware of the inevitable cross – which
he could have avoided if he wished – looming up, drew upon
the symbolism and poetic riches of the suffering servant to
make plain that his death was for others. Other passages of
Scripture point in this direction, too. The Last Supper, for
example, was not a theatrical ending to a good life but was a
commemoration with theological meaning of great depth. It
is generally accepted by scholars that the supper which Jesus
shared with his disciples shortly before his death was a 'kind
of' Passover meal. There were two factors which ruled it out
as a typical Jewish Passover. First, Jesus held it on the day
before the Passover (see Mark 15:42) and, secondly, no lamb is
mentioned. This latter is a most striking omission because this
was a central feature of the Jewish ritual at the time of Jesus,
representing as it did God's deliverance from the hands of the
Egyptians when the angel of wrath 'passed over' the Israelites.
The blood of that first lamb had been painted on the lintels
of the doors as a sign of the covenant people, and ever since
the people of Israel had eaten the flesh as a commemoration
of their salvation. It would be foolish, then, to deny that the
story of the Last Supper is of the greatest significance in
understanding the mind of Jesus shortly before his death.
The bread was taken and Jesus said, 'Take it; this is my body'
(Mark 14:22). We must leave aside, for the time being, the
interesting question about whether the bread 'represented',
'means' or literally *was* his body. 'This' is obviously the
bread in his hands and it is most likely that we have here
an acted parable, similar to many prophetic actions in the
Old Testament. Using more than a symbol, Jesus anticipated
the bloody actions of the following day when his broken body
would, indeed, be life for humankind and made available for
them. Then the cup was taken and Jesus said, 'This is my
blood of the covenant, which is poured out for many.' The
images awakened by such words as 'blood', 'covenant' and

'for many' force the sacrificial system of the Old Testament to our attention. 'Blood' may echo the blood of the Passover victim, through whom the people of God were saved. If this is so, Jesus might have been referring to himself as one who delivers all people from a more dreadful fate and his cross as a 'new Passover'. Or, the reference could be to the blood of the covenant sprinkled on altar and people after Moses was given the law (Exod. 24:6–8). Whatever the most dominant influence upon the mind of Jesus, there can be little doubt that Jesus saw himself as a sacrifice for others and his body and blood as being offered up for men.

Thus a very strong 'sacramental' colouring is discerned in the passage. Jesus does not invite his disciples to eat his flesh or to drink his blood – nothing could be more repugnant to Jews, who were taught by the Old Testament Scriptures to regard blood as sacred and not to be consumed – but to eat bread and drink wine as symbolising his life surrendered for many. The bread remains bread and the wine remains wine but they are now charged with a greater significance, power and meaning. They are not *just* bread and wine any longer.

Although we shall take up the meaning of the cross for Jesus in the next chapter, we see that it is impossible to dismiss it as being irrelevant to Jesus' ministry. It is there, we have argued, at the centre of his understanding of the kingdom and we make Jesus more mysterious, not more intelligible, if we insist that his followers read it back into their master's career. Jesus did not come with a 'theology' of the cross. He was himself the theology and in his life and teaching the cross lay latent and only became totally explicit after his death.

WHO WAS THIS MAN?

It is now time to tackle a problem hinted at the beginning of this chapter. It is true that the followers of Jesus and the people regarded Jesus as a man. Perhaps at the start it did not dawn on anyone to question this. Even when he did mighty works (and remember that 'Jesus as a healer' belongs not only to the earliest traditions but was the witness of contemporary secular writers) they were amazed, saying, 'Where did this man get these things?' (Mark 6:2). But it is clear from the gospel narratives that Jesus did not fit ordinary categories. True: he was 'one of us' but his way of talking about God, his teaching, his poise, his attitude to life, his miracles, his love for others, his sympathy for their needs, his understanding of his role – all of this, and more, disturbed his followers and forced them to ask: 'What kind of man is this?' (Mark 4:41).

Gradually, then, his followers began to think the unthinkable – that their dear friend, leader and master was, in some shape or form, God! Jews, with their strong doctrine of monotheism, were not in the habit of ascribing divinity to every Tom, Dick or Harry. Unless we grasp the extreme unusualness of their action, we will not be able to understand the impact of Jesus. But over a period of time their understanding of him changed from that of a man, a teacher and a healer, to 'the Christ, the Son of the living God' (Matt. 16:16). Of course, this development was only completed after the resurrection, which blazoned forth the specialness of Jesus in no uncertain terms.

HUMAN AND DIVINE

With these two words the followers of Jesus down the ages have confessed the uniqueness of Jesus of Nazareth. He is incomparable in his humanity and matchless in his divinity. We need both to make sense of his ministry. If he is just one of us – lost in trespasses and sins – he is no more than any other messianic figure in history who has tried to rescue humanity from the alienation within. The saviour of men has to come from God's side to have any authority. As the television personality Kenneth Robinson once said: 'Without the divinity of Christ, his teaching has no more authority than a landlady's list of "don'ts" for the bathroom.' If Jesus is not in any real way 'God', the bridge is broken at the other end. But a saviour has to be human as well. How can there be any real salvation if the redeemer does not represent us in our sin and evil? A totally divine saviour cannot save and neither can one who is totally human. The one because he cannot represent and the other because he has no right.

Of course, we have to acknowledge that we shall not in this life understand fully the mystery of this person who is for us both God and human. The task of theology in every generation is to think out the meaning of this conviction that God was incarnate in Jesus. This may, indeed, be just mere rhetoric to some. How can you know, they ask, that Jesus is who you claim? The answer, for most of us, is through experience – through meeting him ourselves as the one who saves us from our sins and enters into the loneliness of our existence. Philip Toynbee, reviewer, writer and struggler after truth, expressed it movingly in this way: 'I call myself a Christian because I discern in the New Testament a man whose life, death and central teaching penetrates more deeply into the mysterious reality of our condition than anyone or anything else has ever done. In the Gospels, Acts, and the Epistles, I find a total view of what man is, of what he could be and ought to be, which evokes a response in me such as no other writings have ever done.'[7] Such is the impact of the central figure in Scripture. But is it necessary to believe in the virgin birth?

To be sure, there are Christians who do not accept the virgin birth. They view it as a theological construction on the part of Matthew and Luke to explain that Jesus comes from God. The Bishop of Durham in 1984 attracted national attention by dismissing the stories of the virgin birth as 'fairy tales'. The last thing I want to do is to impugn the scholarship, sincerity and Christian commitment of those who cannot accept the virginal conception of Jesus but we must not, equally, be bullied or press-ganged into dismissing an article of faith which has been central to the story of Jesus from the earliest days. As I believe this is important for our study of the incarnation, let us consider some of the arguments from both sides.

Professor Wolfhart Pannenberg believes that the virgin birth is an aetiological legend, that is: its reason (*aetia*) or purpose is to explain how a certain state of affairs has been reached. In this case, argues Pannenberg, the virgin birth explains how Jesus was called the Son of God. That Jesus, as the Son of God, was not born like other men would have seemed highly plausible to people of the Hellenistic period,

'After all, the pagan myths also recorded the divine origins of important men and great heroes.' Pannenberg advances two further points. First, that only two writings in the New Testament, Matthew and Luke, appear to know about it. Secondly, the assertion of Jesus' virginal conception seems to militate against his true manhood: 'Nor can we see any longer why Jesus as Son of God should come into the world in a different way from anyone else.'[8]

A number of points can be made from the more traditional side of Christianity. We can readily concede that the virgin birth is not as central to the Christian faith as the resurrection. But Pannenberg's argument from frequency in the New Testament, if taken as a conclusive tool, may have repercussions beyond the virgin birth. For example, the Church is not a familiar concept in the New Testament – and the Trinity is never mentioned. Furthermore, should we not also on this basis dismiss the accounts of the ascension in Luke 24 and Acts 1 as aetiological legends, explaining how he returned home?

But what about the link with pagan mythology? Dr Alan Richardson argues that pagan mythology is 'full of legends of a supernatural hero born of intercourse between a god and a human woman. But this is scarcely a virgin birth and there is no real parallel to the story of the birth of Christ in pagan literature.'[9] Furthermore, Professor Pannenberg does not explain how Jewish writers, who would have been revolted by the idea of physical intercourse between a god and a woman, so cheerfully adopted such an idea. I find this objection particularly telling. I can understand an aetiological legend developing well away from Jewish soil, but Matthew and Luke (especially Matthew) are intensely Jewish. The idea of the Son of the most holy, transcendent Lord of the universe taking up his abode in a stable, born of a woman, would be scarcely credible to a Jewish writer unless he was convinced *it happened*.

Last of all, what about the argument that there is a theological purpose in all this, that the intention is to explain that Jesus is the Son of God? The fact of the matter is that both Matthew and Luke tell the story in a matter-of-fact way, they offer no explanations and draw no conclusions. The gospel accounts 'simply relate an historical happening and leave the matter without any form of explanation'.[10] But is it, in fact, the case that to reject the virgin birth is much better theologically? Are we then left with a real man and a real redeemer? I don't believe this is so. Rather, we are left with further problems. If Jesus were the child of Mary and Joseph, wherein lies his divinity? How does he acquire it? Are we not led to espouse a form of adoptionism, which the Church rejected long, long ago, whereby Jesus the man, through some inexplicable process, was given the Holy Spirit in full measure and made the Son of God? Is it, in fact, the case that to accept the virgin birth leads to a diminution of Jesus' personhood? I really cannot see how this is the case. What the virgin birth protects is not an emasculated personhood but a sinless one. It brings together two wonderful insights: that Jesus through Mary is fully human – he was born a baby, born of our flesh, he was poor and learned obedience – and through the seed of the Holy Spirit, this Jesus is truly the Son of God. No: we can't explain it fully. But what I find convincing about the story is that long before the Church got around to formulating the two-nature theory of the person of Christ, here in the simple narrative of the infancy story we are given insights which anticipate later conclusions.

5

The Cross in
the Earliest Preaching

In this chapter we are going to examine the place of the death of Jesus in the teaching of his followers and consider the Acts of the Apostles and the letters of Paul.

Only an extremely blinkered sceptic would refuse to acknowledge that Jesus' life and death triggered off 'something'. There have been many great teachers in history who have been commemorated because of what they have contributed to human destiny. Jesus figures among such men and women – but 'Jesus as a teacher' does not even begin to explain him. He started a missionary movement which exists to proclaim that the true meaning of life is to be found in him; that his death is the means to life; that he is Saviour and Lord; that eternal life commences when he is followed; that he forgives sins and bestows the Holy Spirit. This is at the heart of the earliest preaching.

THE PREACHING IN ACTS

Professor C. H. Dodd excited students of the New Testament some years ago when he suggested that the early preaching in Acts, which he called 'the *kerygma*', had a common shape to it which emphasised that:

i. The prophecies are now fulfilled and the new age has dawned.

ii. Christ is born of the seed of David.

iii. He died according to Scripture, to deliver us from this age.

iv. He was buried.

v. He rose on the third day according to Scripture.

vi. He is exalted at the right hand of God, as Son of God and Lord of the quick and the dead.

vii. He will come again as Saviour and Judge.[1]

I think that Dodd is substantially correct about this and it shows the way the pattern of the earliest preaching imprinted itself on the mind of the Church and was recorded by the writer of Acts years after the events. However, from the point of view of our more precise interest in the preaching of the cross, having looked very closely at six passages in Acts where a sermon outline is given (chapters 2, 3, 4, 10, 13, 26), it seems that five significant things are emphasised about the cross. Let us consider the first passage as our example and then go on to look at the others. In Acts 2:22–39 the apostle Peter makes five points.

A. The life and character of *the man* Jesus of Nazareth – he was blameless before man and God (v. 22).

B. He was *delivered up* – that is, he was the innocent victim of a plot but it was according to God's *plan* (v. 23).

C. He was *crucified* (v. 23).

D. God *raised* him up (v. 32).

E. He was *proclaimed* as Saviour and Lord (v. 36).

Placing the passages side by side, we can see the astonishing agreement:

The Man	Character	Plan	Crucified	Raised	Proclaimed
Acts 2, Jesus of Nazareth (22)	A man. Mighty signs and wonders (22)	Definite plan and foreknowledge of God (23)	You crucified and killed (23)	But God raised him up (24)	Lord and Christ (36)
Acts 3, Jesus of Nazareth (6) Servant (13)	Holy and Righteous (14)	Prophets foretold (18)	You delivered up and denied (13)	God raised from the dead (15)	Author of life (15) His name (6, 16)
Acts 4, Jesus of Nazareth (10)	Holy (30)	By the mouth of our father David, did say (25)	You crucified (10)	God raised from the dead (10)	No other name (12) Healer (30)
Acts 10, Jesus of Nazareth (38)	Doing good and healing (38)	Word sent to Israel (36)	They put him to death by hanging from a tree (39)	God raised on the third day (40)	Good news of peace by Jesus (36) Lord of all (36) One ordained by God (42)
Acts 13, Jesus of Nazareth (23)	Nothing deserving death (28)	God promised a saviour (23)	They asked Pilate to have him killed (28)	But God raised from the dead (30)	A saviour (23) Good news (32) Forgiveness of sins (38)
Acts 26, Jesus of Nazareth (9)		Prophets and Moses said would come to pass (22)	Christ must suffer (23)	First to rise from the dead (23)	Darkness to light (18) Forgiveness (18) Light to Jews and Gentiles (23)

Looking at these passages, then, we can see the outlines of a gospel which was indeed 'Good News' to the first believers and to those who found faith through their preaching. We note the emphasis upon Jesus – Jesus of Nazareth (2:22); this Jesus (2:32, 36); his servant Jesus (3:13); Jesus Christ (2:38); 'your holy servant Jesus' (4:27, 30). As we might have expected from the earliest preaching, we discover here a primitive Christology. They are working from Jesus' humanity rather than his divinity, and the human-ness of the Messiah is emphasised. Attention is paid to the character of the life of Jesus. With confidence Peter was able to preach that Jesus was a man 'accredited by God' (2:22) and that he was 'Holy and Righteous' (3:14). Although this is, as yet, an unshaped doctrine of Jesus, we find in this preaching the elements of much deeper teaching. Jesus is the Son of David (2:25–30); he is the author of life (3:15); he is the Anointed One (4:26); he is the Christ (2:38); he is Lord and Christ (2:36).

The last verse cited has been greatly discussed because of its claims for Jesus. It used to be said that the statement that God 'made' him both Lord and Christ smacked of adoptionism – that is, before his resurrection Jesus was merely God's faithful servant and after it God adopted him as Lord and Christ. It is much more likely that it means 'vindicated'; that is, the resurrection, far from making him Lord and Christ, demonstrated it in power. It proclaimed that Jesus of Nazareth, all along, was God's Anointed One. But the application of 'Lord' to Jesus is of the greatest importance because it gave him a status and dignity which could only be construed as 'divine' because the term Lord (*kurios*) was normally applied to God himself.

The other points we can only mention briefly. The first preachers referred to Christ being 'delivered up'. The frequency of this phrase suggests that it was used greatly in the early Church to drive home the point that Jesus' death was planned by God. The crime of Jesus' death is laid squarely at the feet of the Jewish people (2:23; 3:14; 4:27). There may be in this a sublime irony – that Jesus was crucified for a so-called crime against God, namely blasphemy, yet his accusers 'murdered' God's Chosen One, an even greater blasphemy. It is important to observe that this accusation against the Jews gives no encouragement for anti-Semitism. The first disciples were themselves Jews and it is very likely that they were laying the crime at the feet of disobedient men who had the chance to accept the claims of Jesus but wilfully refused. A 'representative' aspect therefore emerges. In an important way they represent the whole of disobedient humanity. Their crime was also our crime.

But even if the death of Jesus was a terrible crime, the *kerygma* stressed the plan and foreknowledge of God in it all. The first disciples, being Jews, saw it as all of a piece with the history and destiny of the Jewish people. It is there in Peter's emphasis upon David (2:25ff) and it is also there in Stephen's defence before the high priest (ch. 7). In his speech Stephen argued that the whole of Old Testament history pointed ahead to the coming of Christ. The rejection of Jesus was typical of Jewish stubbornness and wilfulness. Aptly, Stephen accuses them of having 'uncircumcised hearts and ears' (7:51).

The fourth element in the *kerygma* is the resurrection. It is sobering to compare modern preaching with its occurrence in Acts. There is no half-heartedness here: the passages throb with the excitement, joy and victory of the resurrection. Indeed, it may be said to be the dominant doctrine in Acts. This is precisely what we should expect. We are not surprised that there is no carefully formulated doctrine of the cross yet. The cross is preached firmly and clearly, certainly, but as befits a situation where all would know of the death of the carpenter from Nazareth, the resurrection becomes the firm basis of the preaching and gives it conviction and confidence. But that is not all. The resurrection is not merely the ground of Jesus' ministry, it is also the sign that God is ushering in his kingdom. The resurrection is the start of the 'last days'. It is clear that because of this most Christians at that time thought they were living in the last days. We cannot blame them for assuming that the end of all things was at hand, but in another way they were quite correct – Jesus' rising to life was the commencement of a new age which would end with his coming in judgment and victory.

Thus the last element in the preaching was to offer an invitation to accept the claims of the crucified Lord. The 'good news' included two aspects: the forgiveness of sins through repentance and faith, and the Holy Spirit being given after baptism to those who believe.

While, then, the preaching about the cross in Acts is very rudimentary, what we find of significance is that it is Jesus Christ who is preached as one who confronts men and women as Saviour and Lord and demands their allegiance. It is left to other writers and teachers to work out the message of the cross.

PAUL – 'WE PREACH CHRIST CRUCIFIED'

Paul was the entrepreneur of the apostolic Church. A man of great energy, ability and resourcefulness, he, more than perhaps any other apostolic figure, made the tiny Christian body a force to be reckoned with. His letters, written between AD 47–62 to numerous churches which he had either founded or was instrumental in developing, reveal him to be a caring and anxious pastor and teacher. We will not find in them fully rounded statements of Christian belief. If there is such a thing as Pauline theology, it has to be gleaned from the letters which, in the main, deal with pastoral matters. Although his concerns were of course theological, Paul was not an 'ivory towered' theologian. His theology flowed from a passion for Christ. This was the driving force of his ministry: 'I have been crucified with Christ and I no longer live, but Christ lives in me' (Gal. 2:20). Paul's theology, said A. M. Hunter, 'is the theology of a converted man'.[2] He had encountered Christ on the Damascus Road and life could never be the same again. The Nazarene, whose followers he had spent years persecuting, was thereafter the absorbing centre of his life. This Christ was uplifted in the most exalted terms. He was not only the Son of David, he was also Son of God (Rom. 1:3–4), Lord (1 Cor. 12:3), head of the Church (Col. 1:18), the image of the invisible God (Col. 1:15) and the agent of creation (1 Cor. 8:6). What is perhaps even more remarkable, this Jesus Christ, together with the Holy Spirit, is part of a Godhead – the shadowy outline of a Godhead that would later be called the Trinity.

The heartbeat of Paul's teaching was that through the cross and resurrection of Jesus Christ, God was busily engaged in reconciling the world to himself. The task of Paul and every Christian was to be an ambassador crying out the message of the cross to a needy world and proclaiming, 'Be reconciled to God' (2 Cor. 5:20–1). So, while we must be careful not to separate the resurrection from the death of Jesus, it must be said that the cross was *the* decisive event in Paul's theology. It is a window into the character of God's love and the only way to interpret God's revelation in the Old Testament. It changed Paul's attitude to three important things.

The cross changed Paul's idea of God

Paul, as a Jew, would have grown up with a strong sense that the God of the whole earth had chosen the people of Israel to be a holy nation. Most probably, before his conversion his concept of God would have been that of a stern, just deity whose demands in his law were inexorable. He was a God to be adored, feared and worshipped. One would hardly think of such a God as being in a warm, personal, fatherly relationship with his people. Although there was much in the Old Testament to encourage this belief, the accent fell upon his greatness, awfulness and holiness. With this extreme awe went a fear of his judgment.

Paul's doctrine of God underwent a significant change when he became a Christian. First, to the rightful attention to God's justice, holiness and sovereignty there was added an emphasis upon his character as a loving and merciful God. He learnt that God's glory was to be seen in the face of Jesus Christ: 'For God, who said, "Let light shine out of darkness," made his light shine in our hearts to give us the light of the knowledge of the glory of God in the face of Christ' (2 Cor. 4:6). This striking linking of the two creations – the creation of the world and the new creation

– shows how Paul's understanding of God was deepened by his encounter with Jesus. He now worshipped a God with a human face.

But he also took into his conception of God an understanding that in Christ God had come to save humanity. Now, it is a fact that Jews believed that God was a Saviour, but normal Jewish theology believed that God 'saved' by working through intermediaries such as the prophets. Not so Paul now. In Christ God has made himself known as the saving God. Paul did not drive a wedge between God and Christ, as if Christ does something on humanity's behalf and offers it to God. On the contrary, God does something through Christ and offers it to men and women. Paul's statement that 'God was reconciling the world to himself in Christ' (2 Cor. 5:19) speaks of his discovery that God was personally involved in the cross and resurrection of his Son. The incarnation of Christ was the activity of a 'down-to-earth' God. This, as we shall see later, is of the greatest importance in understanding how the New Testament views the death of Jesus.

It changed Paul's understanding of sin

The thinking and experience of the pre-Christian Paul was dominated by three awful tyrants who held sway over him. Although Christ had broken 'the power of cancelled sin and set the prisoner free', the attention Paul gives to the power of sin, the bondage of the law and slavery to demonic forces shows that he saw them as central to the experience of everybody.

The power of sin

For Paul, sin was the tyrant through whose rule all other enemies gained their entrance into the human race. We are 'sold to sin' (Rom. 7:14). Paul's concentration was not so much upon sins as upon sin. It is not merely that we do evil deeds but that sin dwells in us, compelling us to do things that we would rather not do. Sin reigns over all and no one can free him or herself from its tyranny. Broadly speaking, Paul's argument in Romans 7 is from his own experience but he is asking in it: 'Is this not your experience also? Why is it that our ability to do good things is so weak and our desire to do evil things is so strong? Why cannot we conquer sin?' But sin reigns and results in a threefold bondage:

1. It results in *death*. 'The wages of sin is death' (Rom. 6:23). This is a frequent note in Paul's letters and is part of God's condemnation of sinners. It would not have been in Paul's mind to distinguish between spiritual death and physical death, although we would want to do so. For him it was all of one piece, although the spiritual side would have been uppermost in his thinking – sin's legacy was eternal death and, therefore, separation from a holy God.

2. But it also resulted in the *destruction* of the relationship between God and people. People without God were all alone in the world, separated from their true existence as spiritual beings made for God's embrace. Using modern terminology, there is a strong sense of existential despair in Paul's description of people separated from the family of God. He refers to them as being 'dead in your transgressions and sins', 'foreigners . . . without hope and without God in the world' (Eph. 2:1, 12).

3. Finally, it results in *despair*. We cannot overcome the power of sin. Romans 7 testifies to Paul's frustration as a helpless sinner trapped in the web of his own choosing and discovering that sin had found him out. In a real way we 'know' ourselves in our sin because, as well as finding out about human weakness, and our own in particular, what we also discover is that sin is not at all external to us – though most people assume that this is the case – but that it dwells within us. We *are* sin or, as Malcolm Muggeridge once put it, 'I am the dark little dungeon of my own darkness.'

The bondage of the law

By the law Paul did not mean the traditions of the scribes
which Jesus so trenchantly criticised, but the Torah of the
Jews enshrined in the Old Testament covenant, which had
at its heart the ten commandments. The Torah (law) was
an Israelite's greatest treasure. We must not think of it as a
compilation of legalist rules, of 'do's and don'ts'. It certainly
included these in some measure, but the heart of the Torah
was the covenant between God and men and women. The
Torah made of Israel a nation, and it was believed that the
keeping of the Torah would lead to a pure and holy life that
would bring glory to God. So Psalm 119 extols the Torah:

> Blessed are they whose ways are blameless,
>   who walk according to the law [Torah] of the land.

> (v. 1)

The Torah, in fact, was like a road – it kept a person from
falling into sin:

> How can a young man keep his way pure?
>   By living according to your word [Torah].

> (v. 9)

The Torah, indeed, was a light and a guide by which the faithful were led. Of course, this involved the people in obeying the
statutes and keeping to the rules.

One can perhaps see, then, that the gospel of Jesus Christ
was a threat to the Jew in the first century – and possibly still
today – not simply because it attacked the 'works' of the law
but because it replaced the Torah by another way, by another
guide.

Such then is the background to Paul's attitude to the
law. And it helps to explain what we might think at first
to be his contradictory conclusions about it. For example,
he calls it 'holy' (Rom. 7:12) and says that its purpose was

to give life (Rom. 7:10). Yet he talks about the 'curse of the law' (Gal. 3:13). How can these opposing statements be reconciled? The explanation is that the law – meaning God's moral framework for humanity – belongs to God's holy purpose for our lives. As such it is holy and good. And from this point of view, gospel and law are not in opposition. The law makes clear God's demands upon people. Paul says in Galatians that it is like a school-master who leads us to Christ. On the other hand, legalism, which is our attempt to find salvation by obeying the law and doing so in our own strength, is condemned because it is self-centred and not God-centred.

Paul thus came to three distinct conclusions concerning the law. First, the law exists to make clear God's moral demands upon us. In other words, it is like a signpost which indicates where we stand before a holy and righteous God. The gospel needs the law if there is to be any coherence about needing a saviour. Secondly, the law – on its own – cannot save anyone. It is a clear signpost but it is powerless to save. 'For what the law was powerless to do in that it was weakened by the sinful nature, God did by sending his own Son . . . He condemned sin in sinful man' (Rom. 8:3). Thirdly, while the law is prominent in its role of witnessing to the holy standards of God, insofar as its purpose in the work of salvation is concerned, it is preparatory. Its role in God's plan is to lead men and women to Christ, through whom alone we may find freedom from the power of sin and the demands of the law.

Demonic powers

It may seem strange to modern people that Paul believed that, because of sin, humanity was in bondage to the powers of darkness. He believed that the natural person was subject to the 'ruler of the kingdom of the air' (Eph. 2:2). He warned Christians that even after their conversion to Christ, a 'warfare' was going on between the kingdom of God and the powers of darkness (Eph. 6). But he also asserted that through the cross of Christ the powers of evil have been overthrown and the final victory of Christ is now inevitable. In a wonderfully dramatic passage in Colossians 2, Paul writes of the principalities and powers being spoiled, saying that Christ 'made a public spectacle of them, triumphing over them by the cross' (v. 15).

It is common these days to scoff at such a belief. Surely, people say, we can no longer accept the reality of the demonic in the world? But before we dismiss such a notion as part of the mythology of a bygone age, let us remember that Jesus himself shared the conviction that his ministry was in opposition to the powers of darkness. On what grounds, then, would we sweep away such ideas as 'nonsense'? We must add to this that there have been many serious thinkers who have postulated the existence of the demonic, not only because it is referred to constantly in Scripture, but also because it makes sense of a world which is shot through with evil and sin. The idea of good and evil in steady combat, both in the spiritual realm as well as in the physical order, echoes human experience. C. S. Lewis once remarked: 'I have always gone as near dualism as Christianity allows, and the New Testament allows one to go very near.'

It changed Paul's idea of salvation

We have seen, therefore, that basic to Paul's teaching is the view that humanity is under the tyranny of sin. This has made us subject to other tyrannies – the law and the 'powers of the universe'. We are consequently helpless, condemned and defeated. But Paul writes about this bondage from a post-conversion point of view. He now *knows* that Christ has brought deliverance to fallen humanity. He *knows* that the cross is good news of a new creation, of a new society and a new world. His whole conception of the Christian faith is now dominated and determined by his experience of the cross. But it is useless to look in Paul's epistles for a precise and logical statement of a 'doctrine' of Christ's death. He presses into service many varied metaphors in order to draw out the riches and extent of its meaning. We shall now consider some of the key ideas in Paul, using the following diagram as our guide:

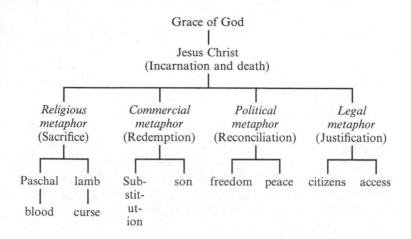

Christ as sacrifice

Considering that Paul was a Jew, steeped in the Old Testament and alert to the possibility of connections between Jesus and the old covenant, it is remarkable that there are few direct references to Christ's death as sacrifice. However, it is clear that Paul did regard the death of Jesus as sacrificial. For example, in dealing with abuse of fellowship in the Corinthian assembly, he refers to the tradition received about the Last Supper of Jesus. The bread broken symbolises the sacrificial offering of the Lord (1 Cor. 11:24) and the cup is 'the new covenant' in his blood (v. 25). Indeed, the logic of his argument in 1 Corinthians 10:14–21 about the eating of sacrificial offerings to pagan deities suggests that for him Christ is the sacrifice *par excellence* and that compromise is unacceptable. Ephesians 5:2 points us in the same direction, 'Christ loved us and gave himself up for us as a fragrant offering and sacrifice to God'. The words 'fragrant offering and sacrifice' are religious terms linking Christ's death with Old Testament sacrificial ideas.

However, in 1 Corinthians 5:7 we do find a direct reference to the Old Testament cultus when Paul mentions that 'Christ, our Passover lamb, has been sacrificed'. This, of course, is an incidental remark made in the context of advice to Christians whose lives were not as God-glorifying as they ought to be. Yet it shows how Paul's mind turned naturally to Christ's offering when talking about Christian discipleship (see also, 1 Cor. 6:20; 10:16ff; 11:27ff; Phil. 2:5–11). As the Paschal lamb, Christ's offering was seen as doing something which brought about men and women's salvation.

But in a passage which has been the subject of extensive learned examination, Christ's offering is also treated by Paul as a sacrifice which 'propitiates' God or 'expiates' our sin. In this passage, Romans 3:23ff, Paul states of Christ that he had been presented by God as a 'propitiation' (*hilasterion*) through faith in his blood (3:25). Until C. H. Dodd's book *The Bible and the Greeks*,[3] the Greek word *hilasterion* was generally interpreted to mean 'propitiation', thus denoting that in some way Christ's death propitiated God. Dodd, however, examining the evidence, came to a different conclusion. As Paul used the Greek translation of the Hebrew Bible, called the Septuagint, an examination of its uses of the verb *hilaskomai* should determine Paul's meaning. His conclusion was that as *hilaskomai* keeps company with words like 'grace, mercy, love' and not words like 'anger or punishment'; a better translation would therefore be 'expiation', that is, Christ's death removes sin. While accepting Dodd's general verdict, the theologians T. W. Manson and D. Daube suggest that the root idea in Romans 3:23 is the *mercy seat* image of the Old Testament – that is, just as the covering of the ark in the tabernacle was the place where God's mercy was shown, so the cross is the place where we find forgiveness.[4]

The Australian scholar Leon Morris disagrees with Dodd's conclusion. In his view Romans 3:23 and the Septuagint follow the traditional Old Testament idea that to 'propitiate' is to 'atone'. In a very detailed examination of the texts in the Old Testament Morris tackles the central issue, namely, whether atonement is an action directed towards God or towards the offence. If it is the former, 'propitiation' is the word we should use; if the latter then we should choose 'expiation'. Morris quotes Horace Bushnell with approval: 'We propitiate only a person and expiate only a fact, an act or a thing.'[5] As Morris points out, Dodd's argument on this issue is all of a piece with his statements concerning God's wrath. Because Dodd rejects any suggestion that 'the wrath of God' is personal, but rather belongs to the realm of cause and effect, so, argues Morris, Dodd cannot accept the notion that God's justice and holiness require satisfaction.[6]

All this may seem an unnecessarily erudite and specialist discussion and not at all relevant for ordinary Christians. This, in fact, is not the case. A great deal hangs on what conclusion one comes to. We shall be returning to this issue later when we come to discuss in greater depth the meaning of the death of Jesus. But for the moment two observations must be made. First, scholarship has not given sufficient credit to Leon Morris for his contribution to this subject. Probably because he concludes in favour of 'propitiation' – a most unpopular doctrine – his work has been brushed aside and its depth and penetration ignored. I am personally convinced that Morris's conclusions are sound and that he has made a strong case for the argument that Romans 3:23–5 is in line with the Old Testament idea of atonement. But, secondly, it appears to be the case that when 'propitiation' is used in this verse and elsewhere in the New Testament (1 John 2:1, for example) we have new content to it. No longer is it people offering something to God and trying to avert his wrath and disgust at human sin, but we have God setting forth Christ as the propitiation. We must, therefore, keep to the Old Testament categories in order to understand what Paul is saying in Romans, and we must not brush them aside as if they no longer count.

But we are left in an exegetical dilemma, however, because neither propitiation nor expiation is wholly satisfactory: expiation is too weak because it makes God's action too impersonal and seems to leave out that it is God himself who is doing the atoning, and propitiation appears to be deficient because if pushed to its conclusion it could be interpreted to mean that Christ 'propitiates' God the Father which, we must say emphatically, is not what Paul and the other New Testament writers believed.

What comes across from the passage, however, is Paul's amazing conclusion that God set forth Christ as our atoning sacrifice; that in some mysterious way the whole Godhead was involved in a 'rescue operation' to bring us back to God.

Christ our redeemer

It may seem at first that the idea of 'redemption' is totally foreign to modern life. But a little thought will show that although the words 'redeemer' and 'redemption' may be little used, the idea is far from uncommon. Take its commercial links. Hire purchase agreements work on a 'redemption' model. A down-payment, perhaps, and you walk away with your stereo or computer and spend the next few years paying back so that you can truly say 'It is mine'. If you are unfortunate enough to fall into the hands of money-lenders, you must hand over a treasured possession in return for cash, and your possession will not be 'redeemed' until you have bought it back. In the political arena it is, sadly, all too common these days for innocent people to be caught up in political situations and be made hostages of terrorists, and even governments, in order to force the countries of those held prisoner to comply with the demands of the oppressors, in order to redeem them. Thus, Paul's rich metaphor, that Christ in some way redeemed us (bought us, set us free), is not as remote as we might have first thought.

At the heart of redemption is 'freedom'. The first-century world was riddled with social inequality, most clearly expressed in the institution of slavery. To a large degree this was the bedrock of the social system and the Roman Empire depended upon it for its life and smooth running. The rich and cultured classes led a free, contented and pleasurable existence because their slaves cocooned them from the harsh realities of life. But it was possible to purchase your freedom if you were a slave. The release money was called a 'ransom', the process was called 'redemption', and anyone who gave a slave his freedom would be called a 'redeemer'. The transaction, in the ancient world, was normally done in the local temple where, before the legal owner of the slave, the temple official would witness the payment of the ransom and the slave would be set free. Although the owner would receive the payment, the ceremony was done as though the slave was being purchased by the deity. As far as we can tell, it was normal for such an important event to be inscribed on the temple wall. A. Deissmann gives this example of such a transaction: '(Date.) Sosibus sold to the Pythian Apollo a female slave named Nicaea at the price of three minae of silver for freedom. (Witnesses.)'[7]

What this means is that Nicaea had saved the three minae of silver that was her price and had paid it into the treasury of the temple and had been 'sold to the god' for freedom. We can imagine her walking away from the temple, a freed woman, now about to begin a new life in society. She was set free, she was *redeemed*.

It was against this rich background of meaning that Paul introduced the message that Christ is redeemer. Although Christ had himself spoken in these terms in Mark 10:45, saying that the Son of Man had come as a 'ransom' for many, it was Paul who maximised this theologically. We should note three aspects of the redemptive motif.

First, that God in Christ has redeemed us. Ephesians 1:7 talks about Christ offering us 'redemption through his blood, the forgiveness of sins'. Similarly, Romans 3:24 speaks of being 'justified . . . through the redemption that came by Christ Jesus'. In both passages the Redeemer is Christ, the redemption is what he achieved on the cross and the results include forgiveness and justification. We cannot avoid the implication of this, that the atonement was *objective*, that is, Christ did something that we could not do for ourselves. Indeed, this is reinforced by one of the most remarkable references to Christ's redemption in the New Testament, namely Galatians 3:13: 'Christ redeemed us from the curse of the law by becoming a curse for us.' There is no escaping the force of this language – that we were released from the condemnation of the law because Christ, somehow, took the full force of the law's condemnation and became accursed for us. Again, this is the raw material for a later chapter but it is imperative to bear in mind that it seems as if Christ's death is viewed by Paul as being 'penal' in some form (that is, he is condemned as somehow 'guilty') and that he is our 'substitute' (that is, he takes our place).

Second, Paul stressed the costliness of our redemption. It is through the precious blood of Christ that we are redeemed. Paul does not cease to marvel at the wonder of God's love shown in Christ: 'Christ's love compels us, because we are convinced that one died for all, and therefore all died' (2 Cor. 5:14); 'but God demonstrates his own love for us in this: While we were still sinners, Christ died for us' (Rom. 5:8). In other words, this was a not a sacrifice-less redemption but something which cost the redeemer everything. It was common at earlier periods of Church history to ask at this point: 'To whom was the ransom paid?' Some theologians answered 'To the Devil' and some offered ingenious theories how the ransom tricked the Devil. Gregory of Nyssa, for example, offered a fishing analogy in that the hook was like a cross – that the flesh of Christ was the bait and the deity was the fish-hook. The Devil gulped down the bait and was trapped. It would appear, however, that the New Testament writers were wiser than such fathers of the Church because there is no hint given in Scripture that the ransom is paid to anybody. What we have here is a metaphor to illustrate the wealth and wonder of the cross. It is God, after all, who is doing the paying. This does not weaken in any respect the meaning of redemption. What the picture language is saying is that the death of Jesus was not just a good example or even an inspiring act of martyrdom – but it was a death which set us free.

This leads into our third point: redemption is to be lived. 'You are not your own; you were bought at a price' (1 Cor. 6:19; 7:23). Here Paul, drawing on the analogy of being bought from slavery, emphasises that the Christian has been set free from sin, death and the law but he or she is now a slave of Christ. 'It is for freedom that Christ has set us free. Stand firm, then, and do not let yourselves be burdened again by the yoke of slavery' (Gal. 5:1). The follower of Jesus is under new ownership and this is expressed in the character of the redeemed life – love, joy, peace, long-suffering, etc. – which later in that chapter Paul describes as the 'fruit of the Spirit'.

There is one final point we should notice about redemption. Although the transaction is complete and final, in that Christ has died and is risen, as far as humanity is concerned the tangible reality of the new life, its complete redemption, is still in the future. So Paul talks of Christians waiting for 'the redemption of our bodies' (Rom. 8:23; see also Eph. 4:30).

Christ is our reconciler

It is not surprising that many modern theologians believe that 'reconciliation' is by far the best New Testament word to use of the cross because of its relevance to social and political life. We live in a divided world where reconciliation is needed at every level of human existence. Of course, when talking about reconciliation we make a natural assumption that the two warring factions need to resolve their differences and we often say that there are 'faults on both sides'. Paul's use of the reconciliation model for the work of Christ shows how he draws upon human experience but brings into play something very new and exciting.

The background to Paul's doctrine of reconciliation is alienated humanity. As we have noted on more than one occasion, his teaching about the work of Christ takes its driving force from the two poles of people's sin and God's love. Humanity, since the fall, has been in bondage: 'alienated from God', enemies in their minds through 'evil behaviour' (Col. 1:21). Men and women, made for harmony with God, are now at issue with him and, to all intents and purposes, his enemy. This, then, is the background to Paul's teaching about reconciliation. It is clear that reconciliation cannot be achieved by humanity. Before Christ came we were 'powerless', objects of 'wrath' and 'enemies' of God (Rom. 5:6, 9, 10). Effective reconciliation could only come from God himself.

Paul makes two important points about reconciliation. First, it is God's work. God is never the object of reconciliation – he is the reconciler. 'God was reconciling the world to himself in Christ' (2 Cor. 5:19). So James Denney observes: 'When reconciliation is spoken of by St Paul the subject is always God and the object always man. The work of reconciling is one in which the initiative is taken by God and the cost borne by him . . . we never read that God has been reconciled.'[8]

The second point is that reconciliation was achieved through the death of Christ. 'We were reconciled to him through the death of his Son' (Rom. 5:10). Concerning the divisions between Jew and Greek, Ephesians asserts that through Christ 'our Peace' the wall of partition has been destroyed for ever because both have been reconciled to God in 'one body . . . through the cross' (Eph. 2:16). Colossians, in a parallel passage, echoes the same theme: God reconciled all things to himself 'by making peace through his blood, shed on the cross' (Col. 1:20). We must observe that reconciliation is not a process which goes on inevitably unto the end of time. Rather it is an act by which humankind is delivered from sin and death. It is true that, as far as the Church is concerned, it has the task of proclaiming the message of reconciliation, and this will certainly go on until all is accomplished, but the Church proclaims a finished work. God offers us peace and hope and we pass from being enemies to his dear children and as such we have 'access' into his presence (Rom. 5:2).

Christ our justifier

Our fourth metaphor and cluster of related concepts appears to come from the language of the court room. 'Justification by faith' is one of Paul's favourite ways of describing a Christian's relationship to Christ. Luther, in Reformation times, saw the doctrine of justification by faith as so central to the Christian faith that he called it 'the leaven that leavens the lump'. We shall not be considering the controversial aspects of this doctrine which divided Catholic from Protestant four hundred years ago, because many of the issues are irrelevant to the main thrust of our enquiry.[9] Luther's famous dictum, however, shows that millions of Christians have seen justification by faith as summing up the Christian heritage in Christ and expressing succinctly what the gospel is all about. What, then, is it saying?

The Old Testament word for justification (Hebrew *tsadeq*) comes from a root which probably means 'that standard which God wants to see in the world'. The verb 'to justify' has a definite legal meaning, that is, 'to declare righteous'. This is undeniable in Deuteronomy 25:1: 'When men have a dispute, they are to take it to court and the judges will decide the case, acquitting [justifying] the innocent and condemning the guilty' (see also Exod. 23:7; Isa. 43:9; Ps. 143:2). The sense here is that the good people (the righteous) are declared innocent and the wicked are sentenced. Justification takes place on the basis of the obvious goodness of the righteous. But there are passages in the Old Testament where it is suggested that when men and women are brought into a right relationship with God, the status of *being right* is conferred upon them. In Genesis 15:6, for example, Abraham believed in God's promise and 'he credited it to him as righteousness'. Now, what does this mysterious verse mean? It means, surely, that Abraham's faith in the word of promise was regarded as the equivalent of a meritorious life. God delighted in this swift and courageous act of believing what seemed to be impossible and he rewarded it by saying, as it were, 'I accept this kind of commitment.' Similarly, in Psalm 106:31, Phinehas's act of removing sin from the congregation stayed the plague and, we are told, 'it was credited to him as righteousness'. This aspect of righteousness is sometimes called *imputed righteousness* because it is a status given to someone on the basis of their faith or trust in God.

It is important to remember when we approach Paul's theology that justification by faith is not the whole of his theology but, rather, one important element among others. If we try to interpret everything else in the light of this doctrine we run the risk of getting the whole out of focus. What we must constantly keep in the foreground is the work of Christ and then we shall see that justification by faith is a beautiful and exciting analogy and metaphor which demands careful exploration.

It is clear, for a start, that for Paul the cross is the basis of justification. So he writes: 'But God demonstrates his own love for us in this: While we were still sinners, Christ died for us. Since we have now been justified by his blood, how much more shall we be saved from God's wrath through him!' (Rom. 5:8–9).

Furthermore, the means of justification in Paul is always faith. 'We have been justified through faith' (Rom. 5:1). As we observed earlier, central to salvation are two things: our helplessness and God's love. What we could not do, God does in Christ – he offers us salvation freely and generously. Faith reaches out and accepts the offer of life.

Now, there are many questions which people will want to raise concerning justification at this point. A common objection is this. If justification doesn't mean *really* being righteous, aren't we in danger of making it a pretence like Hans Christian Andersen's fable of the king who thought he was beautifully dressed when all the time he was stark-naked? Not at all. Paul's metaphor, we must recall, is taken from the courtroom. Justification means that we are declared 'Not Guilty' – on the basis of the work of Christ. It is not an ethical quality that Paul has in mind, but a status and a relationship. It is certainly true that when we are justified through the work of Christ a new life begins, which entails that we live a holy and God-glorifying existence. But this is the fruit and not the root of salvation.

Jesus – our sacrifice, redeemer, reconciler and justifier

So then, in these four graphic pictures we find the outlines of Paul's teaching about the death of Jesus of Nazareth. Paul was not systematic in his treatment and this is perfectly understandable because he was not writing theological treatises but letters to small Christian communities to build them up in the faith. His major concern was to show that in Jesus Christ God had made himself known as Saviour.

6

Glory and Sacrifice

Two of the greatest New Testament interpretations of the cross of Jesus are the writings ascribed to John and the epistle to the Hebrews. Both contribute significantly to the witness of the New Testament and each must be considered carefully.

JOHN – THE GOSPEL OF GLORY

It should be obvious by now that the New Testament bears the imprint of Jesus of Nazareth. His character, deeds, dying, death and resurrection give the New Testament accounts their unmistakable ring. There is unity in their chorus that Jesus Christ is Saviour of the world although, from different perspectives, testimony is given to what he means individually. And to a large degree, testimony is what it is all about. Although each writer was conscious of writing the truth about Jesus, no gospel is history in our meaning of that phrase. None was writing down factual history in a chronological order and in a clinical manner. We would have loved to have had more detail of the extraordinary life and career of Jesus – what he looked like, his early life at Nazareth, his growing sense of call – but these and many other intriguing questions are passed over in favour of meaning. 'This is what Jesus means to me,' appears to be the dominant theme of each gospel; 'This is how I make sense of his amazing impact on people.'

There isn't a richer or more exciting book in the New Testament than the gospel of John but it presents the serious student with some intractable problems. For a start its approach to the story of Jesus is completely different from that of the other gospel writers. Many of the familiar stories are missing and are replaced by Johannine stories: seven great miracles or 'signs' are the only miracles referred to, there is no story of the institution of the Lord's Supper, the cleansing of the temple is placed at the start of Jesus' ministry – and so we could go on. But there is a second difference, too. Whereas Jesus in the other three gospels is reticent concerning his identity, in John he is open about it – he confronts men as God's only begotten Son.

How does one account for these differences? It is pointless discussing which of the two, the synoptic gospels or John, is the more historically accurate because both are concerned with presenting Jesus Christ as Saviour and Lord. Both are concerned to present the truth and both are engaged in a process of interpretation. Think how impoverished the Christian Church would be without the gospel of John. This fourth gospel has penetrated the human heart in a way that the others cannot equal, and its understanding of Christ takes us down into a deeper knowledge than the others go. Little wonder that Clement of Alexandria said long ago that the fourth gospel was the 'spiritual gospel'. A secular parallel to this might be the biography of Winston Churchill written by his personal doctor. This intimate account of the great politician shed information on the man in a way that more objective accounts of other biographers never did, going behind the public face of Churchill's career.[1] Similarly, John's account goes 'behind' and takes us, as it were, to the very heart of God's concern for humankind.

One of John's most important words is 'glory' (*doxa*). Just as a schoolboy might concentrate the sun's rays through a magnifying glass, so John sees God's glory centring in Jesus: 'We have seen his glory, the glory of the one and only Son who came from the Father' (1:14). John shows how Jesus manifested his glory in the miracle at Cana, in the raising of Lazarus, in his dying on the cross and in his resurrection.

Indeed, this word 'glory' is a very fitting one to express John's treatment of the work of Christ.

The glory of an obedient life

While the cross and resurrection remain the glorious peak of Christ's ministry, John stresses that the life of Jesus showed forth his glory also. 'The Word became flesh' (1:14) and this 'flesh' (*sarx*) became the receptacle for Christ's glory. 'Flesh' denotes human nature in all its weakness, limitations and earthiness and it is all the more surprising that John commenced his gospel with the affirmation that Jesus was the Word of God and by nature one with him. This glory continues into Christ's obedience to the Father's will: 'I seek not to please myself but him who sent me' (5:30). In fact the fourth gospel makes it plain that Christ's work should be seen in the whole movement of his ministry as he enters into his Father's work and faithfully embraces all he is commanded to do (5:17, 26). In John the cross is never isolated from the life of Jesus. The incarnation of God's beloved Son is the supreme proof of the love of God which is pre-eminently and most gloriously expressed in all its simplicity in the sufferings and death of Jesus. But what is this work into which Christ enters? John expresses it in terms of 'life' and 'light' which, up to chapter 13, are two dominant ideas in the first half of the book. The coming of Christ is to give light and, in so doing, to bring life to men (3:16–19). Indeed, in the last passage 3:16 almost sums up the message of the fourth gospel in the four verbs which express the meaning of Jesus: 'For God *so loved* the world, that *he gave* his only Son, that *whoever believes* in him shall not perish but *have eternal life*.' Obviously this is to anticipate the full expression of the gospel after the resurrection, but John wants to ram home the meaning of Jesus for his readers and to show what it is all about.

But the glory is in his actions too. Chapter 13 is the start of a second great division in the gospel, when words such as 'life' and 'light' fade away, to be replaced by 'love'. This love Jesus shows in an astonishing example of humble service as he takes a towel and washes the feet of his friends. Here, perhaps, we have one of the greatest signs of the incarnation of Christ as he stoops so low to do what was the work of a paid servant. Little wonder, then, that Christ in his 'high priestly' prayer in chapter 17 can say with confidence: 'I have brought you glory on earth by completing the work you gave me to do' (v. 4). It is true that in one sense the work was still to be completed on the cross, but from another perspective we are reminded to see that Christ's incarnation was as much a part of the work of reconciliation as his death.

The glory of his hour

Even though the life and ministry are seen as part of Jesus' redeeming work – it is not a 'deity-filled' Jesus who comes floating from heaven just before the crucifixion and who floats back following the resurrection – John's gospel makes much of the fact that Jesus looked ahead to his destiny on the cross. There is frequent mention of 'his hour' or 'time' which is to be the moment of his triumph and glory. The occurrence of 'his hour' (7:30; 8:20; 12:23, 27; 13:1; 17:1) or 'his time' (7:6, 8) indicates that Jesus believed the whole course of events was in his hands. Far from being a leaf blown here and there by the wind of fate, Jesus was the master of his own destiny and in calm control of the situation. This is reinforced by the support of Scripture in the fourth gospel. There is not so much direct citation of Old Testament Scriptures in John as in the synoptics, but it is still an important aspect. Thus his outspoken comments about the temple (2:18ff) were linked later in the disciples' memory with the testimony of Scripture. But Jesus was confident that students of the Scriptures would soon be led to accept the validity of his claims: 'You diligently study the Scriptures because you think that by them you possess eternal life. These are the Scriptures that testify about me' (5:39). He is even dimly foreshadowed in the story of Moses: 'Just as Moses lifted up the snake in the desert, so the Son of Man must be lifted up' (3:14).

The glory of God's gift

A third prominent element in John is the conviction that the

Saviour of the world is God's gift to humanity. He does not work back from what Jesus did to who he is. On the contrary, the meaning of what Christ did is tied up with his identity as the 'Logos', and particularly as the 'one and only' Son of God (3:16). Such is God's love that he gave his very best for humanity.

But more can be said. This gift is a sacrificial gift which takes the gift from the giver to an altar. John, more than any other writer, emphasises the notion of Jesus as the Paschal lamb. Jesus comes on the scene in the fourth gospel with the cry of John the Baptist ringing in his ears: 'Look, the Lamb of God, who takes away the sin of the world!' (1:29). There has been much dispute about the origin of this saying and what the significance and meaning of the word 'lamb' is,[2] but there can be little doubt that John saw this as referring to Christ's sacrificial offering on the cross. As has often been observed, it is very striking that the fourth gospel represents Jesus dying at the very moment the Paschal lambs were being slaughtered in the temple. A more profound symbolism cannot be found than that the Lamb of God dies for sinners outside the Holy City's walls and makes redundant the offerings within.

As John sees it a divine necessity also rules over the gift of the Son of God. 'For them I sanctify myself' (17:19) are the words of Jesus in the often-called 'high priestly prayer' but at this point the priest is also victim. Like a lamb being offered in sacrifice, he makes himself ready for the offering. All this picks up a quiet theme running through the gospel – that it is required of Jesus to lay down his life in death. 'Unless an ear of wheat falls to the ground and dies, it remains only a single seed. But if it dies, it produces many seeds' (12:24). Death even intrudes into the story of the good shepherd. Four times Jesus spells out the message that the good shepherd lays down his life for the sheep. Here is found an astonishing reversal of affairs. No human shepherd, however committed and good, would willingly die for the animals in his care. Circumstances, of course, may force him to die accidentally for the sheep. But the good shepherd chooses to die for those in his care (10:11, 15, 17, 18). All this is in obedience to his Father who desires that all people receive the eternal life which is made available through his Son (10:25, 28, 29).

The glory of the cross

The fourth gospel does not minimise the cross as the place of humiliation and shame but, more so than any other gospel, stresses its glory aspect. This is anticipated by Jesus' words following Judas' departure to inform the Jewish authorities: 'Now is the Son of Man glorified and God is glorified in him' (13:31). His being 'lifted up from the earth' (12:32) will be his moment of triumph; his hour of glory (12:23), though misunderstood by the world, will be recognised by those with the eyes to see. Even Pilate had a part to play in the coronation of his Saviour. His entitling of Jesus as 'King of the Jews' – the blasphemy which sent Jesus to the cross – is a veiled statement of what is, in fact, the truth, even though Pilate himself did not understand! The climax, of course, came with the great and triumphant cry from the cross: 'It is finished [*tetelestai*]!' This is the moment of glory for Jesus, when his work reached its tremendous conclusion in his act of self-oblation.

But John does not give us a theory or a theology of the death of Jesus. As we might expect from a book which sees the whole ministry of Jesus as a 'sign', we are left with clues which we must sift to figure out the glory of the cross. With confidence we can say that for the fourth gospel Jesus' death was *vicarious*, that is, he died for others. This is clear from references to the 'laying down' of his life. It may be that even a *substitutionary* motif may be discerned in Caiaphas' words that it was expedient that 'one man die for the people than that the whole nation perish' (11:50). The fact that the fourth gospel picks this up again as Jesus is led away to Caiaphas (18:13) must surely suggest that John is thinking of Jesus' death in substitutionary terms, even though it is unlikely that this is more than a hint. What we can certainly say is that the death Jesus died is God's moment of victory over the powers of darkness and sin (12:31–2) and all who believe in him have eternal life (3:16). Thomas' confession that the risen Jesus is 'Lord and . . . God' (20:28) is one the early Church shared, that the crucified Jesus with the wounds in his hands and side is the Lord of Glory and worthy of the greatest confession that can pour forth from the mouth of any man or woman.

Before we leave John's Gospel we must glance at two other writings which are part of the Johannine corpus – 1 John and the Revelation of John.

1 John, in some respects, continues themes explored in the gospel. The death of Jesus is the supreme revelation of love. This is the basis for his oft-repeated words that Christian love is shown in action (2:5, 10). God's love is shown in that he 'laid down his life for us' (3:16), which is an imitative principle for Christians. The cross is also operative in daily life: 'the blood of Jesus . . . purifies us from every sin' (1:7) because, as Saviour of the world (4:14), his death has a timeless efficacy. He is humankind's advocate (2:1) and the 'propitiator' of our sins (2:2). No attempt is made to work out these ideas theologically – they are simply expressed in the context of Christian living to show the relevance of the cross. As such they are important statements because they show how the first Christians viewed the death of Jesus, and how central it was to their thinking.

The Revelation of John, written towards the end of the first century, is peculiar to the New Testament by reason of its style. Writing in the apocalyptic tradition of Daniel, the author sees the immediate human activities against the backcloth of the immense conflict going on in the heavenly places between God and Satan. The whole book bears witness to Christ who, by reason of his triumph, is Alpha and Omega, the beginning and the end. Central to the author's vision of the divine victory, which is absolutely certain, is that of the 'Lamb who was slain' (5:6, 12). The destiny of all pivots on humankind's attitude to the Lamb. To those who belong to him there awaits the new heaven and the new earth; for those who do not there is the certainty of the 'wrath of the Lamb' (6:16).

HEBREWS AND THE ROYAL PRIESTHOOD OF CHRIST

No one knows who wrote the epistle to the Hebrews, but it was clearly written by a Jew to a Jewish group, probably between AD 60–70. Some scholars suggest that the readers lived in Rome and were one of the growing number of Christian groups springing up in the ancient world. What the book reveals is that this particular congregation were not at all certain that they had done the right thing in following Christ. They had started to question the wisdom of turning their backs on the privileges of being the chosen people. It may be that Jewish neighbours and former friends were mocking the name of their Saviour and discouragement and opposition were beginning to wear down their resistance. The purpose of the writer was to encourage and to remind these Jewish Christians of their inheritance in Christ. If the Jews could pride themselves on their many privileges, Christians had much more to shout about. The word 'better' is at the heart of the writer's claim. Christ is better than the angels (1:4); better than Moses (3:3); and he offers a better covenant (7:22) and a better priesthood (8:6).

There are, in fact, two central themes in Hebrews which the author concentrates upon to show the superiority of Jesus – namely, covenant and priesthood. First, with reference to *covenant*, the epistle claims that the old covenant was valid in its day but now a new covenant has arrived, sealed with blood and based upon better promises. Whereas the old covenant was established by Moses and sealed with the blood of bulls and goats, the new covenant is sealed with the blood of Jesus, who is the author of a new agreement with God. The former had to be renewed annually (9:25) and even then it was ineffective in removing sin (10:4). But Jesus is the mediator of an eternal covenant which puts sin away for ever (9:26; 10:16–22).

It is central to the writer's purpose to show the inadequacy of Jewish priesthood. Why was it that the ritual could never remove sin? The epistle offers two explanations: first, that every priest and high priest were sinful men who needed atonement for themselves; secondly, that the sin offering lacked the one essential qualification which marked a satisfactory offering – namely, free will. Both of these were damning deficiencies and against them the once-for-all sacrifice of Jesus is seen in all its richness.

Now in a number of respects the epistle to the Hebrews deepens our understanding of the cross. At the centre of the

writer's thought is the great act of worship which took place
on the Day of Atonement, the Yom Kippur. On that day the
high priest stood before the people as their representative. All
he did in the worship was in their name and on their behalf.
This was symbolised by the fact that he bore their names
engraved on his breastplate as a 'memorial' before Yahweh.
Before the ceremony he consecrated himself by liturgical acts
and by the sacrifice of an animal. Then came the great moment
when, bearing their names, he laid his hands on the creature
and vicariously confessed the sins of all Israel. The victim
having been slaughtered, some of the blood was taken into
the holy of holies and there the high priest interceded for
the people of Israel. The worship over, he returned to the
people to give them his blessing; which reassured them that
atonement had been made. All this, for the writer, is a shadow
of the eternal covenant and priesthood made by Jesus. Jesus'
whole life of obedience (5:8) and love he offered in death so
that he might be the Lamb of God which takes away the
sin of the world, and seal the new covenant with his blood.
However, Hebrews does not call Christ 'lamb' and, indeed,
is careful not to align Jesus with any particular animal. The
point of the argument is that he offered himself a full and
free sacrifice for humanity. What is of special interest is that
the writer does not question the motive of the old covenant.
There is tacit acceptance of two things:

1. When the high priest entered the holy of holies all
Israel was present in his person. The high priest had a
representative character.
2. When he confessed the sins of the people, bearing
the blood of the sacrificial victim, God accepted not
only the high priest but all Israel through him. We
shall call this, then, *vicarious* representation because the
representative came bearing the offering.

These two important ideas are developed very helpfully in
Hebrews as the writer attempts to show that Christ's death
was a final and totally satisfactory sacrifice for the sins of
all.

First, Jesus is truly man and represents us in our humanity. As with other New Testament writings, Hebrews has a very high doctrine of Christ and this is the starting point of its understanding of the death of Jesus. He comes from God (1:2) and shares his nature (1:3) and may even be called God (1:8). Even though he shares such a glorious estate he is made lower than the angels and goes through suffering to a cross of shame. Jesus is indeed seen as an exemplary and perfect person, but it is not perfection given (although there must, of course, be an element of that) as much as gained – gained through obedience and testing (5:8), and as such he has earned the right to represent humankind before the Father. His life, insists the epistle, was one long period of obedience which is summed up in citation of Psalm 40:8 and in chapter 10:9: 'Here I am, I have come to do your will.' It is important for Hebrews to highlight the humanity of Christ because the incarnation is seen as central to the mission of the Saviour. His lowliness, obedience and quiet endurance coincide with similar themes already noted in Paul (Phil. 2:5–11) and John (5:17ff).

Secondly, unlike the high priest who must stand before God as a sinner and have his own sins to confess, Jesus the high priest enters the presence of his Father as the pure and holy one to make a perfect confession on behalf of others. 'How much more, then,' the writer exclaims, 'will the blood of Christ, who through the eternal Spirit offered himself unblemished to God, cleanse our consciences from acts that lead to death, so that we may serve the living God!' (9:14) For the writer, then, Christ's sacrifice is final. The phrase, for example in 10:10, is emphatic – 'once for all' (*eph-apax*). It is most important to note the definiteness implied in this statement. Unlike the Aaronic priesthood which must continually offer its sacrifice to God, Jesus' offering is finished: atonement has been made and there is nothing more to offer. Further, we should note, this Jesus is more than the willing victim, he is the eternal high priest who was both priest and victim. In his own person he joins men and women to God.

Thirdly, while it is true that the offering was a perfect and final act of redemption for humanity, the epistle adds a point which is unique in the New Testament, that the high priestly work of Christ continues in heaven: 'he always lives to intercede for them' (7:25). Whereas the earthly high priest entered once a year into the holy of holies, Christ by the power of his sacrifice has entered into the true, although spiritual and invisible sanctuary. There he lives to intercede for his people. The writer certainly does not intend this to be taken to mean that the sacrificial act of Christ was somehow incomplete. It would be an erroneous interpretation of the epistle to the Hebrews to believe that it is suggesting that Christ's death is, somehow, finished on the historical plane but on the supra-historical level (i.e. in heaven) Calvary is still being repeated before the Father and that the Church on earth enters into this offering every time it celebrates its eucharists. That cannot be right, simply because the epistle's intention is to argue that Christ's sacrifice is finished. His work over, he has 'sat down' on the right hand of God (10:9–12). Intercession, while it includes prayers, means much more than that. It also conveys the idea of someone representing and standing for us in another realm. We might think of it in terms of someone who, going ahead of us to another land, has already staked out our place and is making it ready for us. Because he is there we can be sure of a certain destiny and of a hope which passes human understanding.[3]

PART THREE

THE CROSS
EXPLAINED

7

Can a Death Atone?

During the war, the wife of the American President, Franklin D. Roosevelt, kept this prayer in her purse. It became a constant reminder to her of the sacrifices being made by others:

> Dear Lord, lest I continue
> my complacent way,
> Help me to remember
> Somewhere out there
> A man died for me today.
> As long as there be war
> I then must
> Ask and answer
> Am I worth dying for?

As Mrs Roosevelt realised, the death of any man or woman who fights for another is essentially 'vicarious'; that is, the death represents a life laid down for others. Any nation or people who send others into battle on their behalf has to ask that same question: 'Are we worth dying for? Do our values, or our freedom, or our national pride, require the death of *one* soldier, let alone many thousands?' At every Remembrance Service this question returns to haunt the free world. Its most awful memory is that of the First, or Great, World War where millions of young men threw themselves on to the barbed wire of places like Ypres, Neuve Chapelle and the Somme in the name of their Mother and Fatherland. Kitchener's accusing face and pointing finger with the commanding words: 'Your country needs you' called many hundreds of thousands to hurl themselves into a bloody and pointless war. A popular print which found its way into thousands of working-class homes showed a handsome Tommy sprawled in death at the foot of the cross. It was called 'The Great Sacrifice' and it invited comparison with the death of Christ. Far from being blasphemous, as many thought at the time, that dreadful war which left most families in Britain, Germany and France grieving for their young, gave to those communities a tangible understanding of the nature of sacrifice. It may have been pointless and utterly stupid – nevertheless, it expressed powerfully the costliness of love and the devotion which drove many to offer themselves as glad victims on the altar of patriotism. To the question: 'Was it really necessary?' millions would have replied, 'Necessary or not, our country required it and it was our duty to obey.'

If we find it difficult to understand the necessity of such human sacrifice, how much more does the death of Jesus seem to us at first sight to be an utterly pointless and unnecessary death. 'Why should God require the death of anyone, let alone his only Son? Couldn't he have just forgiven us?' is a question which leaps easily to our lips. An ordinary working man put it to me in these words: 'When one of my family, or perhaps one of my mates at work, offends me, after sorting the matter out I just forgive them or I don't forgive them, as the case may be. I don't expect either them or me to end up on a cross!'

That seems to be a perfectly logical point of view. However bad sin is, and however desperate the human condition, surely God could have found another way! The idea of the Lord God of the universe sending his beloved 'Son' to a lonely cross strains human credulity and makes it harder, rather than easier, for people to believe in the Christian faith. That may well be the case. I have made no attempt in this book to claim that the cross has been seen by people as a compelling and attractive symbol of reconciliation. As we observed in Chapter One the cross, as a symbol of faith, was laughed out of court by sophisticated pagans of the day. And through history it has been an embarrassment to those who have desired a faith which is readily acceptable to the intelligentsia.

But let us now consider the reasons why Christians, rather than being embarrassed by the cross, have through the ages seen it as their greatest jewel and most sublime delight.

IT IS A SIGN OF GOD'S IDENTIFICATION WITH HUMANITY

We acknowledge that there is no earthly reason why the non-Christian should see the death of Jesus as the centre of God's purposes for humankind. What appears to the outsider to be the death of faith is seen by the Christian as the start of it. It is, from a Christian perspective, the point of departure for humankind. Whereas for those outside the Christian family it is a 'nonsense' which appears to block the way to faith, it is for the Christian the place where God is at last understood and experienced. For example, let us take the often expressed viewpoint, 'Why couldn't God have simply forgiven us our sins?' This cry is deficient in two main respects. First, it conveys an unsatisfactory idea of the reality and extent of sin. Instead of seeing sin and evil as a terrible blot on humanity which has penetrated into our hearts and lives and has deeply affected the whole of creation, it sees sin as something external to us which can be brushed aside by a simple word of forgiveness. But as an answer to the reality of sin it is only plausible in the most trivial of human wrongdoing. Of course I will forgive the person who wrongs me, but when that wrongdoing spills over into areas of human justice which involve others, forgiveness and wrongdoing must meet at the tribunal of justice. This is at the heart of human justice and why should we assume that God's is any different? Putting it the other way round, theologians wrestling with the concept of justice have argued that human models of justice reflect and express the divine. That is, God's world is moral – at the heart of a moral universe is an implicit understanding that injustice must pay recompense for the injuries it has caused. In everyday life it is sometimes the offender who realises and acknowledges this most particularly. In my dealings with prisoners I have discovered a profound awareness of the reality and power of sin – with its accompanying control over people. One of my students who became a Christian in prison, when he was serving seven years for a kidnapping offence, remarked that it was 'good' people who found sin so difficult to grasp. He observed that people 'inside' know only too well the power of sin and young children and teenagers can grasp it, too. But 'good' people, especially churchgoers, seem to brush it aside as if it has nothing to do with them – sin affects other people. But moral failure cannot be washed away as if it were external to us. It is graven into our very being and penetrates that part of our nature which we call spiritual.

The second aspect missed by the simple, 'Why doesn't God just forgive?' is that the incarnation is God's way of showing the depth of his care. If, in fact, God simply waved his hand and sin was removed as a handicap, we would be no wiser about God. He would remain the transcendent and basically unknowable God. Dr J. H. Oldham once said: 'If we want to make a thing real we must make it local.' That is precisely what God has done in Christ. The cross reveals God's staggering commitment to the human race. He enters so fully into the human situation that he is prepared to die for it and a cross becomes his throne. No wonder this is a scandal to many! Yet again, doesn't this costly way of caring express all that we believe about the nature of goodness and love? Perhaps the most wonderful thing known to us in life is when one person takes another's load upon himself or herself freely. This is done in many trivial, although to the receiver very precious, ways in ordinary life. It might be a helping hand or a generous, unsolicited gift – whatever it is, the action tells us profound things about the giver. Above all, the relationship is never the same afterwards. A special bond unites giver to recipient. By localising himself in the incarnation, God has shown in action how far he will go to rescue humankind from its sick and dying condition.

THE CROSS IS A SIGN OF GOD'S LOVE FOR HUMANKIND

Without any shadow of doubt, love is the quintessence of humanity. If we were asked to compare a civilisation which had arrived at its very peak of technological achievement with a society which was truly loving and accepting, without any doubt we would choose the latter as the most advanced society, because love is the basis of all human values and ideals. Without it people are intelligent animals, concerned for themselves only; with love they become moral beings concerned for the true welfare of others. In George Orwell's disturbing nightmare of the future, *1984*, one of the characters comments: 'Once a man has reached the stage of only caring for himself – sacrificing even the one he had loved most to his own advantage – then he ceases to be a man.' It is a fact that the nature of love is to be unconcerned about oneself. Vicariously, it inserts itself into the miseries of others and makes them its own. Ask any parent why they are prepared to put their money, energy and time into the lives of their children and they will look at you with utter astonishment for asking such a stupid question. Because love does not need to justify itself – it simply pours itself out in self-giving.

In a much more profound way Christians have seen in the cross of Christ the extent of God's love in caring for humanity. But what is it that makes it the supreme revelation of the love of God? For a start the death of Jesus is not the death of a good man or even of God acting in an outstanding man, because that could be said of the prophets. Rather, what we have in Jesus is God coming to us as man. The incarnation means that in Jesus we have to do with someone who is truly God and who is truly man. This staggering conclusion which the New Testament writers come to, means that Jesus does not merely reveal the love of Jesus, but rather the total love of God. The good news of the gospel is the good news of a loving God who personally intervenes and saves. 'To claim that Jesus Christ is not God himself become man for us and our salvation', writes Professor Tom Torrance, 'is equivalent to saying that God does not love us to the uttermost.'[1] Indeed, if God's love stops short of Calvary we may have a God who loves – but not one whose love is complete. As such he remains mysterious and aloof *behind* the love of another. We can now begin to see why the early Christians fought so tenaciously for the doctrine that Jesus was truly God, because any other option spells the death of atonement. Jesus does not need to be God to set me a moral example; he does not need to be God to be a brilliant and inspiring teacher. But he does need to share the nature of God if he is the Saviour in the sense of reconciling humanity to God and restoring us to our former dignity. At this point we can, perhaps, begin to answer Bultmann's famous question: 'Does Jesus help me because he is the Son of God or is he the Son of God because he helps me?'[2] It is clear that New Testament Christianity and the faith of the early Church would reject the functional approach of the second part of the question and emphasise the first. Jesus saves humankind because of who he is. He is not made God because of what he does.

The cross, then, is not only an astonishing sign of God's love; it is also the incredible revelation of a pardoning God. But we can say more than that. It is the sign of a *suffering* God. Dostoevsky in *The Demons* makes a very penetrating point that 'a God who cannot suffer is poorer than any man', that is, an Unmoved Mover – or a God unable to get close to people in their pain and misery – is not one who truly loves. But the God of the Bible is one who not only says he cares – and this is a constant theme in Scripture – but he shows that love by plunging into a world shot through with sin and evil.

But by saying that we are confronted with yet another radical question: how can the immortal God suffer and die on a cross? This was an issue which haunted the early Church and split it between the Arians and orthodox believers. The Arians could not believe that God could suffer and endure pain. He is the eternal, changeless Lord and, accordingly, it is wrong to suggest that he directly endured suffering in Christ. Orthodox Christians correctly saw this as opening up a chasm between an unchanging God and a changing

Christ. If God cannot enter into human pain and misery, then his salvation stops short of real involvement with the causes of human sin and wrongdoing.[3] If, however, Jesus Christ truly represents God among us, then he saves and heals by opening up the dark and twisted passages of our humanity and by entering fully into it, cleansing, restoring and reconciling from within. 'That which was unassumed,' said the ancient theologian, Gregory of Nazianzus, 'is unredeemed.' He meant by this, against those who argued for a kind of hybrid Saviour who was neither the unchanging God nor a real man, that only a Saviour who was both God and man and who really became incarnate in a suffering world could save to the uttermost.

THE CRUCIFIED LORD IS A CHANNEL OF GOD'S GRACE

Christian theology is constantly haunted by the question: 'Why was the cross necessary?' We shall never be able to answer this fully because as frail, fallible people we can never see or understand the whole story of redemption from God's point of view. We are *in* the story (that is, like characters in a drama which is still going on, we are attempting to grasp the wholeness of the story as if we were outside) and our interpretation is obviously very limited. However, one thing is clear – any attempt to bring two sides together requires someone who can reconcile the two estranged groups. But more is required than that. He must have such authority as to 'represent' both sides fairly. There are examples we can draw upon from secular life. In Britain we have ACAS (Arbitration, Conciliation and Advisory Service) which performs a valuable task in negotiations between employers and trade unions in order to restore normal relations. Such an analogy, however, has its weakness when we apply it to the death of Jesus because we could so easily fall into the trap of supposing that Jesus is the negotiator who reconciles people to an angry God and who brings us together. We must remember where we got to: Jesus is God incarnate who restores us to fellowship. As we saw earlier, in the New Testament God is never the object of reconciliation; he is always the subject. He is the one who reconciles.

Thus, the cross does not procure God's grace – it flows from grace. It is grace which shapes the entire history of Jesus; grace was expressed in his ministry and grace took him to his death. The result of his sacrificial dying is that God's grace now flows freely into the life of the Church and out into the unreconciled areas of human life. Christian teaching, very properly, has seen Christ's work in terms of representation. In order that they may return to fellowship with God, men and women need a vehicle for their penitence, and in order that God can show the fullness of his acceptance he too must have a vehicle for his love. As our *representative* Jesus Christ stands before the Father and takes responsibility for our sin and evil. He is our 'sin offering' and our perfect high priest, blending the two together in his matchless life and death.

Although we shall see in the next chapter that 'representation' does not exhaust the significance of Jesus, we can observe that it is a splendid way of understanding the meaning of his life and death. In normal life a representative is often able to do many helpful things for us. It is not always possible for the entire group – a workforce, organisation or company – to deal directly with the management, so we elect delegates or representatives. We normally choose our best people for this important task. They have authority to 'stand in for us', and when before the management they speak in 'our name'.

The New Testament makes it clear that in a deep and analogous sense Jesus, too, was our representative. Jesus' recasting of the 'Son of Man' idea in terms of the Suffering Servant of Isaiah 53 indicates that he thought of his destiny in terms of 'standing alongside' and 'standing for' others. This, as we also saw, is a dominant note in the epistle to the Hebrews. He represents us before the Father as our full, final and eternal offering for sin. He was, we might say, 'inclusive man' – in his suffering and death he has done what no one else could have done, but into which every person may enter. This representative note is struck in John Newman's famous hymn, 'Praise to the Holiest in the Height':

> O generous love! that he who smote
>   In Man for man the foe,
> The double agony in Man
>   For man should undergo.

Representation, then, is a very helpful way of understanding the profound mystery of God's love which the cross expresses. Of course, it does not give us the whole story because although Jesus Christ stands 'for' humanity, he also stands 'apart' by reason of his difference from us. But leaving that aspect to one side for the time being, Jesus as our representative takes humankind with him into the presence of God and opens the way to fellowship and peace. And it is important to realise that this ministry continued throughout his entire life. This is at the heart of his obedience to his Father from his youth on and is picked up by the epistle to the Hebrews as a mark of his Sonship (5:8). 'This Jesus, who was so supremely Man at his highest', declared Max Warren, 'became Man at the very apex of his humility.'[4] Yet, we have to confess, we are no nearer to understanding fully why it was necessary for Christ to be our representative. Try as we may to break this mystery into categories which we can understand, we find that we meet an ultimate mystery which defies our attempt to master it. It is said that someone once asked Pavlova, the great dancer, what she meant by a particular dance she had performed. Pavlova replied: 'Do you think I would have danced it if I could have said it?' We have to recognise the fact that even Christ, the great teacher, did not explain the cross in so many words. It had to be taken up – lived and died. And, then, we find to our amazement, that instead of our explaining the cross, it explains us and shows why we cannot really live the kind of life God intended for us without his salvation.

But, of course, this is the real beauty of the cross. It expresses a God who cares so much that he gives of his best and whose love is shown in the humility and shame of incarnation. G. Studdert-Kennedy, known affectionately as 'Woodbine Willie' to many thousands of soldiers during the Great War, found that for many of them the cross was the only symbol which made any sense about God in that

pointless war. In his poem 'The Comrade God' he compares
two ways of looking at God:

> Dost Thou not need the helpless sparrow's falling?
> Canst Thou not see the tears that women weep?
> Canst Thou not hear Thy little children calling?
> Dost Thou not watch them as they sleep?
>
> Then, O my God, Thou art too great to love me,
> Since Thou dost reign beyond the reach of tears,
> Calm and serene as the cruel stars above me,
> High and remote from human hopes and fears.
>
> Only in Him can I find a home to hide me,
> Who on the cross was slain to rise again;
> Only with Him, my Comrade God, beside me,
> Can I go forth to war with sin and pain.

No wonder that millions of people have found in this 'down
to earth' God the end to their searching. We may be left
with residual questions concerning the mystery of the cross,
but there is no arguing about the reality of his love. In
Jesus God is made translucent.

CAN A DEATH ATONE?

Well, it all depends on whose death we are talking about.
When Yvonne Fletcher, a young policewoman, died in a
tragic shooting incident outside the Iranian Embassy in 1984
no one jumped to the conclusion that her death was an
'atoning' sacrifice. Very properly, she was later commemorated for doing her 'duty' and people saw this death as part
of the 'sacrifice' entailed in the profession, the 'thin blue
line' which keeps evil and crime at bay in society. But let
us take another example. When the Polish Jesuit Priest Fr
Maksymilian Kolbe took the place of a man who was one
of ten prisoners sentenced to starvation in the notorious
Auschwitz, his sacrificial death certainly 'saved' the man,
Franciszek Gajowniczek, from death. He gave his life for

another. Yvonne Fletcher's death was sad and unnecessary, Fr Maksymilian's was a heroic and deliberate 'surrender' of life so that someone else might live.

But the death of Jesus overshadows them both because it was a deliberate, sacrificial death which reconciled men and women to God. As God and man, Jesus restored the harmony which had been wrecked by sin and thus made 'at-one-ment' through his sacrificial death on the cross. Down the centuries, Christians have contemplated the cross as the place where Jesus, the Son of God, has really taken upon himself our sin and guilt, our violence and pain, our wickedness and shame, so that through his own atoning sacrifice he might do away with it completely. Inevitably it is in the language of poetry that we begin to comprehend the staggering scale of God's love:

> And God held in his hand
> A small globe. Look, he said.
> The son looked. Far off
> As through water, he saw
> A scorched land of fierce
> Colour. A light burned
> There, crested buildings
> Cast their shadows; a bright
> Serpent, a river
> Uncoiled itself, radiant
> With silver.
> On a bare
> Hill a bare tree saddened
> The sky. Many people
> Held out their thin arms
> To it, as though waiting
> For a vanished April
> To return to its crossed
> Boughs. The son watched
> Them. Let me go there, he said.

(R. S. Thomas, 'The Coming')

8

Ways of Understanding
the Cross

In the three chapters which follow we shall be considering a number of the theories which have emerged in Christian history to explain the death of Jesus. But it is worth observing, before we do so, that the Church has never arrived at a definitive understanding of the cross, as if to say, 'This is what Christians must believe about the atonement.' Whereas the Church spent nearly five centuries hammering out the doctrine of Christ, the death of Jesus was not at all a subject of controversy or debate. Everybody in the Church accepted that Jesus' death was 'vicarious'. Sunday by Sunday, for the first thousand years of the Church's life, the sacrifice of Christ was celebrated in the churches of Christendom as God's victory over sin and death, and this appeared to be sufficient.

It is when we approach the second thousand years of Christian history that we observe the atonement beginning to replace Christology as the centre of interest. A number of reasons explain this shift of emphasis. First, in the later Dark Ages 'schools' of theology developed which produced analytical descriptions of God's ways with people. Theology wasn't content to leave questions unanswered; everything had to be explained. Alongside this tendency went a second development – namely, a greater interest in the meaning of the central part of the Holy Communion rite when the priest takes the bread and wine and blesses them. Whereas it was sufficient for Christians of an earlier period to believe that Christ was 'really' present and leave it at that, the Church of the thirteenth and fourteenth centuries considered it extremely important to work out as precisely as possible the meaning of the service. Inevitably this led to a tighter identification of the relationship between the sacrifice of Christ on the cross and the service which commemorated it. Thirdly, the period from about AD 1000–1500 was a time of great spiritual upheaval which took its theoretical basis from the nature of man. Although its secular expression was the 'Renaissance', its spiritual counterpart was the 'Reformation' of the Church. The overt issue at the time was the nature of authority, but the spiritual issue was in fact: 'How may a person be saved?' Atonement, therefore, was at the very heart of the Reformation crisis.

Out of the many theories of atonement which have emerged in Christian thought there are five we shall consider briefly in this chapter. Although some may fall short of an adequate explanation of the cross of Jesus, each of them has something to offer us today and merits our full attention.

THE CROSS AS GOD'S TRUMP CARD

Although, as I pointed out above, there was no one single way of understanding the death of Jesus in the early Church, it appears that there was one way which was extremely popular. According to this view, Jesus' death was a victory over the powers of evil which held sway over the minds, wills and bodies of men and women. So Irenaeus, Bishop of Lyons towards the end of the second century, put forward the theory that Jesus' death 'ransomed' humankind from the Devil. Irenaeus was a great lover of 'types'. Christ, the second Adam, overcame the sin of the first Adam by dying on the tree of life, which is an anti-type of the tree of knowledge, which was the downfall of humanity. Similarly, Mary, the mother of Christ, was an anti-type of Eve. Whereas Eve, through disobedience, led Adam and all humankind astray, Mary's dutiful obedience led us back to God through the offering of her Son. For Irenaeus, the story of redemption was seen as a fight against the Devil and powers of darkness which resulted in Christ 'recapitulating' all that God had originally attempted to achieve through Adam, and leading humanity on to life and light.

Although Irenaeus does not state how Christ's death 'ransomed' humanity from the clutches of the Devil, the image was taken up by later writers, especially Gregory of Nyssa (335–95) who made it into an elaborate theory of redemption. According to this viewpoint, the incarnation was God's method of striking a mortal blow at the Devil, who held people in bondage. The Devil, seeing the goodness and purity of Jesus, sought to destroy him and contrived his death on the cross. 'Hence it was that God, in order to make himself easily accessible to him who sought the ransom, veiled himself in our nature. In that way, as with a greedy fish, he might swallow the Godhead like a fish-hook along with the flesh, which was the bait.'[1]

Although Gregory was aware of the moral problem with this divine 'trick' – how do you reconcile absolute justice with a deceit, even against your greatest rival? – he believed that the deceit was, in fact, a crowning example of divine wisdom because the Devil could not be defeated in any other way. God paid back the Devil in his own coin. He who deceived human beings in the beginning now gets paid back with vengeance because he is made captive. The cross, therefore, was the Devil's 'come-uppance'. But this ingenious theory received short shrift from the pen of his friend Gregory of Nazianzus (329–89). 'Was the ransom then paid to the evil one? It's a monstrous thought. If to the evil one – what an outrage! Then the robber receives a ransom, not only from God but one which consists of God himself.'[2]

Although this theory was deficient in several respects, not least in its idea that a ransom was paid to the Devil, it has been revived through the study of the Swedish bishop Gustav Aulen in his fine book *Christus Victor*.[3] He argued that Luther himself was profoundly influenced by the 'classical' motif of the early Church, that Christ had ransomed humanity from the power of evil. Aulen, of course, had no intention of taking the ransom idea literally. He saw it as a dramatic symbol of a tremendous paradox the Church should take seriously – that of the conflict between God and evil, between the dark, hostile forces of sin and the redeeming love of God. Indeed, what Aulen has drawn attention to is the aspect of malevolence at the heart of the evil with which God struggles. This is an element modern people are likely to overlook or, perhaps, rationalise. Even though we are likely to avoid the suggestion of a 'deceit' played by God upon the Devil, and also that of sharp dualism implicit in the theory, we are reminded to take seriously the nature of a cosmic struggle which the 'classical' theory emphasises. Perhaps we cannot say much more than this.

THE CROSS AS A 'DUE' OR 'HONOUR' OWED TO GOD

Anselm, Archbishop of Canterbury from 1093 to 1109, gave the Church its first theory of salvation. His book *Cur Deus Homo* (Why did God become Man?) was written as a defence of the Christian faith, to explain to thinking people the logic of Christianity. Anselm dismissed the 'classical' idea that the Devil held 'rights' over humankind. Because the Devil himself was a rebel, he cannot be said to possess rights over anybody. Only God holds rights over us. This, in fact, is fundamental to *Cur Deus Homo*. He rejected the notion of Christ as a ransom paid to the Devil, but replaced it with the idea that redemption was something demanded by and paid to God the Father.

Yet, how is it possible for God to be owed anything? Drawing upon the categories of sovereignty and honour that were current in his day, Anselm interprets the atonement as a 'satisfaction' paid by Christ to the Father. Sin, consequently, is essentially a refusal on the part of God's serfs to render to God his due, thus comprising an outrage to God's honour which must be satisfied. By our sin, then, not only do we owe to God absolute obedience that is his to expect, but we must also pay him back for the honour he has been robbed of. Sin, then, is a debt owed by every person but it is one that no one can pay. Even if we could make recompense to God for the present, there remains the enormous debt of the past. The sum is so vast that no one but God can pay it – but it is our responsibility to pay. This is the reason 'why God became man'.

How did Anselm, therefore, view the atonement? Salvation could only be achieved by a Saviour who is both God and a representative of the human race: truly human and truly God. On the cross he paid the debt owed by humankind and he closed the account. But he did more. Anselm, at this point, develops the idea of extra merit, or works of 'supererogation' as it is sometimes termed. In his sufferings and death, Christ not only paid the full price for us, but his sacrifice was so abundant that it acquired superabundant merit for humankind – thus giving us eternal life as well.

This brief sketch does less than justice to Anselm's theory, which held sway for hundreds of years, but enough has been shown to illustrate its extreme inadequacies. His idea of sin, dependent as it was on a feudal idea of 'honour', results in a very poor understanding of its nature. It is more than debt. But sin, as we have observed elsewhere, is the breakdown of relationship between a loving God and dependent humanity and requires much more than the payment of a debt or the satisfying of God's honour. Because Anselm ties himself too completely to an analogy, he ends up making sin an external reality. But secondly, *Cur Deus Homo* distorts the relationship between Father and Son. Jesus, on this reckoning, is our champion, who redeems humanity from a debt owed to God the Father. Although, to be fair to Anselm, salvation is the work of God, the very fact that he expresses it in terms of feudal categories makes God appear as a feudal baron who has such an almighty sense of offended honour that salvation seems to be the work of the Son entirely.

While space does not allow a more penetrating criticism of Anselm, two final things must be said. On the one hand, to Anselm's great credit he did at least attempt to put across the message of atonement in terms which his contemporaries understood. He drew upon insights in the society of his day which might become ways of understanding the mystery of the atonement. On the other hand, however, this became part of Anselm's negative legacy to the Church. His theory, sometimes called the 'Latin' or 'satisfaction' theory, only encouraged the Church further along the lines of legalism and law which formed the backcloth to the unfortunate break-up of the Church in the sixteenth century.

THE CROSS AS OUR EXAMPLE

We now come to a theory which has all the signs of being a modern, progressive idea and, yet, it goes back to an eleventh-century Frenchman, Peter Abelard (1079–1142). His tragic love for Heloise, their secret marriage (even though he was a monk and she a nun), their enforced separation and his lifelong quarrel with authority, has all the ingredients of a breathtaking novel, which indeed, it became.[4] His understanding of the atonement, however, uninfluential during his own day, has now become a popular theory among some theologians for the way it shifts atonement from God's action to ours. As such, it is often described as a 'subjective' theory because of its effect on us rather than upon what Christ achieved. The question he put to the issue of atonement was: what possible act of expiation could come of an act of murder committed against Christ? Justice cannot flow from injustice was Abelard's firm conclusion: 'Indeed, how cruel and wicked it seems that anyone should demand the blood of an innocent person as the price for anything . . . still less that God should consider the death of his Son so agreeable that by it he should be reconciled to the world.'[5]

Abelard, therefore, rejected a transactional theory and put in its place a view which stressed the cross as depicting the nature of God's love. The example of the sacrifice and death of Jesus is that which calls from us a like response. Abelard explains it: 'Now it seems to us that we have been justified by the blood of Christ and reconciled to God in this way; that through this unique act of grace manifested to us – in that his Son has taken upon himself our nature and persevered therein in teaching us by word and example even unto death – he was more fully bound to us himself by love; with the result that our hearts should be enkindled by such a gift of divine grace . . . '[6]

For Abelard, then, the life and death of Christ was a long and inspiring story of God's self-giving and sacrificial love which wants nothing back but love. The cross thus becomes a timeless and universal visual aid which declares, 'This is how much God loves you!' and which excites our love in return. To quote Peter Abelard again: 'I think that the purpose and the cause of the incarnation was that he [God] might illumine the world by his wisdom and excite in us a love to himself.'

This simple and immediately recognisable theory of God's love has been taken up by two more recent thinkers, Hastings Rashdall and R. S. Franks. Rashdall's important book, *The Idea of Atonement in Christian Theology*,[7] was a trenchant defence of the 'example' theory, asserting that this is at the heart of the New Testament. He denied that Jesus had ever taught that sin could only be forgiven through his death. His death, true, was a sacrifice, but one that any disciple might make. Christ's concept of atonement was that of forgiveness and this, he pointed out, was at the heart of the Lord's prayer: 'Our Father . . . forgive us our sins as we forgive those . . . ' 'There is not the slightest suggestion,' he went on, 'that anything but repentance is necessary – the actual death of a Saviour, belief in the atoning efficacy of that death or in any other article of faith, baptism, confession to any but God, absolution, reception of the holy eucharist, Church membership – not a hint of any of these. The truly penitent man confesses his sins to God, receives instant forgiveness.' Insofar as the cross has any meaning, it is to be found in the doctrine of free forgiveness. Because love is the highest thing in human life, we find in the 'death of the Supreme Revealer a pledge or symbol of the forgiveness he had preached and promised'.[8]

Dr R. S. Franks' *The Atonement* reinforced Rashdall's conclusion, although from a more thorough and reasoned basis. Whereas Rashdall finds the centre of atonement in free, divine forgiveness which only wants the sinner to return, Franks sees the centre in love itself. This is the first principle of theology, which determines how one sees the rest. God's love is manifested in such a way as to induce penitence: 'The sacrifice of Christ is the offering of Himself up to God on the Cross to be the means of revealing the divine love.'[9]

This 'exemplar', or 'moral influence' theory as it is some-times called, initially seems to be a most attractive and persua-sive theory. It seems to offer a most positive reason for the atonement with none of the drawbacks of other theories which tie atonement with judgment, holiness or sin. God, simply through his Son's cross, says 'Come' and it is a mere matter of returning home. Now it is a fact that this theory is of importance for Christians. Combined with other ideas, the cross as God's 'love appeal' to the heart of humanity is part of the gospel. The mistake of Abelard, Rashdall and Franks, however, is to make it the *whole* of the gospel, and this is its fatal flaw because it is an inadequate and dangerous argument which has as much chance of creating despair as life. Let us consider why. First, the theory seems to say to people, 'The life of Jesus is how you should live. Come as you are to him, follow his example and you will live a truly happy and fulfilled life.' Whatever it is, such an exhortation is obviously not Good News, even though it may be very good advice. The 'example' theory is very simple to understand but very difficult to live.

This leads into a second more serious problem with the theory. What significant difference is there between Jesus, the master of moral perfection, and the law discussed in Romans 7, which condemned Paul's sin and weakness? Well did T. O. Wedel ask: 'What can Jesus as mere Master of human perfection really do for you? The Sermon on the Mount as a vision of Mount Everest of moral striving can beckon to a life of ethical heroism. But woe to those who drop by the wayside in that upward climb.'[10] Indeed, we are back with the heresy of Pelagius, who believed that we can save ourselves. But the testimony of human weakness is that mere encouragement to persevere in the climb of following Jesus, without a radical change of heart and life, will do nothing. What human beings need to know, even more than that Jesus is perfectly human, is that as *Saviour* he has dealt with the power of sin in their lives. It is not enough, then, to say that the cross reveals God's love – unless it also deals with our sin it is as worthless as a food shop is to a starving child who has no money to buy.

Thirdly, Abelard's theory takes too cheap a view of sin. There is no sense of the heinousness and power of sin in the writings of these theologians, and no appreciation of human despair in trying to live a good or holy life. Fourthly, one wonders if the 'exemplar' theologians, by avoiding the cross as the place where atonement takes place and where God and men and women are truly made one, miss the very heart of God's love. Their Saviour goes to his cross almost as by accident, as a great example of self-giving love. But the Christ of the gospels is called by the magnet of the cross to lay down his life for the sheep as an act of sacrifice for them, bearing their sin and evil and nailing them to the cross. This is love indeed, which knowingly bears the sins of humanity from cradle to grave.

THE CROSS AS MAN'S PERFECT RESPONSE

One of the most important theories about the death of Christ to emerge from the Reformation was a theory known as 'penal substitution'. We shall examine this notion more closely in the following chapter. For the moment we must note that principally through the theology of John Calvin, the idea of Christ as our substitute sin-bearer quickly became orthodoxy among Protestant Churches. By emphasising the sacrificial aspects of the atonement, Calvin was able to show that Christ bore the character of a sinner and, consequently, took upon himself the curse of the law. This curse, which was properly ours, was transferred to him so that we might be released from sin's power and condemnation, 'He bore in his soul the tortures of condemned and ruined man.' But, whereas Calvin combined penal substitution with other ways of understanding the cross, his followers tightened up his teaching so much that substitution became the exclusive idea, and the sufferings of Christ the morbid yet all-important centre of the system.

Two theologians who reacted against the quasi-orthodoxy of this view, John McLeod Campbell and R. C. Moberley, rejected the notion of substitution, believing this to present a warped and unChristian theology of God. Their common ground consists in their understanding of Christ's ministry for humanity. In John McLeod Campbell's case, Jesus offers 'the perfect confession'; according to R. C. Moberley, Jesus makes for men and women 'the perfect penitence'.

McLeod Campbell's book, *The Nature of the Atonement*,[11] marks the start of modern theology as far as the atonement is concerned. Campbell was a Presbyterian minister in Calvinist Scotland and was thoroughly dissatisfied with the legalist and penal views of atonement which seemed to separate God from Christ. It was impossible, Campbell believed, that God would want to punish his own Son for the sins of others. Rejecting, then, penal theories of the death of the Lord, Campbell saw the heart of forgiveness in the free and unconditional love of God. But he also rejected any idea of an easy atonement: love, he insisted, which is worth anything must necessarily suffer a great deal for others, 'Infinite love can only be expressed at infinite cost.' If, then, there is no punishment for sin, where does Campbell find the centre of atonement? Whereas many of Campbell's contemporaries considered the heart of atonement to lie in the actual pains and torments of Christ on the cross, Campbell put the emphasis upon Christ's vicarious penitence and confession which flowed from his life and was expressed supremely in his death.

Now, three important ideas emerge from Campbell's theory of the atonement. First, he brought the incarnation into it. It was important for Campbell's theology to emphasise that Jesus Christ was truly human and truly one of us. The whole of his ministry was to bring erring sons and daughters back to God. God is eternally forgiving love and is always ready and waiting to forgive. All of Christ's life was a witness to the fatherhood of God and the sonship to which we are all called. Secondly, Christ makes atonement through his perfect confession of our sin and weakness. As we noted, Campbell rejected any notion of penal suffering for sin, even though he was committed to the idea that people need to be reconciled to God. As perfect human being, therefore, Jesus Christ's atonement took the form of a perfect confession of our sins. He responded to the divine wrath by expressing, on our behalf, penitence and grief. Campbell emphasises the point he is making: 'The sufferings and tears are no more penal than the sufferings and tears that a parent might experience over a wayward child.' Thirdly, Campbell stresses the prospective aspect of the cross of Christ. The present immediate effect of the atonement is justification and the acquisition of the righteousness of Christ in us, and the remote effect is eternal life. The moral and spiritual qualities we see in Christ's life and death are to be repeated in the lives of all the redeemed.

What are we to make of this theory? Few of us would doubt that we find in this picture of atonement a sensitive and moving appraisal of Christ's work. Many of Campbell's insights, such as the importance of the incarnation and God's work in Christ, are worthy of our close attention. The major objection we must bring against the theory, however, is that the cash value of his splendid idea of Christ as our perfect confessor, who offers a perfect 'Amen' to our contrition, is exactly nil. How can someone who is perfect and without sin make a confession for others? If he is not really bearing our sin or 'becoming sin' for us, how can we make sense of someone confessing sins we have committed? The second criticism is that Campbell evacuates the atonement of any 'objective' content. Christ did not die as 'a substitute' or as a 'punishment' but as a moral and spiritual sacrifice for sin. His sufferings were not the measure of what God can inflict, but the revelation of what God 'feels'. We have here, incidentally, a variation of the 'moral influence' theory considered in the last section. The real atonement takes place when, with the same attitude and response of Christ's perfection, obedience is seen in us.

R. C. Moberley's book, *Atonement and Personality*,[12] took up many of Campbell's ideas and themes and explored them further. As the title of the book suggests, his intention was to relate the work of Christ to the problem of human personality. He argued that no real understanding of the atonement could be reached without knowledge of personality – nor could 'personality' be explained without exploration of the nature of the atonement. In his first chapter he examines the nature of punishment and arrives at an understanding which affects his conclusions about atonement. He observes that punishment can only have meaning to creatures who have personhood. The lower one goes down the evolutionary scale, the less meaning punishment has. Similarly, Moberley continues, 'penitence' and 'remorse' only have meaning for beings with personality. But there is this significant point – the more a person is corrupted by sin, the less meaning he will find in penitence and the less possible it will become. Moberley thus arrives at an important and profound understanding of the power and influence of evil: 'The reality of sin in the self blunts the self's power of utter antithesis against sin. Just because it now is part of what I am, I cannot, even though I would, wholly detest it.'[13] The legacy of past sin, therefore, prevents true repentance.

With 'punishment' and 'penitence', according to Moberley, we have the two poles of atonement. Because people are corrupted through sin, they cannot offer true penitence; the sinner, as a moral being, must be punished (because this is of the essence of 'personality'). And, yet, how can this be, because it is the nature of God's punishment to lead sinners to repentance? Moberley finds the answer to this dilemma in Christ as the 'perfect penitent'. Perhaps more than any writer before him, Moberley anchors the atonement in the incarnation. Although he never says that Jesus' incarnation *was* the atonement, he comes very close to this idea. Christ's life was that of unceasing obedience to the Father and that obedience produced in our Lord the kind of personality which could make the perfect act of penitence on our behalf. The problem of atonement, according to Moberley, is how to get one who is unholy to be holy. He answers this question by insisting that atonement is made (a) when the mediator does so out of love and freely, (b) when he is closely related to the guilty person and can be his true representative, (c) when his sacrifice produces the contrition and sanctification of the guilty person.

Before we criticise this theory there are two points to draw out. First, Moberley's notion of punishment is largely non-retributive. Punishment is largely restorative and its meaning must be sought in the end it seeks to achieve and not the satisfaction of the punisher. Secondly, Moberley, perhaps more strongly than any other writer before him, stresses the work of the Holy Spirit in the work of atonement. Whereas Campbell's theory lacks a doctrine of grace, Moberley's connects the work of the Spirit with the work of Christ and thus unites the life of Christ with Pentecost.

But, in the final analysis, Moberley's theory is damaged by the criticism we applied to Campbell – if a 'perfect confession' is impossible for the sinless Son of God to make, so is a 'perfect penitence'. 'Personal guilt Christ could never confess,' argued P. T. Forsyth, 'there is that in guilt which can only be confessed by the guilty: "I did it." That kind of confession Christ could never make.'[14] For that reason, vicarious suffering is one thing but vicarious penitence is quite another. In the film *Airport*, based upon Arthur Hailey's book, we may recall that one of its sub-plots concerns a deranged Italian who decides to blow up the plane and claim insurance. The plane lands safely although a number of people are badly wounded. The wife of the Italian meets the crew, passengers and injured people crying, 'Oh, I am sorry; I'm so sorry!' No one could question her sense of shame and penitence – she was innocent yet she felt guilty. That is quite understandable. But if we were to apply this to Moberley's theory we would have to take it further; the wife's remorse and penitence would have to become an 'atonement' for her husband's crime. But this is not logical in life and it is difficult to understand how any feeling, however powerful, can be vicarious.

THE CROSS AS 'REPRESENTATION'

It is time now to consider a theory which was mentioned briefly in the last chapter – namely the idea that Christ's death was a representative act on behalf of all people. This is perhaps the most widely accepted theory of all and is the basis of most Church confessions. The theologian we shall look at is the great Methodist scholar Vincent Taylor, who has bequeathed to the study of the atonement his trilogy on the subject: *Jesus and His Sacrifice, The Atonement in New Testament Teaching* and *Forgiveness and Reconciliation*.[15]

It is extremely difficult to summarise Taylor's view in a few lines; the richness and comprehensiveness of his thought defies such a reduction and I fear that its life will be lost through over-savage surgery on his masterly contribution to our theme. But the attempt must be made if we are going to have any form of overview. In *Jesus and His Sacrifice*, Vincent Taylor studied the teaching of Jesus against the background of the Old Testament's thought concerning the kingdom, messianic hope, sacrifice and the Suffering Servant. He concluded that Jesus believed his sufferings would fulfil the Father's will for reconciliation with humanity. He died 'vicariously' for all people and established a covenant-relationship between God and people.

How was this done? Jesus Christ identified himself with sinful men and women in the greatness of his love, 'entering into the consequences of human sin and bearing them upon his heart'.[16] As Suffering Servant he stood in a representative relation to his own, voicing their penitence, obedience and submission to the will of God. In his second great book, *The Atonement in New Testament Teaching*, he continues his study of the atonement, taking his investigation into the rest of the New Testament data. He argues that they are of one mind with the gospels in the conviction that the death of Jesus was the fulfilment of God's purpose and that it was messianic, vicarious, representative and sacrificial. The New Testament writers, suggest Taylor, recognised the momentous significance of the death and resurrection of Christ and they started to link it with suffering (1 Peter 2), sacramental communion (1 Cor. 11), faith (Gal. 2; Heb. 11–12) and love (1 Cor. 13).

In the concluding part of his trilogy, *Forgiveness and Reconciliation*, Taylor declares that the best New Testament word to describe the purpose of the atonement is 'reconciliation'. The root meaning of the word atonement – at-one-ment – says it all, the purpose of Christ's incarnation and death is to make humanity one with God. The consequences of reconciliation are no less momentous – we are forgiven and therefore restored to God – placed in a new relationship with our heavenly Father. There is a three-fold aspect of the doctrine, Taylor suggests. It is *vicarious* – that is, Christ died for me; it is *representative* – he stood in for me in his obedience, penitence and submission to the Father; and it is *sacrificial* – he made there a sacrifice of himself for others.

We must draw out a few significant aspects of his teaching. First, it is vital for Taylor to affirm the unity of the Trinity in the salvation of humankind. This is so strong that it must rule out any idea of vindictive punishment. This does not mean that Taylor is against retributive punishment – indeed, he finds it difficult not to accept that all punishment, as well as being disciplinary, implicitly carries with it an aspect of retribution. Justice must be done; accounts must be settled. He can readily accept, then, the notion that Christ's sufferings on the cross were 'penal' – not in the sense that God was angry with him as though he were a sinner, but penal in the sense that in his representative role for humanity he submitted to the divine judgment against sin. We shall be considering this again in the next chapter, but it is worth reflecting whether Taylor is not having his cake and eating it at this point. It is important for him to argue for Christ's identity with us in all respects except sin, and that he bears our sins on his heart and takes them to the cross. His death was 'penal' and 'vicarious'. But God was not angry with him, nor was he punished in our stead. In a stirring passage he presents his case: 'Jesus entered into the blight and judgment which rest upon sin, and bore its shame and desolation upon his heart. Because he loved men so greatly he became one with them, entering into the situation in which they stood, sharing the pain of their disobedience, and feeling the pressure of their sins. Such suffering is penal because it is the fruit of the judgment which rests on sin.'[17] Fine. But did he or did he not become 'sin' for us, to use Paul's phrase (2 Cor. 5:21)? It would seem not, because the judgment falls not on Christ but upon sin. This, I fear, is a fatal weakness in Taylor's careful exegesis. He wants to show that Christ is identified with us in every respect but he pulls away when the logic of his argument leads him to say that Christ bore our sin and was identified with it.

My second observation on Taylor's magnificent contribution follows closely from the last point. Vincent Taylor is unable to take Christ in any closer to identification with sin because he rejects the notion of 'substitution'. He admits that

Paul's theology comes within 'a hair's breadth' of substitution,[18] but repudiates it because of its punitive overtones. He finds it difficult, if not impossible, to hold because it drives a wedge between God and Christ so that it seems that Christ, a loving Saviour, offers to God a sacrifice for sin to appease his wrath. Fundamental to Taylor's thesis is that Christ died not in order that God might *now* be able to forgive sins, but his death declares that God *does* forgive and the cross is God's way of removing the barrier of sin. Calvary is the incredible revelation of a pardoning God. It proceeds from grace, assures us of God's gracious pardon and gives us life and peace.

Such, in brief, is Vincent Taylor's contribution. Much of it I wholeheartedly agree with and find extremely helpful. Yet, probably by over-reacting against the implications of certain primitive and crude presentations of the theory of substitution, he has deprived himself of some rich insights the theory would have given to him. It is to this much maligned idea we now turn.

9

Jesus our Substitute?

In the last chapter I advanced the suggestion that any theology of the cross without the idea of Jesus as our 'substitute' deprives itself of significant insights and understandings which are there at the heart of New Testament faith. There are many versions of this concept of 'substitution': some are very primitive and crude in their understanding of Jesus as substitute; others, however, are more sophisticated and moderate in approach. But common to the theory are two main elements: that Jesus Christ was humankind's substitute on the cross and that it was a penal substitution for sin that was properly ours.

OBJECTIONS TO SUBSTITUTION

My contention, however, runs counter to a great deal of scholarship which has already concluded that this notion is wrong. So G. W. H. Lampe asserts: 'It is high time to discard the vestiges of a theory of Atonement that was geared to a conception of punishment which found nothing shocking in the idea that God should crucify sinners or the substitute who took their place.'[1] In the United States, Horace Bushnell parted company from Calvinism on this issue: 'If penal substitution is all there is to the doctrine,' he declared, 'there was a great deal to disgust us in God's method of squaring accounts.'[2] In his view the justice satisfied is satisfied with injustice. A more recent theologian, David Edwards, criticises penal substitution for its distortion of God: 'Such pictures portray the Eternal as morally inferior to any human father ... no father would today be admired if he was so enveloped in his own interpretation of the moral code as to demand "satisfaction" for every breach of it by his children before he would show them love.'[3]

These comments are very forceful and come from respected theologians, for whom the love of God and his unity in the work of the Son are paramount. What, we must ask, do they particularly reject in the theory of substitution? There are two main criticisms we must consider.

It separates the Father from the work of the Son

It is said that one of the main problems with the doctrine of substitution is that it drives a wedge between Father and Son. The Father is seen as a holy, righteous deity concerned with matters of justice and the Son is viewed as one who 'propitiates' God's wrath and appeases him. So God himself is polarised between the Father, who is viewed as a stern law-giver and judge, and his Son, who 'saves' humankind from the righteous demands of God's law. Not only does this appear to set Father and Son against each other, but it also suggests that Jesus did something to change the attitude of God to sinners. Such a theory appears to insult God and make him seem to be an angry, implacable God more concerned about his wounded pride than the real interests of his creatures. This kind of picture, as Edwards declared above, falls a long way short of even our ideas of fatherhood, let alone the loving Father of all. We must readily acknowledge that there have been versions of the substitution theory which have led to that conclusion. I have no wish to defend any notion which removes God the Father from his active role in salvation. *He* takes the initiative; it is *his* Son who is the mediator; it is *his* love the Son expresses; it is *he* who reconciles humanity to himself.

But is there any reason why the unity of Father with Son rules out the notion of Christ as substitute? Let us consider the difference between 'representative', which many scholars agree is a helpful idea, and that of 'substitute'. Both theories are, essentially, objective theories – that is, the cross achieved something. According to the former view, Christ is the perfect man who stands for me before God and represents me there. His death did something for me which I could not do for myself. But according to the 'substitutionary' view, Christ died for me, he took my place and took my punishment upon himself.

Let me attempt to illustrate this by way of something that happened ten years ago. One day a young man in Durham asked my help. He had to appear before a trade union tribunal to answer a certain charge. He was extremely agitated because not only was his job at stake, but if the appeal was lost he would also lose his 'tied' cottage as well. According to the union rules he was allowed to have a representative. He was an ordinary working man and knew that he would be out of his depth confronted by his employers, who were skilled at argument and debate. So I was approached and I agreed to represent him. But there was more to it than that. He could have asked anybody, his best friend or someone more conversant with the Employment Act, but he didn't. He chose me because I represented the Church as well, and my presence as a representative of the Church, as well as being his personal representative, counted for something. But however much I sympathised with his position and was, indeed, happy to give my time and energies on his behalf, I was always an outsider. It was his problem, not mine, and if we failed in our appeal it was his job and house that would have been lost, not mine.

Applying this to Christ's atonement, the New Testament insists that Christ was no mere external representative whose participation was basically 'costless'. Instead, it asserts, such was his representative act that he identified so closely with our suffering, sin and hopelessness that he made them his own. Representation, then, appears to have been translated on to a plane very different from our use of the word.

Proponents of the representative theory, indeed, speak in such a way of the nature of Christ's representative act that makes us wonder if the term fits the description. P. T. Forsyth, for example, speaks of the way Christ entered into human sin and suffering: 'Christ, by the deep intimacy of his sympathy with men, entered deeply into the blight and judgment which was entailed by man's sin, and which must be entailed by man's sin if God is holy and therefore a judging God.'[4] Vincent Taylor, similarly, speaks of the 'self-offering of Jesus in his perfect submission to the judgment of God upon sin ... no offer of penal suffering as a substitute for his own will meet his need, but a submission presented by his Representative before God becomes the foundation of a new hope.'[5]

But such is the degree of commitment by this 'representative' that one has to ask: 'At what point does a representative become a substitute?' If Jesus, my representative, enters into the despair and loneliness of sin on my behalf, and tastes death for me and us all, so that we might have life – then no careful circumlocution can avoid the fact that we are talking about a substitute! A. M. Hunter quotes Winer's dictum: 'In most cases one who acts on behalf of another takes his place.'[6] And James Denney, commenting upon P. T. Forsyth's avoidance of 'substitution' while insisting that Christ's death was 'vicarious' (in my place), argues: 'If Christ died the death in which sin had involved us – if in his death he took the responsibility of our sins upon himself – no word is equal to this which falls short of what is meant by calling him our substitute.'[7]

But there is another reason why 'representative' seems to fall short of New Testament description. A representative is one of us, he may be better, wiser, more eloquent and good – but the essential thing about a representative is that he shares our humanity. Now, Christ is all of this – but much more. He is certainly our representative and this is New Testament teaching, but he is *more than that* because he comes from God and represents all that is holy and true. Denney made this point nearly seventy years ago: 'The fundamental fact of the situation is that, to begin with, Christ is *not* ours, and we are *not* one with Him ... we are "without Christ" ... a Representative not produced by us, but given to us, not chosen by us, but the elect of God, is not a Representative at all in the first instance, but a Substitute.'[8]

It seems, then, that not a lot is gained by calling Christ our representative. Not only do we risk confusion because of the evident overlap between the two terms but, more importantly, we lose the force of substitution with its implicit suggestion of someone who takes away my sin, grief, despair and suffering and makes them all his own. He enters so deeply into our predicament that we are made free through the gift of his death. There is no reason why we cannot use this language of Christ in God because Father and Son are inseparably connected in the work of salvation. Christ does not appease a Holy God and he certainly does not change his attitude – because God's attitude from the beginning of time has always been that of love and mercy. What Christ does in some unfathomable mystery which lies beyond the reach of our language (although not our spiritual understanding) is to provide God's answer to the issue of justice. The cross became the place where sacrificial love took within itself the rebellion of humankind with its consequent despoiling of God's holiness in creation, society and human life.

The Christ paid our penalty

The sharpest objection to the theory of substitution is the notion that Christ so bore our sin on the cross that he became accursed by God. Our penalty he made his. The first to criticise this theory on moral grounds was the Unitarian Faustus Socinus who, in his polemical book *De Jesu Christo Servatore* (Of Jesus Christ the Saviour), refused to allow the transfer of moral blame. It is quite in order for someone to pay a debt of money for another, he argued, but moral bankruptcy is another matter. If it is not expiated by the one who has incurred it, it is not expiated at all. According to Socinus, then, it would be unjust of God to punish the innocent for the guilty because it is against God's moral laws. A modern theologian, David Edwards, has put it equally clearly, rejecting the penal-substitutionary theory because of our modern awareness that it is unjust to punish a substitute:

'Justice must be addressed to the individual concerned. An individual is responsible for his own virtues and mistakes – and only for his own virtues and mistakes.'[9]

I think there are three observations we can make on the rejection of the penal view because of its so-called moral deficiency. First, at the heart of a rejection of substitution is the denial of a retributive view of punishment. Now obviously there are many strands in a theory of punishment. If punishment is only retributive, our society could quickly become a vengeful, bitter and warped community bent only on exacting just rights. But, equally, if society views punishment simply in terms of discipline and rehabilitation, it may lose sight of values and standards because concentration has shifted from 'What has he done wrong and how can he pay recompense?' to 'How may we help him to be a better person?' Both questions must be held together if we are going to have a balanced view of punishment. Indeed, a great deal of confusion in the Prison Service today has been caused by a refusal to acknowledge the retributive element in punishment.[10] Not only is punishment only punishment when it is deserved (if it is undeserved the victim is not being punished, he is guiltless and remains a free man even in prison), but punishment must be retributive in order to be reformatory. I mean by this that a criminal is hardly likely to be reformed if he did not believe he was guilty and deserved to be punished. Before he can become the kind of person society wants him to become, he must acknowledge his guilt and the justice of the penalty and then, and only then, has he a chance of turning his back on the past and living again. A lot of our problems, in fact, stem from our reading of retribution as an unjust 'eye for eye' or vindictive punishment. I suggest that we should reject such ideas and replace them by an understanding of punishment as the just recompense for our wrongdoing. The Bible, without any apology, has both strands in its teaching. Punishment is both *retributive*, because I have sinned and broken God's laws and deserve to be punished, and *corrective*, because God wants offenders to come back to him. The cross has both these elements. It expresses God's judgment on sin and is the means whereby we are made new people.

Our second observation is that the criticism that moral blame is not transferable rests upon a doubtful understanding of human guilt. Its base is individualistic. I must pay for my sins, you must pay for yours. But the theologian Wolfhart Pannenberg has subjected this notion to intensive investigation and has shown that morality doesn't work that way.[11] It cannot be compartmentalised and categorised according to individual responsibility. This is where modern insights have revealed the truth of the Bible's teaching about human solidarity. Sin cannot, any more than disease, be kept within the bounds of an individual life. Everyone is woven into community life and our actions interact with others. It is part of the social character of human existence for individuals to have responsibilities which extend to others. Take a fairly ordinary incident which happened in Bristol some years ago. One morning, for no apparent reason, a driver skidded across a main road and hit a milk-float. The shattered bottles caused a pile-up, a number of people had to go to hospital with minor injuries, some cars were badly damaged, a few commuters missed their trains, some were late for work and school. Using our imagination we could speculate that, perhaps, the driver's error of judgment was caused by the previous night's late meal, resulting in indigestion, tiredness and lack of concentration. A tiny incident with consequences for scores of people the following morning.

Such is the stuff of human life. Why should it not be so in the matter of human responsibility? Pannenberg answers that it is indeed the case: 'The structure of . . . life . . . has the character of representation, which always includes an element of substitution.'[12] Pannenberg cites the case of the German people who had to bear the consequences of the war to varying degrees, especially in its division of East and West.[13] Here the analogy with original sin is an apt one. Hitler's monstrous crimes against humanity resulted in his own people's separation and hurt. If this is clear as far as evil is concerned, there is no logical reason why this should not apply to good. Pannenberg's point is that individuals or groups can, indeed, bear guilt for others vicariously because such is the inter-penetration of human life that abstraction of the individual from society is impossible. Mind you, the substitution theory is not exactly helped by crude illustrations which make the whole concept unbelievable. One very popular sketch with youth evangelists is that which shows God as a stern judge sentencing man because of offences committed. In the sketch, because the offender is unable to meet the demands of the law, the judge himself steps down from his seat and takes the guilty person's place. The problem with this illustration is that it makes a stupendous and basically mysterious thing too banal and ordinary. By reducing it to a simplistic level of courtroom analogy, an enormous credibility gap is created because, in our experience, judges just don't do things like that and our judicial system doesn't work that way! What we have to hold on to is the fact that a very real substitutionary element runs through human existence, from the way parents often sacrifice themselves, their money and careers for their children, to the surrender of lives for others. Once one accepts that the fabric of human life makes it very understandable for good and evil to be borne vicariously for others, the notion that Jesus Christ entered into the depths of human weakness, sin, guilt and despair and took them so deeply into his experience that he can be said to have atoned for them, is not as scandalous as some have claimed.

Our third observation on the criticisms of those who object to penal substitution centres on their understanding of God. What they share is a common conviction that this is, decidedly, *not* God's way. There is horrified reaction to the idea that Christ became 'sin for us', even if Paul put it that way (2 Cor. 5:21). 'Yes,' they will say, 'our sensitivities go out to the one who stands in for another and allows himself to be mocked, beaten and crucified for others. That God's Son should choose to stand alongside me is a wonderful identification of God with our sickness and sadness. But, of course, it cannot be that Christ died to meet the demands of the law and to become a "curse" for us.' Yet doesn't 'substitution' reveal something wonderful about the nature of God and the wonder of his love that he, in the person of his Son, was willing to take our place to die our death and suffer for our misdeeds? Doesn't 'substitution' call out adoration and praise from hearts excited by such a love which stops short of nothing? This is not the heroic death of a theologian's 'representative' who, blameless and innocent himself, intercedes for us in the sight of God. This is the blasphemous death of the Lord of Glory, who takes his death a stage beyond 'representation' to that of being our substitute for sin. So the great hymn of substitution proclaims:

> Man of Sorrows! what a name,
> For the Son of God, who came
> Ruined sinners to reclaim!
> Allelujah! What a Saviour!

The closest we shall ever get to understanding substitution is in worship, when we dwell upon the wonder of God's love for fallen people and contemplate that in his love he stooped as low as that to bear upon his heart our offences and sin.

THE CASE FOR SUBSTITUTION

For the sake of clarity I must repeat what I mentioned earlier, that I am not arguing a case for substitution only. Other theories are indeed of great value for us in understanding the nature of the cross. What I am contending for is that the greatly despised doctrine of substitution has much to commend it. It is time to present the case for this.

Substitution has strong biblical support

It is acknowledged even by those scholars who reject substitution that the idea is present in the New Testament. Vincent Taylor admits that 'a theologian who retires to a doctrinal fortress guarded by such ordinance as Mark x:45, Romans vi:10f, 2 Corinthians v:14, 21, Galatians iii:13, and 1 Tim ii:5f, is more difficult to dislodge than many New Testament students imagine'.[14] He admits that Paul came within a 'hair's breadth' of the doctrine of substitution. And it is not hard to understand how such a responsible scholar as Vincent

Taylor arrived at this conclusion, because Paul's language is certainly explicit in a number of passages. We shall now consider a few of the key passages.

Romans 3:21–5

Paul shows here the abject helplessness of men and women before God as sinners. But in the mercy of God, Christ has been set forth as an expiation or propitiation for our sin. We have already seen the controversy surrounding the meaning of the Greek word *hilasterion*, translated 'propitiation', 'expiation' or 'mercy seat'. We must not get bogged down in trying to solve that problem, but rather concentrate upon the meaning of the passage as a whole. First, we note that salvation is God's work. He sent his Son forth. Even if we hold that propitiation is the correct word, we have to admit that it is not a question of Christ propitiating God as such, because it will not do justice to the fact that the action is God's. Secondly, atonement is sealed through blood – that is, just as in the Old Testament it was the blood that atoned, so here the life of Christ offered in death established the new covenant between God and humanity – with the initiative coming from God's side. Thirdly, through this act the righteousness of God is declared.

Now, what does that mean? Here we might find Paul's response to the question: 'Why couldn't God simply forgive us?' This option is inconceivable to Paul because such a response overlooks the holiness of God. God's righteousness properly requires that he should condemn sinful humanity. But to do so would vitiate his purposes for creatures upon whom he has lavished, and continues to lavish, his love. So it was necessary for his righteousness to be shown and his justice made manifest. This he did, not by winking at sin, nor by requiring payment from the hands of those who deserved to be punished – but by demonstrating through the death of his Son that he is righteous. That is, God has not overlooked human wrongdoing, and brushed it aside as though it were nothing. Rather, he has acted justly by allowing his Son to take upon himself the whole force of the law. Paul, we should note, does not explain how this is done. Neither does he explain how Christ can do this on God's behalf. He finds it sufficient simply to state the facts of the matter – the death of Christ is an expression of God's righteousness.

There is, indeed, a great unity in Paul's thought about the righteousness of God. Everything has its source there. God's salvation springs from it; the death of Christ has its roots in it. The faith of those who believe in him originates in righteousness and continues to it. But their righteousness is not their own: it is God's and is a gift, 'so as to be just and the one who justifies those who have faith in Jesus' (v. 26).

It is, then, extremely difficult to avoid the fact that whatever else we might find in this profound passage, Paul is clearly stating that Christ's death altered our destiny. He took our place of condemnation, and the righteous judge saw his death as a necessary and satisfactory atonement for us all.

Romans 5:8

'God demonstrates his own love for us in this: While we were still sinners, Christ died for us.' We see clearly in this verse Paul's secure hold upon the unity of Father and Son. Nevertheless, Paul is not afraid to speak of the death of Christ as something which is done for us. It is true that the preposition used for 'for' is *huper*, which means 'on behalf of', rather than *anti*, which is usually translated 'instead of', but New Testament language is rarely that precise. Those who believe that Paul views Christ as representative in this verse, and not substitute, must decide whether that weaker understanding can be substantiated by the context of the verse. I doubt that it can. Paul goes on to say, 'Since we have now been justified by his blood, how much more shall we be saved from God's wrath through him!' (v. 9). The note of penal substitution beats clearly in this verse. The wrath of God is averted by the death of Jesus – through the cross we are reconciled to God (v. 10). It is striking to observe that Paul, in the space of two verses, can talk of God's *love* being the motivating force of Christ's self-offering which saves humankind from God's *wrath*. Obviously Paul did not believe that wrath and love were two diametrically opposed principles in God, but that wrath was his righteous judgment upon sin and not a vindictive hatred of sinners. Yet, we must observe, even though Christ effected man's salvation, there should be no talk of effecting a change in the mind of God through the atonement, because the atonement is to Paul the work of God.

Romans 6:10

'The death he died, he died to sin once for all.' What is this death which involved the sinless Son of God in dying to sin? Sin in Romans is not basically about moral short-comings but a power under whose bondage men and women live. The character of sin is a hostile force which tyrannises humankind. Central to Paul's thought, then, in Romans 6 is that Christ has cast sin down from its throne. He met it head-on and vanquished it. Again, we must press home the question: what does it mean to say that Christ died to sin? The clue to understanding this mysterious phrase lies, I believe, in what Paul says about the meaning of baptism. We see in Romans 6 that Paul is contemplating the two-fold relationship humankind has with Adam and Christ. Through Adam we are children of wrath and alienated from God's presence. Even though we are descendants of Adam, we still stand in relation to him and bear the consequences of his sin and guilt. In the same way, Paul argues, baptism unites us with Christ. Through baptism we are incorporated into the death and resurrection of Jesus Christ. We share his death – a death to sin – and we participate in his resurrection and the fruits of it. There is a two-way movement here. We are sinners and are, therefore, dead – Christ entered into our death by dying for us and we now live in him. There, I suggest, is the clue. 'He died to sin' means that Christ entered into our death for sin; he took our sin upon himself and identified himself with it – and *substituting* himself for us and *representing* us, died a death that should have been ours.

Galatians

Paul's argument in Galatians is similar to that in Romans. He is adamant that humanity's situation was so serious that only God could save – the result of this now being that salvation is a free and unmerited gift. A particular pastoral matter in the Galatian church raised for him a number of important theological issues. The church of Galatia he had founded was being tormented by Christian Jews who insisted that Gentile believers should be circumcised and take upon themselves the law. Apparently they believed that Christ had not intended the law to be set aside. Paul meets this grave problem with an emphatic insistence upon the sufficiency of Christ's death. We are not justified by works of the law, he states (2:16), but by faith in what Christ has done. Salvation is not what we earn but is something which is done. The Christian life, consequently, is a participation in Christ's victory. Paul expresses it majestically: 'I have been crucified with Christ and I no longer live, but Christ lives in me. The life I live in the body, I live by faith in the Son of God, who loved me and gave himself for me.' Again, we note the two-way movement: Paul sees his solidarity with Christ's sufferings, death and resurrection because Christ has entered into his.

In Galatians 3 Paul explores more fully the implications of the gospel of Christ. Verse 13 is astonishing in its force and clarity: 'Christ redeemed us from the curse of the law by becoming a curse for us, for it is written: "Cursed is everyone who is hung on a tree".' Paul is talking about the curse of the law (v. 10) – that all who have not kept the law of God are under condemnation. His thought is, therefore, quite explicit; the curse from which Christ redeemed us was *our* curse. It represented our disobedience from the holy requirements of the law. But because we were weak and helpless the curse was transferred from us to him. Paul's vivid language conveys the idea that our sin has been dealt with fully. He stood where we should have stood and died a death we should have died. If that is not *substitution*, I don't know what it is.

But, perhaps with the idea of Christ as 'accursed' we have a clue concerning the meaning of the terrible cry from the cross, 'My God, my God, why have you forsaken me?' Some find this cry so unpalatable that they find refuge in the idea that it expresses simply Jesus' feeling of loneliness. 'God was there all the time,' they say. 'Jesus in his humanity felt forsaken.' Others accept that he said it and say that it shows that he had no awareness of his death effecting anything. Both theories must be summarily dismissed. The first because it is a projection of our experience. Yet there is no evidence in the gospels or elsewhere that there is a difference in Jesus' experience between fact and feeling. The second we must reject because it ignores the sense of purpose and destiny that flows throughout Jesus' ministry. It makes his death a clumsy mistake and not as it truly was, the cornerstone of history. No: let us take the statement as it stands, as a reality to Jesus. So Emil Brunner agrees: 'The trembling and horror of Gethsemane form part of this sacrifice, and, above all, that last cry on the Cross: "My God! My God! why hast Thou forsaken Me?" It is real suffering: there is nothing make-believe about it.'[15] It is remarkable that only at this point in his ministry does Jesus cry: 'My God!' instead of 'My Father'. Could it be that at this point Jesus does take upon himself all the sin, all the muck, all the dis-ease, all the crime, folly and passion of humanity and bears it alone before and unto God the Father? The fact that it is also recorded that darkness fell as Jesus died reinforces the idea that in some mysterious way Jesus accepted the curse and weight of sin.

2 Corinthians 5:14-21

In this magnificent passage Paul talks about the new creation in which Christians share when they are in Christ. A number of astonishing statements are made about the nature of Christ's death in this passage. First, Paul states that 'we are convinced that one died for all, and therefore all died' (v. 14). The substitutionary character of this verse can scarcely be denied. He took the place of others so that they might live (v. 15). As a result of this transaction, all those who believe in him are members of his new creation and live according to his new life.

But Paul does not stop there. He goes on to clarify the reconciling work of God. He emphasises that 'God was reconciling the world to himself in Christ' (v. 19), to stress the unity of the Godhead in the work of salvation. Then comes a verse that many modern scholars, if they had their way, would have preferred Paul not to have said: 'God made him who had no sin [Jesus] to be sin for us, so that in him we might become the righteousness of God' (v. 21). What does this curious expression mean? Socinus' view, mentioned earlier, was crystal-clear – moral guilt is not transferable, therefore God cannot transfer sin from us to Christ. But that, in fact, is what Paul is saying. And neither can we avoid the force of it by arguing, as some have suggested, that Paul is talking about Christ taking sinful human nature upon himself, so that all Paul is saying is that Christ came into a sinful, fallen world and identified with sinners. Attractive as this is to some, its drawback is that Paul could have said 'he became man' (Phil. 2:8) or 'he is human' (2 Cor. 5:16) – but he did not; he said 'he was made sin'. Indeed, the interpretation which tries to suggest that it is merely saying that Christ identifies with sinners tends to overlook the phrase 'him who had no sin' – that is, the righteous stands in for others and bears what we cannot bear.

The substitutionary element in 2 Corinthians 5:14–21 is also emphasised by Karl Barth, who makes reference to what he calls the 'exchange' motif in the passage. 'On the one side, the exchange: "He hath made him to be sin for us (in our place and for our sake), who knew no sin" . . . On the other side, the exchange: He does it, He takes our place in Christ, "that we . . . might be made the righteousness of God . . . in Him".'[16] A. M. Hunter says, in a forthright way, about this verse: 'The "penal" element in that statement is not to be eliminated by any exegetical legerdemain, and no doctrine of the Cross which rejects it can claim to be Pauline.'[17]

Hebrews

Although the theme of sacrifice runs throughout the New Testament, it is the epistle to the Hebrews which makes it central with its application to the work of Jesus as our high priest. The essential feature of priesthood, according to Hebrews, is that of mediation. A priest stands between humanity and God. The unusual feature of Jesus' priesthood is that he offers *himself* as a perfect sacrifice for sin and for an atonement which is full and eternal. The language used shows that the writer has a transactional view of atonement – namely, that the cross achieved reconciliation with God. Thus, in Hebrews 2:17 (RSV) we read: ' . . . that he might become a merciful and faithful high priest in the service of God, to make expiation for the sins of the people'. Yet the verb is actually 'to make propitiation' and the sense appears to be that sins are removed through the work of the high priest. He makes the necessary propitiation so that sin is dealt a mortal blow.

In a variety of other ways the author of Hebrews indicates an understanding of the death of Jesus as effecting the removal of sin and that he, as priest and victim, is God's *representative* and man's *substitute*. So, Hebrews 9:28 speaks of Christ having been 'sacrificed once to take away the sins of many people'. The verse clearly speaks of the decisive event of Calvary which now becomes the definitive event on which human destiny rests. Other verses also speak of Christ's work in relation to sin. He appeared 'to do away with sin' (9:26) and he offered 'one sacrifice for sins' (10:12). The writer emphasises the perfect nature of our high priest (4:15) who offered himself as a sacrifice for sin (7:27). Indeed, the imagery taken from the Old Testament cultus imagines Christ entering into the holy of holies, taking not the blood of animals but his own blood, 'thus securing an eternal redemption' (9:12, RSV).

1 Timothy 2:3-6

In common with other New Testament writers, 1 Timothy underlines the point that salvation comes from God. Atonement is not made to him but comes from him. So, God is the Saviour 'who wants all men to be saved and to come to a knowledge of the truth. For there is one God and one mediator between God and men, the man Christ Jesus, who

gave himself as a ransom for all men.' Here a clear exchange
is in mind. Jesus stands as mediator between the God who
wants everyone to come to him and sinners who cannot
come because of their sin. His offering of himself is seen as
a ransom (*antilutron*) for everyone.

And so we could go on, piling up references to this strand
of New Testament teaching. It is there in other parts of
the New Testament, such as 1 Peter 2:24; 3:18; 1 John 2:2;
4:10; Revelation 5:9. But my concern has not been to prove
that substitution is the only theory worth considering. Indeed
not: rather, my concern has been to show that it is an essential
element in New Testament teaching and should be united
with other theories to give us a balanced doctrine of the
cross. Brunner is prepared to acknowledge this: 'The idea
of substitution gathers up all these elements into one. If the
Cross really means the dealing of God with humanity, then
we cannot interpret it in any other way than in the sense of
the doctrine of substitutionary atonement.'[18]

Substitution has a powerful appeal

As we have noted on more than one occasion, one of the
central reasons why scholars are reluctant to give 'substitution' its proper emphasis is because of a genuine concern that
we should not make God out to be a vengeful, less than human
deity who metes out punishment and to whom a ransom is
made. They have also been very rightly concerned that any
interpretation of the cross should not separate the Father's
involvement in atonement, nor polarise love and wrath, or
justice and salvation. These are desires I share, too. But it is
surely equally important that any interpretation should not
say less than what the Scriptures say (and my complaint is
that modern scholars, by avoiding substitution, have said
considerably less) – neither should we say more. Yet we
are in danger of saying more when we make substitution
the only biblical doctrine of atonement, or when we treat
it as a close – or even as an exact – explanation of how
salvation happened. The New Testament does not give us

the authority to go that far. Even when Jesus (Mark 10:45) and Paul (2 Cor. 5:14f) talk in terms of ransom, reconciliation and substitution, no mention is made of to whom the ransom is paid or how the transaction is made. Such is the direct involvement of the Father in the work of salvation that if we talk of 'ransom', it is clear that it is God who is doing the ransoming; if we talk of 'reconciling', then it is God who is doing it; if we talk of 'substituting', then it is God who is there in the offering of his Son.

It seems to be the case, then, that the New Testament writers use the substitutionary image as a very powerful and meaningful tool to show the wonder of Christ's sacrifice. However, they transcend it and enrich its content by showing that Christ is not merely the means of man's propitiation of God, but God's way of bringing us home to him. He takes our place of condemnation; he takes the full force of the law, and he is made sin for us. It is, in short, God's work and all persons of the Godhead – Father, Son and Spirit – are at work in the plan of salvation. We have to acknowledge, frankly, the element of mystery in atonement. Substitution is not a way of explaining by logical means how we are made one with God, but a way of understanding with the heart what God has done for us in Christ. For this reason Jim Packer prefers to use the term 'kerygmatic model' of penal substitution because it is not an analytical method but a 'pointer directing attention to various fundamental features of the mystery'.[19]

I mentioned earlier that I saw substitution as speaking more to the heart than to the head, with an astonishing power to convict. This dimension is an element which is greatly overlooked. It does, however, coincide with observations made by scholars who would probably consider themselves outside the evangelical movement. For example Robert Paul, commenting upon mission, frankly acknowledges: 'It was largely the churches which were not afraid to preach the older theories of Atonement with clear-cut issues in soteriology and ethics which had the greatest missionary zeal and evangelical success. It has always been admitted that the theory of penal substitution "preaches" well, and its success on the frontier is probably due principally to the fact that those who preached it spoke directly about sin and grace to men who knew themselves to be sinners in need of grace.'[20] Similarly, Frances Young, in her fine book *Sacrifice and the Death of Christ*, speaks of the power of the substitution model: 'Propitiatory sacrifice has provided the key to the Cross for many Christians and it remains psychologically forceful.'[21] And Vincent Taylor admits the power of the substitutionary model: 'The persistence of theories of substitution and of satisfaction in the history of Christian doctrine reveals the immense strength of a felt religious need.'[22]

Yet, strangely, none of these writers, nor anybody else as far as I can tell, has bothered to explore why this model 'preaches well' and why it is 'psychologically forceful', and whether there is something here that the Church should learn. I think there is and I suggest that there is a three-fold message in it for the Church: it is simple, intelligible and compelling. *Simple*, because it can be grasped easily and quickly; *intelligible*, because it resonates with human experience of sacrifice and 'laying down of life for another'; *compelling*, because millions have found in the substitutionary model the overwhelming picture of the extent to which God is prepared to go to rescue humankind from sin and despair. The love of a representative is generous enough, but the love of a substitute, who takes my sin and makes it his and who becomes 'Godforsaken', is beyond the reach of human language but, thankfully, not worship. Churches which combine substitution with other models and other pictures will be able to draw upon a way of understanding the cross which has been forceful and very effective since the start of Christian preaching.

The Glory of the Cross

In the last chapter I emphasised the importance of the substitutionary 'image', a term I prefer to 'theory' because, as we saw, the New Testament nowhere explains *how* Jesus died in my place as a ransom to God, but simply states that God offered Jesus as my ransom. That is, the Scriptures, by using the language of substitution, transcend it by making it the work of God himself. But what we have to heed is that no one is saved by a theory, image or theological speculation. I may believe in 'substitution', you may believe in 'representation', she may believe in the *Christus Victor* model – but a theoretical model cannot bring a person home to God. Only a Saviour saves; only a Redeemer redeems; and only a Reconciler reconciles. In other words, salvation is a deeply personal transaction and transcends our intellectual grasp of a doctrine. Oh yes, theories and images help. They can make sense of the mysterious and bring home the wonder of God's love. They can act as bridges – but they cannot give life. The work of Christ, then, is not something about which a person must know, but rather something which we must experience in our hearts, minds and lives. To be understood, certainly – as far as we are able; but most important of all, to be appropriated and experienced.

This warning, to see the explanations as bridges or aids to our understanding, helps us to keep the cross in focus as something which is meant to change our lives and not to whet our intellectual curiosity. It releases us to ask: 'How may we understand the cross better in order to discover its power in the lives of men and women?'

I like to think of the death of Jesus as a matchless jewel. Just as an experienced jeweller will take the gem into his hands with a reverence almost approaching awe, so we will observe that as he handles it he will turn it this way and that way to glimpse the exquisite variegated beauty of the precious object before his eyes. As he does so, undiscovered contours, shapes and colours burst into view – and he does not tire of gazing. The cross is like that. Little wonder people have seen different things in it. That is not surprising considering that it is God's answer to the whole of human need. Little wonder men and women have stamped their rights over a particular interpretation – overlooking the fact that all they have done is to approach it with a particular need or from a particular cultural standpoint. Most of the theories are reflected in the jewel of the cross and, from time to time, each will play a part in our understanding of what the Christian life is all about. But how do they fit together? Is there an overriding idea which unites them?

The biblical category which seems to be at the heart of most of the theories and ideas is *sacrifice*. We have seen that it is at the heart of the Old Testament and it stands at the intersection of forgiveness and relationship. God is the one to whom the sacrifice is offered and the thing sacrificed represents the offerer. The essence of the rite consists of a highly symbolic and ritualised act in which the worshipper comes with his sacrifice, acknowledging that he cannot please God as he is but needs to make an offering which is going to satisfy his creator. The interior attitude of the worshipper is that of humility and contriteness; the external aspect consists in bringing a perfect animal to make amends. This Old Testament perspective is, as we saw, at the heart of New Testament faith, too. It is a mistake to belittle the importance of the sacrificial in the formation of the Christian faith. David Edwards, for example, while acknowledging that Jesus spoke of his death as a ransom (Mark 10:45) and referred to his blood as the 'blood of the new covenant' (Mark 14:24), states:

'Such echoes . . . are scarcely enough to give the theme of sacrifice that central position in the teaching of Jesus which it has occupied in traditional Christian doctrine.'[1] But such an assertion ignores the nature of the Last Supper itself, which was clearly sacrificial as Jesus anticipated his bloody and atoning death.[2] Edwards' thesis, if true, would cast serious doubt on the veracity of the New Testament writers as true interpreters of the message of Jesus because they obviously believed that Christ's death was sacrificial. The epistle to the Hebrews, especially, concentrates upon the nature of Jesus as both high priest and victim. It is important to notice this early recognition that Jesus represents God and humankind in his sacrifice. As high priest he is not only perfect human being but perfectly God – 'in the order of Melchizedek' (7:17). Yet, as victim, he is not only God but also perfectly human – 'tempted in every way just as we are – yet . . . without sin' (4:15). The epistle, therefore, brings together these two concepts in a remarkable and astounding way. Jesus, God's Son, accepted the way of the cross willingly and offered himself as a living sacrifice for all men and women. The writer makes the point more than once that as the spotless one Jesus had no need to make sacrifice for himself. But in the act of obedience Jesus represented fallen humanity in himself and went to the cross and accepted death on our behalf. His sacrifice became our sacrifice of redemption and we were set free.

But let us explore the nature of sacrifice a little more closely and relate it to some of the theories and ideas we have considered.

THE CROSS IS THE LOVING SACRIFICE OF A HOLY GOD

As we saw in the last chapter, it is essential that we see the cross as God's action in Christ and not simply as Christ's action alone – as if it were independent of God the Father. The death of Jesus was the Father's rescue operation and was meant to bring people back to God. I suggest that there are two important elements in the work of Christ. First, the cross was not isolated to the last few hours of Jesus' ministry but was the focus and driving force of it. It has been an unfortunate side-effect of evangelical theology to ignore (to all intents and purposes) the ministry of Jesus. Even to this day evangelical preaching tends to see Jesus' ministry as a rather grand and spectacular introduction to the 'real' work on the cross – occasional forays are made into the teaching of Jesus but the main use of the gospels appears to be that they manifest the divinity of Jesus. We need to rediscover the insight of the early Church that Jesus' work of redemption started from his birth, 'you are to give him the name Jesus, because he will save his people from their sins' (Matt. 1:21). He was born Saviour and did not suddenly become one on the cross. To be sure, his death made it effective, but failure to see that his whole ministry was salvific (that is, aimed to restore people to God) makes Jesus' life seem unreal and almost docetic. This means to take the incarnation seriously as part of a doctrine of the cross.[3] It is part and parcel of the work of the Son, whose whole life was an offering to his Father. This is, as we saw, an element very important to the gospel of John and to the epistle to the Hebrews. Both wish to bring together his death and his life to show that the cross was the culmination of a life of obedience and sacrifice. It brought things together to a glorious conclusion.

An incarnational view of the sacrifice of Jesus will stress the obedience of the Son as, indeed, do both the epistle to the Hebrews (5:8) and the gospel of John (5:30). The 'obedience' motif was, in fact, an idea greatly beloved in the early Church and developed into the theory of deification. Just as Adam's essential sin lay in disobedience, so the virtue of the second Adam lay in his obedience. The early fathers developed this into a theory of participation, that as Christ entered into the various areas of human life so he redeemed it by his pure and triumphant obedience. This may sound nothing more than a romantic notion to us and we may ask sceptically: 'How can obedience, or disobedience for that matter, be transmitted to us?' The early Christians did not find this a difficulty because they saw the moral obedience of Jesus pointing to a perfect human response. Obedience, according to this view, is at the heart of people's relationship to God because it depicts a proper love relationship which glorifies God and builds us up. Christ's obedience, then, was a mark of his filial relationship with the Father as well as being a sign of his perfect humanity. And, here again, they discovered in this motif of obedience a clue concerning human destiny. In Jesus we see what human beings ought to be. Not 'more than human', as if we were just a God with human skin, but 'more human than we are ever likely to be' – at least in this life. Jesus, then, in his incarnation, offers to us a blueprint of what is, in fact, our true nature and what will one day be our inheritance. St Irenaeus, who was Bishop of Lyons at the end of the second century and the first great systematic theologian, summed up graphically that God's aim for humankind was that, 'The Glory of God is man fully alive.' Irenaeus' doctrine of recapitulation (that Christ restored us to a greater glory than we would have had under the first Adam) rests upon the obedience of Christ in his life and death.

But it was much more than an act of loving obedience. It was also the loving sacrifice of a holy God. The cross was an objective act of redemption which will be for all time the basis of our forgiveness, and its consequences are timeless. In the words of Wesley's great hymn: 'He breaks the power of cancelled sin and sets the prisoner free.'

Wesley saw correctly that Christ's sacrifice was an atonement which brings humankind home to God, restores us to God and makes us new creatures. To use H. F. Lyte's rich and evocative words, we are 'ransomed, healed, restored, forgiven'. In the light of this great objective event, it is difficult to make sense of Vincent Taylor's words that: 'The New Testament does not teach that Christ died in order that God might be able to forgive sins. The remission of sins is an act of God's free grace.'[4] Denying that the cross makes forgiveness possible, Taylor is forced to make it a symbol of God's forgiveness and not the means of it: 'It might seem, therefore, that our sole need is that we should be assured of his gracious purpose, the significance of the Cross being that it gives us this knowledge.'[5]

But with respect to a fine scholar, Taylor's argument rests upon a half-truth. Of course, God's desire to forgive precedes the coming of Christ and, indeed, is its *raison d'être*, and we would want to say no less emphatically than Taylor that the cross does not change God's mind about sinners as if it transformed his attitude from hatred to love. But we are forced to say, on the basis of the New Testament witness itself, that our standing before God was that prior to Christ's death we were 'unforgiven' and after it we are 'forgiven'. So Ephesians 1:7 claims of the cross: 'In him we have redemption through his blood, the forgiveness of sins.' No amount of sophistication of language can resist the unanimous testimony of the New Testament that before Christ's death we were 'enemies of God', 'unreconciled', 'dead in trespasses and sin' and 'children of wrath'. God's action in Christ was not only to change our attitude to him (that is the first half of the truth, which Taylor and I share) but also to deal with the sin which separated us from him (the second half). That is, before God humanity cannot help asking the vital question: 'How can I, a guilty sinner, come before a holy and loving Father?'

This is where objective theories and ideas such as representation, and particularly the substitutionary element, play their part and shine forth from the jewel. They tell us that such was the helplessness of humanity and such was the generous love of God, that God laid on his dear Son the iniquities of us all. He was on the cross because, by rights, we should have been there. In some mysterious way, which we shall never be able to comprehend fully, through Jesus God made full payment for human transgressions and disobedience. 'A second Adam to the fight and to the rescue came', undoing all the defiance of sin and restoring us to God. 'God made the Cross of Christ at once the throne of judgement and the fountain of salvation,' stated Mozley, long ago.[6] Failure to see the centrality of Christ as redeeming us from the curse of the law ends, I believe, in us minimising the victory of the cross over sin and weakens it as a life-changing message.

Paul Zahl gives a vivid and helpful illustration of the power of the law in his book *Who Will Deliver Us?*[7] He describes the story of a duck hunter who is with a friend in a dry area of

Georgia. Suddenly a cloud of smoke is seen on the horizon and soon the sound of crackling is heard as a fierce wind drives the brushfire towards them. It is moving so quickly that escape is out of the question. The hunter, however, instead of panicking and rushing from the approaching disaster, is busy ransacking his pockets and knapsack. Eventually, he finds what he is looking for – a box of matches. Then, to his friend's amazement, he pulls out a match and strikes it. Standing to the lee side of the wind he lights a fire which quickly scorches the earth before them. Soon, they are standing in a large circle of blackened earth, waiting for the fire to come. Covering their mouths with their handkerchiefs they brace themselves for the arriving holocaust. The fire draws near and sweeps over them. They are completely unhurt because fire will not pass where fire has already passed.

This, of course, is just an illustration and must be used with the greatest of caution. Only in one sense is the law like that fire – none of us can escape the condemnation of God's holy law, which tells me that I have fallen short of God's glory; as I stand before God's highest ideals for me I can only acknowledge my guilt, but if I stand in the burnt-over place where the law has already done its worst, then I escape. The death of Christ is like that burnt-over place. There you and I can huddle, knowing that we are safe.

IT IS THE HEALING SACRIFICE OF A LOVING GOD

The attractiveness of seeing the cross as a mainly past event is that we observe its decisive importance in restoring men and women to God. Its weakness can be a remoteness from Christian living because it is relegated to being a theological symbol. But in the New Testament there is clear evidence that the cross, as well as being a past event in the life of Jesus and in the theological understanding of the Church's redemption, is also our contemporary and daily inspiration. A few passages from the New Testament will help to illustrate this.

To start with we must note what some have called Paul's 'Christ-mysticism' because of his concentration upon Christ

as the model of Christian living. Thus, he writes about the
centrality of Jesus in his ministry: 'I have been crucified with
Christ and I no longer live, but Christ lives in me' (Gal. 2:20).
This remarkable confession which is echoed in passages such
as 2 Corinthians 4:11–12 and Philippians 2:5–11, is most
probably based upon Paul's understanding of baptism into
the death and resurrection of Jesus Christ. It is one of the great
tragedies of modern Christianity that we have lost a sense of
the wonder of baptism as depicting the passing from death
to life and entering into the movement of Christ's victory.
This was brought home to me some years ago when I was
visiting Israel and witnessed a number of young Christians
being baptised in the river Jordan. I was left in little doubt,
not only by the talk given before the baptism, but also
by the evident expressions of joy on their faces, that they
saw this as a turning point in their lives. They were going
down into the waters and symbolically into Jesus' death,
and arising from it into a new life. So Paul in Romans
dwells on the new life and new ethic which results from
following Christ: 'We died to sin; how can we live in it any
longer? . . . We were . . . buried with him through baptism
into death in order that, just as Christ was raised from the
dead through the glory of the Father, we too may live a
new life' (6:2, 4). In other words, Paul was concerned that
the principle embodied in the cross and resurrection should
be worked out in every department of human experience.

But what is this principle? It is that Christ's death is effective
in our lives from the moment of belonging to him. Now
two elements flow from this effective presence. First, the
principle of *imitatio Christi*, the imitation of Christ. So Paul
may tell the wrangling Christians in Philippi to set Christ
before them as an example of obedience and love. 'Your
attitude should be the same as that of Christ Jesus: who,
being in very nature God, did not consider equality with
God something to be grasped . . . ' (Phil. 2:5f). The cross
for Paul was more than just a beautiful symbol of God's
love – it was the spur to the Christian life and to effective
service. So he can exclaim, 'Christ's love compels us, because
we are convinced that one died for all, and therefore all died.

And he died for all, that those who live should no longer live for themselves but for him who died for them and was raised again' (2 Cor. 5:14–15). In 1 Peter, likewise, the writer can encourage persecuted Christians to follow the example of Jesus in his suffering and death (2:21).

In the light of this strong thrust in the New Testament it is not difficult to understand the inspiration the cross has been to Christians down the centuries facing persecution, torture and death. The servant should not expect to face anything less than his master faced and, with that kind of realism, many Christians went to their death rejoicing in a Lord who had gone before. But the victory of Christ not only fed the courage of the martyrs, it was also the life-blood of holiness as well. So Augustine sees the essential link between God and the Christian in terms of following the pattern of love. 'And if it were difficult for us to love God himself, at least it should not be difficult for us to love him in return, when he first loved us and spared not his only Son but gave himself up for us all. For there is no greater invitation to love, than to be first in loving.'[8]

This theme, however, was largely undeveloped until the late medieval period when, through a number of well-known Christians – Bernard of Clairvaux, Peter Abelard, Francis of Assisi and Thomas à Kempis – the inspirational aspect of loving self-sacrifice emerged as a dominant theology. The common element in this teaching was that as men and women meditate upon and follow the sacrificial love of the Son, so they are themselves redeemed from the limitations and defects of humanity and are raised to life with the one they love. Men and women are so moved to become identified with the pattern of Christ that they become united with God in love and obedience.

It is surely important to note the central weakness of this viewpoint, however, which is a failure to understand that as far as salvation is concerned the cross is final and has already achieved its purpose. By making the cross the centre of a mysticism which saves and leads on to a closer identification with the divine, the medieval thinkers were in danger of returning to a doctrine of salvation which rested upon human effort to contemplate the love of the Son. Nevertheless, it is surely crucial that we recognise the value of the theory of Christ as our example. As we saw earlier, Peter Abelard is normally regarded as the arch-exponent of this theory. His mistake, as we observed, was that by rejecting objective theories which stressed what Christ had done for us and replacing them with his subjective notion that the cross only affects us, he makes the cross more mysterious. But, we have to ask, why should we regard the sufferings of Christ as such an overwhelming demonstration of love *unless* humankind was involved in a terrible predicament which affected our eternal salvation? Redeeming love, surely, only becomes meaningful against the desperate and sin-shattered background which men and women are rescued from and restored to God. Abelard's mistake was to remove the background and show us only the foreground. Yet, Abelard is right in emphasising the love demonstrated so purely and beautifully on the cross. Previously, Abelard observes, men and women were motivated by fear – now they may be motivated by love and gratitude, which should be food for the soul. While Abelard's thought is that of Calvary as a gigantic visual aid, it involves much more than that because Calvary is also a constraining and transforming influence upon our lives.

The Reformation led to a swing from subjective and mystical experience to that of the objective basis of the Christian faith. There can be no doubt that this was necessary to sweep away doctrinal aberrations and to restore the Bible to the Church. But the consequence of this, as Dillistone observed, was that: 'Throughout the history of Protestantism the tendency has been to stress the saving activity of God through his Word and the responsive activity of man shown forth in faith and obedience. Feelings have been suspect.'[9] A new form of Christian activism was thus introduced which despised and distrusted the affective life. Contemplation of the cross, with accompanying meditation and inner spirituality, therefore took second place to witness, service and church membership. Rightly emphasising the objective declaration of the cross that 'You are forgiven', the Reformation, unfortunately, lost sight of redemption as addressing the emotional and inner life of humankind, nourishing devotional life and spiritual development. This may account for the fact that, on the whole, Protestant spirituality has been quite poverty stricken compared with Catholic spirituality. There have, of course, been notable exceptions. A number of Puritan theologians had a deep devotion to the cross of Christ and the Moravians, as well, were most influential in keeping alive the contemplation of Christ's example and suffering love. Their role in helping to awaken a discouraged Anglican missionary, John Wesley, led to this aspect becoming a major element in early Methodist preaching. It throbs through Charles Wesley's hymns, such as:

> How sweet the name of Jesus sounds
> In a believer's ear!
> It soothes his sorrows, heals his wounds,
> And drives away his fear . . .

> Jesus! my Shepherd, Husband, Friend,
> My Prophet, Priest and King,
> My Lord, my life, my way, my end –
> Accept the praise I bring.

Aspects, then, of the exemplar model have much to offer the Christian. It puts before us the love of a Saviour who loved us unto death and it encourages us to live and act as he did, thus allowing the model of his humanity to inspire and fire ours.

The second principle which flows from the idea of the cross as the healing sacrifice of a holy God is that the cross *really does* make a difference to our lives. There are objective and subjective aspects to this difference. First, the objective fact is that the cross heals the wounds caused by sin and our alienation from God. This was a favourite concept to some of the fathers of the early Church who viewed Jesus' role as primarily a healing ministry, the divine 'physician' whose cross brought life and health. Later in Christian history the Reformers saw correctly the radical dimension of the cross in bringing peace and healing to the soul of humankind. Their doctrine of justification by faith was a declaration to the hearts of men and women that we are truly forgiven. This doctrine is not the whole of salvation, by any means, but it emphatically declares the reality of our new relationship with God that we are now 'acquitted' and 'declared righteous' through the work of Christ.

In my pastoral ministry I have been greatly surprised by how many Christians there are – many of them evangelical to their finger tips – who believe in justification by faith passionately, and yet whose lives appear to deny the peace and joy it should give them. Instead of that fact permeating their lives, altering their behaviour and making them relaxed and accepting Christians, they appear to be weighed down by a gospel which, instead of being a delight, is – although they would deny it – a burden. One successful businessman confessed to me: 'I was brought up to believe that once I became a Christian I was accepted by God and there was nothing to worry about. I was told that I should not doubt my calling and I should not trust my feelings. This led me to deny my feelings and to privatise my experience of God. I began to feel a sense of burden when I compared my Christian life with others. Why were they all so much better than I was? Why didn't I have their gifts? What was wrong with me?'

In fact, there was nothing wrong with him. What he needed to realise was that justification by faith is more than a doctrine: it is a declaration to our hearts and lives that we are truly accepted by God and there is no need to pretend or compare our gifts with others. Once we are Christians, we are members of the family of God and nothing can remove us from our rightful place in it. The cross says to our hearts, 'You have not only been forgiven and put right with God but it affects your life now. Christ lives in you and has given his Spirit to you. You are accepted!' Many good evangelical Christians still live as though Christianity is a law and that the successful Christian life is achieved by following a host of commands: 'The good evangelical worships twice a Sunday, has a regular Quiet Time, witnesses at work, tithes his money, has at least four church jobs, is a model husband/wife, his children go to church and he has a good 9 to 5 job.' A parody, perhaps, but near enough to the picture for it to sting. But we lose a lot if we fail to realise that the effects of the cross are numerous. The death of Jesus not only heals me but it goes on healing me as I shelter in its shade and allow it to nourish my daily walk with God.

The subjective aspect follows on from this. As I apply the objective fact of Christ's work to my own heart and mind, it will result in a major change in my life. The New Testament clearly expects people to be radically changed after their encounter with Jesus Christ. It affects their walk with God, their personal lives, their relationships – everything, in fact, comes under the Lordship of Christ. This, we must note, does not suggest that legalism is coming in again through the back door because the Christian no longer lives to please God so that he may be saved. *Because* he is saved he wants to please God and his desire is to be the very best for him. Surely this is a goal every Christian will want to aim for.

THE CROSS IS THE TRIUMPHANT SACRIFICE OF A REIGNING GOD

The validity of any sacrifice is related to its result. When Fr Maksymilian Kolbe made his heroic intervention on behalf of another Pole in Auschwitz and offered to die in his place, he had no idea whether his death would achieve its objective. He went to his death in the starvation bunker with no knowledge of the man whose place he took, or whether his sacrifice was worthwhile or futile. It was, in fact, a sheer act of faith, although in the event the 'redeemed' man did survive the war and lived to carry on part of Fr Kolbe's work. Most acts of sacrifice have that element of risk about them. Even when parents sacrifice time and money for their offspring, they have no idea whether their faith will be rewarded. Most of us don't bother, in fact, with such a question and would consider it as being of the nature of love to offer oneself freely, irrespective of the result.

From our perspective in the scheme of things, Jesus' sacrifice for us is not yet final and yet from God's point of view the cross means that the end has arrived. We are able to see some of the fruits of our salvation in the world, in the Church and

in our lives – but in Paul's famous words: 'we ourselves . . .
groan inwardly as we wait eagerly for our adoption as sons,
the redemption of our bodies' (Rom. 8:23). We must try to
put these two aspects together. How do we make sense of a
world which Christians say Christ has redeemed and which
shows so many signs of un-redemption? How do we make
sense of ourselves when our lives show signs of grace – and
yet no one can say with any degree of honesty that our lives
are marked by the beauty and strength of Jesus of Nazareth?
Finality and provisionality are strangely set side by side.

In Christian thought two ideas have been suggested as
bearing upon these important questions: the first emphasises
the victory of Christ over the power of evil, and the second
develops this theme to show that his victory has cosmic
implications.

First, then, Christ as *Christus Victor*. We have already
touched upon this theme in an earlier chapter. As we know,
Gustaf Aulen claimed that the classic theory of the atonement
from New Testament times until the medieval period was that
Jesus, in his death, conquered the hosts of evil spirits that
held men and women captive. By this conquest Jesus secured
deliverance and freedom. It is generally agreed that Aulen's
argument is not as strong as it appears. It does not seem
to be the most fundamental of ideas in Paul's writings, or
as central to Luther as Aulen claimed. Nevertheless, it is
agreed that Aulen has restored to the discussion an aspect
which modern theology was in danger of ignoring, namely
that Jesus' death was a victory over the forces of evil.

Two vivid passages in the New Testament develop this
theme. Colossians 2:14–15 is a breathtaking passage which
likens Christ's victory to the celebration homecoming of an
earthly ruler: returning with the spoils of his conquest and
triumphing particularly in the defeat of his enemies, 'He
forgave us all our sins, having cancelled the written code,
with its regulations, that was against us . . . he took it away,
nailing it to the cross. And having disarmed the powers and
authorities, he made a public spectacle of them, triumphing
over them by the cross.' The imagery here speaks of Christ's
triumph over demonic forces which held sway over humanity.

The important thing to note is that his death is viewed as a divine triumph over cosmic powers. But what was their hold over men and women? For Paul they tyrannised people in two major ways. First, they controlled sinful men and women who could not escape their clutches (Eph. 2:1–3) and, furthermore, they represented death.

The same theme is expressed in our second passage, Hebrews 2:14: 'Since the children have flesh and blood, he too shared in their humanity, so that by his death he might destroy him who holds the power of death – that is, the devil.' The principle assumed here is that the only way to break the power of death is for someone stronger to assume mortality and gain the victory within death's own territory. This is why Jesus' identification with humanity is of such importance for the writer to the Hebrews; it is crucial for his argument to show that Jesus is fully human because, in his view, the power of the Devil could only be defeated from the human side – but only God could do it. The title used for Jesus in the same passage is that of 'Pioneer' (2:10, cf 12:2). Probably the idea behind this choice of title is that of a pioneer who enters an unknown territory on behalf of others. He goes ahead and clears the way. As fully human, he shares in the weaknesses of the flesh and, subject to his Father's will, offers himself as a perfect sacrifice for sin.

It is difficult for modern Christians to have an objective attitude to this concept of conquest over evil powers and forces in the universe. Scholars who try to be faithful to the testimony of Scripture are dismissed as obscurantists for even taking this dimension seriously. But I contend that we must because Jesus, as recorded in the gospels, clearly saw his ministry as a fight against the powers of darkness. What the New Testament leaves us in little doubt about is that the cross was the supreme victory for the forces of darkness – but it turned out to be their place of final defeat. So, then, I suggest that the *Christus Victor* theme is another aspect of our 'jewel' which we must include in order to get a rounded theology of the cross. When we look at our world we do not have to look far to see evidence of the powers of darkness, yet this description of the victory over evil encourages us to see in the cross the sign of God's promised conquest of death, sin and evil.

Our second insight is but an advance on the first – that the cross of Jesus is the beginning of the end; it heralds the coming new age. This, as we know, was at the centre of New Testament preaching. The first Christians firmly believed that with Jesus' death and resurrection, God's day of salvation had dawned and with the second coming of Jesus, God would usher in a new heaven and a new earth. In that day, at the name of Jesus 'every knee should bow . . . and every tongue confess that Jesus Christ is Lord' (Phil. 2:10-11). This gives to the cross of Christ a universal and cosmic significance which is usually missing in these days when we emphasise the individual's response to the gospel. But the individual and the cosmic are the two poles of the cross. If we privatise it too greatly we end up with a gospel which is completely other-worldly and unrelated to life today. Yet, on the other hand, if we universalise its application we lose sight of the necessity of personal response. It is true, as Forsyth was fond of saying, 'We are living in a forgiven world', because Christ *has* paid the penalty on behalf of all men and women. Again, this is another half-truth because this potentially forgiven world has to become the actually redeemed world through individuals accepting the gospel for themselves. While the New Testament does not give grounds for belief in the doctrine of universalism (that all people will be saved), the gospel is universal in its scope and effect. It simply requires the assent of the believer to make him or her a participator in the benefits of the cross.

The cross, then, is the triumphant sacrifice of a reigning God. In the early Church the description of Jesus as 'reigning from the tree' was a very powerful image to Christians. The tree of life is a familiar motif in early murals and frescoes and shows how Christians of the primitive Church saw Christ's death as restoring life to humankind. It goes without saying that this is a concept the modern Church needs to recapture. The death of Jesus did result in the overthrow of the powers of darkness and it will result in his coming kingdom. Eschatology begins with a theology of the cross because the cross points ahead to the glory to be revealed.

THEOLOGIA CRUCIS

Luther's famous definition of Christian theology as *theologia crucis* (theology of the cross), in my opinion, coincides with the testimony of Scripture and the early Church. Fully aware that this was its greatest scandal and stumbling block, the first believers anchored their faith in this unlikely soil of their Messiah who died a criminal's death. This was their confidence and hope; and he was their Saviour and Lord. It was not a sudden hunch which inspired Constantine in the fourth century to set himself forth as a Christian leader under the sign of the cross, with the words 'In this sign conquer' – it was, after all, the testimony of the Church from New Testament times. It is one of those sad ironies that immediately after Constantine's triumph the Church, finding itself in the novel position of having power and influence, fell victim to the false theology of *theologia gloriae*. The problem with any theology which starts from the perspective of 'glory' is that it has to avoid the awkwardness of the cross. But this cannot be done if Christian truth is to remain truth. The fact of the matter is that the cross is the only sign of Christian faith – and its only glory. Luther says again: 'He who understands the Cross aright understands the Bible, he understands Jesus Christ. Therefore this text – "He bore our sins" – must be understood particularly thoroughly, as the foundation upon which stands the whole of the New Testament or the Gospel, as that which alone distinguishes us and our religion from all other religions.'[10]

While this is so, we have already made it clear that there is not one single, definitive way by which we are compelled to understand the cross. I have used the analogy of a jewel to show that the cross is God's act of redemption which speaks to our hearts in many different ways. Failure to observe the richness of the cross – which, after all, is part of its glory – can lead to entrenchment and a poverty stricken theology. Professor Einar Molland, a Lutheran scholar, once observed that the denominations fell into three clear groups according to their dominant theology. Evangelical churches, he said, were Good Friday churches; the Orthodox were

Easter Day churches; and the Church of England was the church of Christmas Day![11] Significantly, he missed out the Roman Catholic Church and the Pentecostal and Charismatic fellowships, which might be called the churches of the Ascension and Whitsunday, respectively. But we need to hold all these aspects together under a theology of the cross. To concentrate solely on Good Friday isolates Jesus from his incarnate work and makes the cross an unrelated peak. But to thrust Easter Day, Ascension or Pentecost forward as dominant theologies for the Church also results in imbalance, because without the cross the resurrection, ascension and Pentecost are meaningless – just as without them the cross would be tragedy instead of victory.

What, then, is the cross? It is a sacrifice – this has been our dominant image but it is much more than that. It is the holy and loving sacrifice set forth by a God who could not bear to see us live without him, and who came himself to bear the weight of our sin so that we might live fully and freely for him. There is, then, a three-fold aspect to the cross – the past is forgiven, the present may now be lived securely, and the future hope is guaranteed.

PART FOUR

THE CROSS
IN CHRISTIAN
EXPERIENCE

11

The Cross and the Kingdom

In this final section of the book we shall attempt to relate the cross to concerns in the Church and the world. We must admit that Christians, in the past, have been guilty of isolating this most central of all doctrines from contemporary situations and problems. Evangelicals, perhaps more than most, have thrown a cultural cloak of privatisation around the cross and have not allowed its radical message to affect all we do and say. In this present chapter we shall consider liberation theology, one of the most important theologies of recent times, to see how it handles the doctrine of salvation and to analyse its weaknesses and strengths.

LIBERATION THEOLOGY

Liberation theology is a stream of theology normally associated with Latin America, although if we were going to be really accurate we would have to include black theology in the United States as well. For the sake of having a manageable entity we shall have Latin America in mind when this term is used. It is, of course, extremely difficult to summarise the main concerns of liberation theology in a few sentences. It is not really a coherent and unified system of theology as such, but a highly diverse stream of Christian thought which shares certain characteristics. First, all liberation theologians write from within societies where the Church is grappling with huge issues of poverty and wealth, un-freedom and freedom, illiteracy and education, violence and order, fascism and democracy. All these issues flamed into life in the all too short career of Oscar Romero as Archbishop of El Salvador. Appointed as a conservative prelate who was outspoken in his condemnation of Marxism and of priests who preached a political gospel, Romero discovered that it was impossible to keep the gospel out of politics. He found himself plunged into a controversy with the government because of its callousness to suffering and its deep contempt for truth. Following the death of a priest who was shot dead for simply speaking out for the poor, Romero became the voice of the poor. He said that his job was to 'put feet on the gospel', meaning by this that the gospel of Jesus Christ affected the lives of ordinary people and it had profound repercussions for human dignity and worth. Shortly before Easter 1980 Romero was shot dead as he celebrated mass in a cancer hospital. He had just read the gospel from John 12: 'Unless an ear of wheat falls to the ground and dies, it remains only a single seed. But if it dies, it produces many seeds.' As he lifted the chalice the shot rang out and struck a main artery. Wine and blood mingled in his sacrifice for the people of El Salvador. Romero was no liberation theologian. He believed in practical Christianity but actions like his typified the background of the struggle and the forces which produced this exciting and committed theology of involvement.

A second characteristic lies in the terminology of liberation theology. Words such as 'alienation', 'liberation', 'exploitation', 'praxis' reveal its indebtedness to Marxist thought. One theologian admitted that 'We are riding on Marx's shoulders.'[1] What we must observe is that this acceptance of Marx's ideas does not suggest an uncritical following of his thought. It is difficult for those of us who have no knowledge of the inner conflict of many of these countries to appreciate the hopelessness and despair which affect thoughtful and sensitive Christians caught up in the struggle for peace. It seems impossible to remove the injustice of society unless society itself is radically changed. Christians, especially Roman Catholic clergy trying to work out the theology of

Vatican II, gradually came to perceive that sin and salvation could not be restricted to spiritual areas of life: sin affects the very structures of society. Alliances between Christianity and Marxism were thus formed, then, not on ideological grounds but from the pragmatic realisation that they were fighting a common enemy, that of oppression, poverty and injustice. I must underline the point that liberation theologians do not view Marxism as a philosophy or ideology of which they approve. Rather, they see it as offering a correct analysis of social illnesses, and some consider it a necessary instrument of social change.

Thirdly, the theological method of liberation theology is radically different from other forms of theology, with its emphasis upon 'praxis'. This newly minted word from a Greek root 'to do' may be translated *action*. That is, the essence of theology is its outcome in society and the Church; there can be no study of theology which is not a critical reflection upon praxis. Just as Karl Marx announced the difference between his views and other thinkers in these words: 'Hitherto philosophers have explained the world, our task is to change it,' so liberation theologians see their task in terms of revolutionary action, too.

Christians, they argue, must no longer take refuge in theology – it is time to obey the gospel. Two particular biblical themes are of crucial importance to liberation theology: the exodus and Christ's life, death and resurrection. The exodus is viewed as God siding with the poor and oppressed. He stands alongside Moses and the other leaders who fight for freedom from exploitation. God, it is argued, does not stand outside this conflict but is active within it. It is through his power that the enemy is defeated and with his encouragement that Israel rises up with a desperate cry of protest which leads to freedom. Inevitably, the struggle is not without violence and bloodshed. This was not something God desired. After all, he did give Pharoah many opportunities to repent. But when appeals only resulted in further stubbornness and increasing repression of Israel, the net result was the slaughter of the first-born and the drowning of the Egyptian army. The second theological motif, the cross, is also cited as an example of God's identification with suffering in the world. Here, they say, is God's great act of commitment to the poor and needy. His only Son took up the struggle against evil and went to his cross. This, they assert, was not a passive acceptance of the inevitability of defeat but was the active surrender of life that others might live.

Suffering and, particularly, violent suffering are important themes in this strand of theology. Violence itself cannot be avoided; it is an inevitable consequence of the class struggle. The Christian, they argue, has little choice in the matter. If he protests that he is against violence he must face the fact that violence is in the structures which imprison people and which restrict their freedom. It is 'repressive violence' which is a crime against the gospel, and whether we like it or not 'the Christian does not decide between violence and nonviolence, evil and good. He decides between the less and greater evil. He must ponder whether revolutionary violence is less or more deplorable than the violence perpetuated by the system.'[2]

With this brief background in mind, let us consider the contribution of one of liberation theology's most important thinkers, Gustavo Gutierrez, a Roman Catholic theologian from Peru.

Salvation according to Gutierrez

Gutierrez rejects any talk of two histories, sacred and secular, as if God is only interested in spiritual reality and that ordinary life is of no concern to him. 'There is only one human destiny,' he observes correctly, 'irreversibly assumed by Christ, the Lord of History. His redemptive work embraces all the dimensions of human existence and brings them to their fullness. The history of salvation is the very heart of human history.'[3] But what does Gutierrez mean when he says that Christ's redemptive work 'embraces all the dimensions of human existence'? For Gutierrez salvation is the central theme of the Christian faith and Christ, the liberator, offers an 'inclusive' salvation: that is, one which takes in the whole of reality. He will allow no reduction in the scope of Christ's work as Saviour.

While Gutierrez fully accepts that Christ redeems us from the power and scope of sin, he rejects any definition of sin which excludes social, political and cultural factors. 'Sin is evident in oppressive structures, in the exploitation of man by man, in the domination and slavery of people, races and social classes. Sin appears, therefore, as the fundamental alienation, the root of a situation of injustice and exploitation.'[4] Sin, according to this way of looking at it, cannot be encountered in itself but only as it appears in concrete situations.[5] This inevitably means that salvation is not simply salvation from spiritual bondage but from all that depersonalises humankind – physical and moral misery, hunger and ignorance, oppression and repression. There is a further implication in this argument; although Gutierrez does not express it this plainly, he does suggest that sin does not come primarily through man's personal choices to affect social structures, but from the social structures to affect personal life and choices. It follows that at the heart of salvation is the transformation of oppressive social structures – change them and we will change humankind. Gutierrez and Marx speak with one voice.

I find two faults in this argument. First, because Gutierrez includes creation in salvation, salvation is defined in terms which are too broad to be in line with biblical teaching. This allows him to present the goal of salvation as the realisation of new ways of overcoming social injustice and all that restricts human development. The exodus from Egypt is seen, typically, as a basically political event which established Israel as a society free from misery and alienation. Gutierrez asserts: 'The God of Exodus is the God of history and of political liberation more than he is the God of nature.'[6] Again, arguing from Isaiah 40–55, he claims that as Isaiah uses the technical term *bara* (to create) of Israel as well as of creation, Yahweh's concern is for freedom, justice and the construction of a just society. The work of Christ forms part of this movement and brings it to its complete fulfilment. He liberates from sin and all its ugly manifestations in the world. His liberation creates a new people which, this time, includes all humanity.

But we must ask whether it is correct to equate creation with salvation in this way. Isn't Gutierrez in danger of misusing

Scripture and looking at biblical themes through the spectacles of a Marxist concept of evolutionary history? Is he not confusing two great acts of God – the God who creates and the God who saves – instead of seeing them (as I think the biblical writers did) as two separate movements, behind which lay the active, personal care of the God of history? Having made this basic confusion, Gutierrez follows this through into the New Testament and makes Christ out to be a revolutionary leader whose sole task is to bring humanity out of bondage into political and social freedom.

But this leads into the second criticism: his view of salvation is not only too broad to be coherent, it is also too narrow to be truly biblical. Because he stresses the structural nature of sin and the nature of salvation in removing injustice, he makes salvation out to be a sociological entity. Too little attention is therefore given to the personal dimension of sin, such as the failure to acknowledge the Lordship of God, which the Bible describes as sin. Although it is true that Gutierrez does not completely overlook the nature of sin as an affront against the holiness of God and as defiance of his sovereignty, this element is so far back in his thinking as to be hardly influential on his argument. He thus provides a one-dimensional treatment of sin which is largely social, structural and political.

Salvation – the work of Christ or men?

It is impossible to deny that Gutierrez emphasises the atonement as the means by which humankind is saved from sin: 'By his death and resurrection Christ redeems man from sin and all its consequences.'[7] Importance is attached to the gift of salvation offered through Christ: he transforms the universe and makes it possible for men and women to reach fulfilment as human beings. This gift makes possible a 'radical liberation' which attacks the roots of oppression. Yet, alongside these very conservative statements there seems to exist a view of salvation which assumes that it is achieved through human effort: 'By working, transforming the world, breaking out of servitude, building a just society, and assuming his destiny in history, man forges himself.' Gutierrez continues, 'To work, to transform this world, is to become a man and to build the human community; it is also to save.'[8] Although Gutierrez never discusses what he means by the atonement, there does appear to be an 'exemplary' or 'psychological' model in the background of his thought. This may be seen in his view of the exodus event which is paradigmatic of God's action in history. It is not just a historical event hidden in Israel's self-understanding: 'It remains vital and contemporary due to similar experiences which the people of God undergo.'[9] It seems then that Christ's death and resurrection perform a similar function for us – there is a motivational link between the cross and the liberation of humanity. We enter into Christ's work of renewal as we identify with his struggle for peace and wholeness. We are still left wondering, however, where the locus of salvation is; is it in the cross or in the revolutionary struggle? Furthermore, 'Does Christ save man from sin or does he merely spur man to save men from sin?'[10]

The implications of this, however, are interesting and serious. Just as we observed in the last section that Gutierrez's concept of sin is open to the charge of being one dimensional, so is his understanding of salvation. The Church is rejected as the centre of God's saving activity and is replaced by the notion of the kingdom at work in the world. The kingdom of God is identical to the struggle of liberation. In fact, a political, liberating event is the growth of the kingdom and a salvation-event. The kingdom will, one day, be finally realised by the in-breaking of God at the end of time, when the oppressed will be totally freed – only then will the process be complete. In the meantime, any liberating event is the historical realisation of the kingdom. The consequences of this are very profound in that evangelism, conversion and spirituality take on a new meaning. 'Evangelism' is to announce the presence of the love of God in the 'historical becoming of mankind'.[11] 'Conversion' is conversion to our neighbour and those who are oppressed – and it is to engage in the struggle for their freedom. 'Spirituality' is likewise similarly redefined in terms of our commitment to liberation. It is a way of living the gospel, not dominating by 'orthodoxy' but by 'orthopraxis' – that is, a spirituality which dares to sink into the soil of oppression-liberation.

Who are saved?

We noted above Gutierrez's blurring of salvation with creation and kingdom with social action. We are not surprised to discover, therefore, that this leads to universalism and salvation becomes 'humanisation'. This leads him to reject what he calls 'the quantitative and intensive' notion of salvation (that people are saved by reference to the preaching of Christ through the Church), which he replaces with 'the qualitative and extensive' view of salvation (that Christ's message and ministry draw all humanity in). He argues: 'Salvation is not something other-worldly, in regard to which the present life is merely a test. Salvation – the communion of men with God and the communion of men among themselves – is something which embraces all human reality, transforms it, and leads it to its fullness in Christ.'[12]

Of course, Gutierrez has a future salvation in mind as well as a present one. While he firmly believes that people are saved to the extent that they are liberated from oppression and freed to realise their full potential, he is aware that by this standard many, many people are not liberated at all. Reading between the lines, it would seem that he holds that such people would experience total salvation when they share in the recreated and liberated world at the end of history.

But by this radical reinterpretation of history, Gutierrez has not only secularised Christian preaching about the atonement, he has also inverted the response of faith. People are saved not by making a conscious affirmation of trust in Christ as Saviour, but by reference to their response to their neighbour. He reaches this conclusion because of his view, largely based on Matthew 25:31–46, that Christ is in all people, even if they do not acknowledge the fact (*A Theology of Liberation*, pp. 196ff.). While there is much to teach us in this 'qualitative' approach, which we shall consider later, there is much that is wrong about it. We need to ask, for example, what is the destiny of someone who is a convinced atheist, yet who is passionately concerned with the needs of the poor and has a sharpened awareness of the value of the individual? According to Gutierrez's theology this person comes within the orbit of salvation and will have his or her part in God's kingdom. If this is so, it would seem that faith in God and belief in Christ as traditionally understood by the Church are basically irrelevant to salvation. What matters is 'orthopraxis'.

THE CROSS AND THE SOCIAL ORDER

We have seen that in many respects the theology of liberation as represented by Gustavo Gutierrez is deficient because of its reorientation towards social and political liberation. Gutierrez's commitment to a single world history – and not one that is separated into profane and sacred – with its sequel in a salvation which is coextensive with the world, means that genuine insights are not balanced with other equally important truths, resulting in, for example, an underestimation of the transcendent and of the individual. Furthermore, Gutierrez is forced to minimise the role of Christ on the cross and to exaggerate the part we play in salvation by our involvement in the task of humanising the world.

Nevertheless, movements such as liberation theology are forcing the Church, especially the evangelical wing, to formulate a doctrine of the cross which includes within it a commitment to the world and to the task of bringing Christ's healing grace to the poor, starving and oppressed. We must reject as unbiblical any attempt to privatise the atonement, as if the only sin from which we are redeemed is personal sin and as if the only salvation that Christ had in mind was spiritual and other-worldly. As Harvie Conn puts it so trenchantly: 'The church is not to be the launching pad for guerilla operations, but neither is it to be the retreat where the pious await the parousia.'[13] Without accepting, then, Gutierrez's thesis of one world history which ends in making the spiritual a rather insignificant element in the task of humanisation, or the opposite error of regarding the cross as having no bearing whatever on the Church's role in society, we must develop a theology of the cross which embraces both. Here are some elements which I believe must be part of our theology and strategy of salvation.

Christ's commitment to the needy

It is obvious that there can be no real conversion to God if there is not a similar reorientation to one's neighbour. Jesus taught this himself at the level of forgiveness: 'Forgive us our sin, as we forgive those who sin against us' (Matt. 6:12). So close, indeed, is reconciliation to God and to our neighbour that one is not sure which is prior (Matt. 5:23–4; 18:21–35). If, as we have been emphasising, the incarnation is part of Christ's work of atonement, we cannot possibly ignore the life of Jesus as if it were irrelevant to the task of redemption. In many of the earliest testimonies concerning Jesus' ministry, the character of his life is emphasised: e.g. Acts 10:38; Philippians 2:5–11; Hebrews 5:7. Indeed, if we were asked: 'Why bother about the poor and needy – after all, our task is to preach the gospel and to make sure that people are given a chance to respond to him?' our answer must be along the following lines. Jesus himself entered human existence as a poor person. He was homeless (Matt. 8:20) and spent a great deal of his ministry with the poor and needy. He identified with those who were regarded with disdain by the aristocracy: prostitutes, tax collectors, Gentiles and women. His opening address at Capernaum gives all the appearance of a manifesto speech with its declaration of concern for what we might call the underprivileged of society:

> The Spirit of the Lord is on me,
>   because he has anointed me
>   to preach good news to the poor.
> He has sent me to proclaim freedom for
>   the prisoners
>   and recovery of sight for the blind,
> to release the oppressed . . .

> (Luke 4:18)

The breaking in of the kingdom in the ministry of Jesus, as expressed in that verse, means that in him the future has already, in part, invaded the present. People are, in fact, healed, freed, converted and made whole. In his ministry we see no polarisation of spiritual healing and physical wholeness. Jesus responds to human need, whatever it is, and ministers his healing grace in accordance with it. Furthermore, he also calls his disciples to identify with his simple lifestyle (Matt. 10:7–12).

But we would also want to answer that Jesus taught that in the final days salvation is marked by compassion to the needy. 'I was hungry and you gave me something to eat, I was thirsty and you gave me something to drink . . . I needed clothes and you clothed me' (Matt. 25:35–6). Those who emphasise the 'verticalist' view of atonement have always found the 'work-ethic' of Jesus' teaching a problem. But it is scarcely a problem if we hold faith and works together and realise that real faith and commitment to Christ and his way result in the fruit of faith, namely, deeds of love and compassion.

The Church under the cross

As we have seen more than once, the coming of Christ into our world was an act of love. He became human, lived among us, caring for the needy, died and rose again so that we might enjoy his new life. The cross and the resurrection are the seal of our freedom. But he who entered this life as a poor man in a poor family calls us to identify with his act of voluntary surrender. St Paul goes to the heart of this when writing to the Corinthians about giving to the poor of Jerusalem: 'For you know the grace of our Lord Jesus Christ, that though he was rich, yet for your sakes he became poor, so that you through his poverty might become rich' (2 Cor. 8:9). In this and other passages of the New Testament, the example of Jesus becomes the paradigm for Christian living. For instance: giving (2 Cor. 8:9); humility (Phil. 2:5ff); suffering (1 Peter 2:21) and discipleship (Rom. 6:4). It is not surprising, then, that Luke tells us that the central characteristic of the early Church was its sharing of goods so that there was not a poor person among them (Acts 4:32, 34). He does not inform us, nor does he need to, where the first Christians got this idea from. From the nature of the earliest preaching, as we saw in Chapter Five, it was clearly the ministry as well as the message of Jesus which had such an impact upon the way the first Christians lived. Again, we must make clear what we are not saying. I am not suggesting for a moment that the act of becoming poor is redemptive, which is certainly Gutierrez's position – instead I am arguing that a consequence of being redeemed is that one is drawn into Christ's ministry to those in need.

It is because we Christians, and especially western Christians, do not take the cross radically and deeply into our own lives, allowing it to affect our lifestyles, giving, jobs, possessions and futures that we earn the stinging rebukes of those who see the contradiction between Christ's way and ours. Gandhi, who had a lifelong admiration for Christ, once said: 'Jesus Christ I admire and revere – but you Christians do not live like him.' And Nietzsche, atheist and nihilist, the son of a Lutheran minister, remarked: 'You Christians will have to look a lot more redeemed before I start believing in your Redeemer.'

Do we not then have to start looking at the New Testament in a new way to rediscover the challenge of Jesus for our own times? Why is it that we have been so blind to the theology of 'giving up' that there is in the teaching of Jesus and in the writers who followed him? Yet Francis of Assisi realised at once that the cross was calling him to emulate Christ's compassion for the poor. He found in Jesus' words to the rich young ruler a word to himself: 'One thing you lack . . . Go, sell everything you have and give to the poor . . . Then come, follow me' (Mark 10:21). Have we been so 'conned' by the affluence of a settled and secure Christian faith on very good terms with secularism that we have separated spirituality from discipleship and service from sacrifice? If the Church has a strategy of the cross it will affect the way Christians live, not only separately but together. It will lead to a positive attitude to 'giving up' for the sake of Christ in order for his care and love to be known through us. It will also mean a willingness to challenge the 'rich man in his castle and the poor man at his gate' philosophy.

At the very least we can learn from liberation theology the necessity to ask critical questions of any society which assumes the God-given right of the rich to get richer and the poor to get poorer. William Temple said years ago that there can be no true human freedom without economic freedom, and he put his considerable ability behind the search for an equitable society in which the poor could climb out of the spiral of poverty to live more useful and dignified lives. Liberation theology is quite right to remind us that this will involve 'praxis'. Praxis took Jesus to a cross and it leads every Christian who is born again into his death and resurrection to embrace his way of living. It is very strange that western Christianity has lost this dimension of radical discipleship. We have replaced it with a following of Jesus which is virtually cost-less. Indeed, some evangelists are guilty of going to the other extreme of offering the carrot that 'If you accept Jesus, he will solve your problems, help you find a good job, husband, wife, peace, contentment, etc.' The motive behind this may be admirable – it is true, after all, that the presence of the Lord is healing – but the result is a 'filleted' Christianity, with sacrifice removed.

The cross and the kingdom

A strategy of the cross will involve any Christian community in earthing itself in the real issues and problems of its social context. Only by so doing will it have any chance of making the link between its preaching and the needs of people. Liberation theology is quite right in its observation that it is not a case of choosing sides. Silence is an actual choice because to do nothing in the face of wrong is in itself an act of injustice. For example, the failure of the churches of Germany (with a few marvellous exceptions) to speak up against the tyranny of Hitler and his unspeakable evil encouraged him and his henchmen to intensify the atrocities. But any church which is under the sign of the cross will identify with the suffering, persecuted and the un-free because this was the way of the master and the disciple is called to follow. This means, however, that such a church will also be a sign of the kingdom because it will represent the values of the King himself. An identification of Church and kingdom is impossible because the Church is always provisional, always reaching forward to its metamorphosis into the kingdom at the end of time. Nevertheless, insofar as it lives under the cross, preaches the cross and expresses the cross daily, it will become a sign of hope to those who live without dignity and freedom. I close this chapter with a number of challenges to the modern Church which come directly from the contribution of liberation theology.

Discipleship

As we have seen, liberation theology takes the Church from the study into the world, from the lecture room into the laboratory. Its emphasis on praxis, action, challenges the Church to a commitment to the cross which is not only deeply personal but which is also deeply social. At the personal level, the question emerges: how may we bring back the power of the cross into Christian living so that we ourselves are tangible witnesses of what following Jesus Christ really means? Western Christians sometimes glimpse the reality of this in the lives and experiences of Third World Christians who, devoid of the excess baggage of western luxuries, reveal a commitment which seems heroic and Christlike.

At the social level, there is an undeniable need to shift the attention of the Church from privatised religion to the arena of political and social commitment. Issues of social justice cannot replace the gospel, but neither are they external to it: they are integral to its message and life. A gospel which shrinks back from the deep concerns of people trapped by unemployment, dehumanised by social structures, crabbed, cabin'd and confined by limited educational opportunities, is not a gospel worthy of the name of Jesus Christ.

Stewardship

If liberation theology sets an agenda for the Church to engage with its world and culture, there is an indirect challenge which comes from the 'holy worldliness' which resists the separation of the secular and spiritual. That is to say, we must challenge the attempt to make of Christianity a 'religion'. The way of religion is that of compartmentalising faith so that it is confined to Sundays or to areas of life marked out as more holy than others. The history of the Church reveals the unfortunate legacy we have inherited – that of religious buildings deemed more important than others, that of Sunday deemed more significant than other days, that of the life of the spirit deemed more important than that of the secular.

However, a commitment to the world, God's world, frees Christians from the demonic separation of the spiritual and secular, and releases us to consider life holistically and without guilt. Most importantly, it releases us to be effective stewards of the whole of God's resources in the world, and to see the ecological as part of God's new creation.

The local church as a 'sign' of the kingdom

As I have remarked, if we are going to have a strategy of the cross which affects people here and now, we must 'incarnate' the message of Jesus in our society. Not only will this mean showing practical action but it will also include identifying with those concerns – social, political, whatever – in our community which will lead to the enrichment of human dignity. This will only seem heretical if our view of salvation is already too privatised and spiritualised for it to have any horizontal relevance. But assuming that we agree that we are called to preach a gospel that is genuinely 'gospel' and yet social in its application to the lives of men, we are forced to ask: what are the issues in this community which dehumanise people and restrict their growth? What Christian insights can we share with our community? How do we balance out the time we should give to purely 'Church' concerns with that we should give to 'community' issues?

Taking up our cross, then, has implications for the individual Christian as well as the Church. We have been led to reject much of the system of liberation theology but what I, for one, do not wish to repudiate is its passionate belief in the relevance of the cross to the needs of our world. To love, to care for the weak, to help the afflicted – in short, to live as Christ lived in the world – will make us question anything which claims to be biblical Christianity if it does not participate in the struggle for the poor and needy. Rather than compromising the gospel and making it more difficult to preach, it will give it a new integrity and purpose.

12

The Cross and the Spirit

As we have already observed, the cross, separated from the context of the Father's love, runs the risk of being interpreted as an act of Jesus to placate a wrathful deity. Equally disastrous is any attempt to explain the cross which leaves out the Spirit. And yet, it is surprising how many books on this subject ignore the role of the Spirit in the work of salvation. I can think of only one substantial book which considers the link in any serious way and that is R. C. Moberley's *Atonement and Personality*[1] which makes an impassioned plea for a recovery of the work of the Spirit in the ministry of the Son on the cross. What Moberley saw very clearly was that although Calvary represented the finished work of the Son (which is done without us and for us), nevertheless without Pentecost Calvary is useless for us. 'An exposition of atonement,' Moberley declares, 'which leaves out Pentecost, leaves the atonement unintelligible – in relation to us.'[2] He saw the inseparable nature of the two: Pentecost could not have happened without Calvary, but Calvary without Pentecost would not have been atonement – to all intents and purposes – because Pentecost represents the reality in human experience of the new birth which Jesus came to give.

In this chapter I want to work out the implications of Moberley's greatly neglected observation because I think he has glimpsed something very exciting about the cross and its effect upon us.

THE SPIRIT IS THE SPIRIT OF THE CRUCIFIED JESUS

Although, of course, we want to stress that the Holy Spirit has an independent life apart from the Son, we should note that in Scripture there is the closest of links between the Spirit and Jesus. For our purposes two interesting facts stand out and demand our attention. First, that Jesus is the bearer of the Spirit.

In all of the gospel accounts Jesus is baptised and the Spirit falls upon him. These are two distinct but very closely related events whose significance is related to the ministry of Jesus. His baptism, Matthew makes plain, is a baptism of identification with human wickedness and sin. The Baptist is aware that by presenting himself for baptism, Jesus seems to be coming as a sinner in need of forgiveness. 'I need to be baptised by you, and do you come to me?' (Matt. 3:14) Jesus' reply indicates his willingness to be one with those he has come to redeem: 'Let it be so now; it is proper for us to do this to fulfil all righteousness' (3:15).

The descent of the Spirit upon Jesus, however, represents not only the beginning of Jesus' ministry in power but also the beginning of the new age. That is to say, through the ministry of the Spirit-filled Christ the new covenant for humanity has come and for which, for the time being at least, Jesus is the paradigm and prototype. He is the bearer of the Spirit who will become, much later, the giver of the same Spirit. So, following the baptism and the descent of the Spirit, Jesus is led into the desert and later into his ministry of teaching and healing and cross-bearing. Professor James Dunn mentions in his important book *Baptism in the Holy Spirit* that 'what the Jordan was to Jesus, Pentecost was to the disciples. As Jesus entered the new age and covenant by being baptised in the Spirit, so the disciples followed him in the like manner.'[3] This is indeed true. But before that could become a reality the cross had to come in between. The gospels make it plain that Jesus, the bearer of the Spirit, is led to embrace death as the way of salvation for all men.

But our second observation is this: Jesus is not only the

bearer of the Spirit – in a very real sense he (that is, Jesus) comes to us. *It is the Spirit of Jesus which is given to Christians!* In our understanding of the gift of the Spirit these days, it is all too easy to leave Christ behind and to assume that the indwelling Spirit is, somehow, independent of Jesus. From this we advance to the conclusion that Pentecost means the coming of the Spirit of power upon the Church and that the cross, as far as we are concerned, belongs to Jesus' past and not ours. But this is not the understanding of the New Testament. Spirit and Son are bound together in an indissoluble unity of mind and purpose. So John talks about the coming of the Spirit following Jesus' departure. 'We know that we live in him and he in us, because he has given us of his Spirit' (1 John 4:13; see 3:24). That is to say, for the disciples it was a comfort to know that they would continue to abide in Jesus through the Spirit of Jesus. And, again: 'It is for your good that I am going away. Unless I go away, the Counsellor will not come to you; but if I go, I will send him to you' (John 16:7). Obviously, then, the departure of Jesus was for their advantage and somehow bound up with their salvation. The Spirit of holiness could not indwell them until humanity was victorious over sin, and the Spirit of reconciliation could not be theirs until humanity was reconciled. The atonement was the essential element which made the coming of the Spirit possible. But the disciples are never given the impression that Jesus ever leaves them. He may leave them physically but he is with them always and not just metaphorically: 'I will ask the Father, and he will give you another Counsellor to be with you for ever – the Spirit of truth . . . I will not leave you as orphans; I will come to you' (John 14:16–18). We should not jump to the conclusion that the disciples are to have the Spirit instead of Jesus. That is not what Jesus was saying. Rather, to have the Spirit is to have Jesus.

This is also the assumption of the rest of the New Testament. The presence of Christ in the Church is the Spirit, and the Spirit given makes it possible for the followers of Jesus to participate in his ministry. This is one of the reasons why it is extremely difficult to separate the persons of Son and Spirit in Scripture. Of course, from one perspective there is a clear separation. Jesus departs to his Father once his work is done and the Spirit falls upon the expectant Church. But the Spirit who comes is not independent of Christ; he applies his work to our hearts and spreads the gospel. People can only receive the Spirit through Jesus (Acts 2:38) and healings are only possible through his name. Peter, filled with the Holy Spirit, said, 'know this, you and all the people of Israel: It is by the name of Jesus Christ of Nazareth, whom you crucified but whom God raised from the dead, that this man stands before you healed' (Acts 4:8–10). The book of Acts does not encourage us to think of Jesus as an absent Lord once his central work is over. The writer draws attention to the dying Stephen's vision of the risen Christ at the right hand of the Father (7:56) and Stephen's last words are: 'Lord Jesus, receive my spirit.' Two chapters later it is Paul's turn to meet Christ on the Damascus road (9:3–5) and we find him and Ananias talking to Christ as if he were physically present with them (see, vv. 10, 13, 15, 17). Later in Acts the writer, Luke, lets slip a very significant remark about the ministry of Paul: 'they tried to enter Bithynia, but the Spirit of Jesus would not allow them to' (16:7). The Spirit, then, whose life throbs throughout the inspiring story of Acts, is not just the third person of the Trinity, but the presence of Jesus with his people, as well. It is as if the writer is saying: 'Jesus is present in his Church and with his people through the Spirit of God.'

The rest of the New Testament is in agreement with this. 'Because you are sons, God sent the Spirit of his Son into our hearts, the Spirit calls out, "*Abba*, Father" ' (Gal. 4:6); 'Now the Lord [that is, Jesus] is the Spirit' (2 Cor. 3:17); 'for I know that through your prayers and the help given by the Spirit of Jesus Christ, what has happened to me will turn out for my deliverance' (Phil. 1:19). In Romans 8, particularly, we find the clearest emphasis upon the inter-relationship of Spirit and Son expressed in such a way that it might seem at first sight as if confusion is the only likely outcome. But this is far from the case. Paul could hardly have written in this way unless his intention all along was to make the point that in the process of salvation and sanctification the Son and Spirit are at work together. To be sure, from our perspective it sometimes becomes very difficult to separate precisely the role of each – but this was obviously no problem to Paul. He was happy to live with the ambiguity. So, for example, salvation is ours through 'Christ Jesus' (Rom. 8:1) and in him is no condemnation. Yet in v. 2 freedom from sin and death is described as the work of 'the law of the Spirit of life in Christ Jesus' (RSV). Indeed, Paul interweaves Spirit and Son throughout the chapter in such a kaleidoscopic fashion that we are dazzled by the sheer richness of the picture before us: v. 1, Christ; v. 2, Spirit; v. 3, Christ; v. 4, Spirit; vv. 5–6, Spirit; v. 9, Spirit; v. 10, Christ; v. 11, Spirit. Verse 9 must surely go to the very heart of the problem: 'You, however, are controlled not by the sinful nature but by the Spirit, if the Spirit of God lives in you. And, if anyone does not have the Spirit of Christ, he does not belong to Christ.' The Spirit indwells the Christian and Christ indwells the Christian (v. 10). We need not go any further to demonstrate the theme in the New Testament that Christ continues his ministry through the work of the Spirit. This should not be taken to read that the Spirit has no nature of his own. Indeed, he has: but his work is to glorify Christ and to make the work of salvation effective in the lives and minds of humankind.

THE SPIRIT OF JESUS IS THE SPIRIT OF THE NEW HUMANITY

If we are right in noting that the indwelling Spirit is, in fact, the Spirit of the incarnate Jesus we can take the argument one step further: in the person of Jesus we see humanity at its purest and best and and, in fact, what God intends each of us to become. He is the pattern of our humanity and in his life we see foreshadowed the nature of our calling. So Paul sees the whole plan of redemption finding its climax in our maturity in Christ, 'until we all reach unity in the faith and in the knowledge of the Son of God and become mature, attaining to the whole measure of the fulness of Christ' (Eph. 4:13). We have to acknowledge that this idea is not clearly worked out in the New Testament. However, the roots are there in a variety of ways in which Jesus is seen as the model of Christian growth. Paul alludes to the destiny of the Christian in the verse just quoted, where the Lord is viewed as the Omega point of redemption. This possibly links in with the striking way Jesus Christ is seen as the first fruits of the resurrection. His rising from the dead is the pattern for our nature yet to be (1 John 3:2; Phil. 3:20–1).

More strikingly, the idea of Christ as the image to which God wants all Christians to be conformed is an element in Paul's thought which merits our attention. Romans 8, a chapter which works out the scope of God's redemption in Christ, moves towards a crescendo in which Paul says that 'we know that in all things God works for the good of those who love him, who have been called according to his purpose. For those God foreknew he also predestined to be conformed to the likeness [image] of his son' (vv. 28–30). Now, what does Paul mean by the 'image of his Son'? In order to answer this let us look at two other passages. Colossians 3:8 is a call for Christian holiness: 'You must rid yourselves of all such things as these: anger, rage, malice, slander . . . since you have taken off your old self with its practices and have put on the new self, which is being renewed in knowledge in the image of its Creator.' In 2 Corinthians 3:18, Paul concludes his famous passage on the identity of Spirit and Son with: 'And we, who with unveiled faces all reflect the Lord's glory, are being transformed into his likeness [image] with ever-increasing glory, which comes from the Lord, who is the Spirit.' These passages help us to see that Paul was aware that Adam had fallen from the glory of God and had either lost the image of his creator or it was defaced in him. But now through Christ the image has been restored. What we lost through Adam has been more than restored to us in Christ. The image is not only a gift and our possession now, but it also remains the fullness of our destiny to be. 'The image of his Son,' therefore, turns out to be God's pattern for each of us and Paul sees a purposeful plan which works for the renewal of life and faith through which it can become a reality.

However, within Protestantism we have greatly neglected the pattern of Jesus as our goal and inspiration. We have already drawn attention to passages which present Jesus as our example (1 Pet. 2; Phil. 2:5ff; Heb. 5; Heb. 12) but, also, it is very likely that the famous passage on love in 1 Corinthians 13 is modelled on Christ and that Paul's teaching on the fruit of the Spirit in Galatians 5:22–3 presents the kind of Spirit-filled life that Christ lived on earth. Indeed, the fact that Paul follows the passage directly with: 'Those who belong to Christ Jesus have crucified the sinful nature with its passions and desires' indicates that he sees anybody in whom the fruits are manifested as living the kind of life that glorifies Christ, and which he lived.

This is the point where we find the atonement making us very uncomfortable. It is all too easy to study it as a doctrine and keep it external to us. But that is not what it is all about. The atonement is not merely a past transaction: it brings to us the Spirit, who is not content until Christ is formed in us and we show in our lives the powerful effect of his presence. One of the reasons why we feel uncomfortable is that we know that our lives fall far short of that reality. 'There are tens and hundreds of thousands,' declared Moberley, 'to whom the simple reality of this belief, if they were able to receive it simply and truly, would absolutely revolutionise present experience. It would alter their interpretation of life.'[4] It is important to see the radical nature of the atonement of Christ. If it means anything at all it must be a real transformation of ourselves so that we are truly 'new beings' in Christ. Certainly, the Scriptures are confident that the cross deals with the past, present and future. The *past* – by dealing with the tragedy of sin and guilt in our lives; the *present* – by restoring us to the Father, with his gift of the Spirit to encourage and heal; the *future* – by giving us assurance of our destiny in Christ. In each of these areas the Spirit works purposefully with the Son in bringing about men and women who have the image of Christ in their lives. How important and necessary this really is for the mission of Christ, as well as for our own good!

To our shame we have to admit that Christianity's greatest and most embarrassing contradiction is the lack of identity between the winsomeness and attractiveness of Christ's life and ours. Although there are many fine exceptions, why do we not expect the acceptance of the cross of Christ radically to affect our lifestyle, our inner lives – our thinking, sexuality, temper – as well as our attitude to material prosperity? Perhaps the answer has much to do with the observation we made in the last chapter: the atonement has been spiritualised so greatly, as only affecting our relationship with God and our future life with him, that the potential power of the healing stream which flows from the cross has been dammed up by the silt of low expectations and bad teaching. I would like to suggest that there are two tools the Spirit uses to make us more like our Lord and it may well be that as we take up these tools and apply them we may find the deepening work of the cross beginning to remove the silt which blocks the fullness of his work.

Grace and justification

Justification by faith is a greatly prized word in the evangelical vocabulary. This idea, mainly to be found in Paul's writings, is at the heart of the New Testament doctrine of salvation. We don't need anyone to tell us what it means. As we observed earlier, it is a legal term meaning 'to pronounce righteous'. Insofar as the person in the dock is not really righteous, it takes on the meaning of 'acquittal', 'amnesty' or 'forgiveness'. It doesn't mean 'to make righteous' but that God has accepted us as forgiven sinners through Christ. Just as a dirty, unshaven tramp might be accepted into the home of the Lord of the Manor because the heir, his friend, brings him into that exalted circle, so God accepts us into his family through Christ, his Son. All we have to bring is our trust, our commitment, our faith and the transaction is made. Although God wants us to be righteous and holy before him, our hold and claim upon his mercies are established by this declaration of 'not guilty' which comes through the redeeming work of Christ. We are now 'in Christ' (Rom. 8:1). We have peace through him and 'access' into the Father's presence (Rom. 5:1–2). The language of the New Testament throbs with the vitality of words like these. The kingdom of heaven which, though a future hope, has been partially realised through the momentous event of salvation is 'righteousness, peace and joy in the Holy Spirit' (Rom. 14:17).

Yet it hardly needs to be said that many Christians believe the doctrine but do not seem to have allowed it to penetrate into their souls and hearts. I have met scores of earnest people, most of them evangelicals, whose lives appear to be marked by the weight of Christianity and not its joy. Their lips say, 'We are accepted,' but the way they live shouts, 'The Christian life is a burden. To live the kind of life God wants, you have to slog away. To enjoy creation is wrong. God wants miserable sinners.' All right, this is another parody, but in my ministry I have met many people of whom this is true. Indeed, if we were truly honest perhaps many of us would have to admit that we have sometimes (often?) allowed a Protestant work-ethic to rule our lives instead of the gentleness and assurance of the Spirit of God. Of course, we believe that we have been accepted in Christ, but our lives cry out for acceptance from the Christian community of which we are a part.

What is the answer to this? I think the answer is to be found in the central role of the Spirit – the creation of life. 'If anyone is in Christ, he is a new creation,' claimed Paul (2 Cor. 5:17). To the Spirit belongs this task of regeneration and growth. 'Since we live by the Spirit,' Paul writes to the Galatians, 'let us keep in step with the Spirit' (Gal. 5:25). For Paul – and, we must say, for the rest of the New Testament writers – this was no flowery, rhetorical message. It was the life-blood of Christianity. For all who are in Christ, life is transformed and takes on a whole new complexion, 'the old has gone, the new has come!' (2 Cor. 5:17). As a result, the destiny of the Christian is rich in Christ: 'It is because of him that you are in Christ Jesus, who has become for us wisdom from God – that is our righteousness, holiness and redemption' (1 Cor. 1:30).

Ironically enough, the passage from which this verse comes reveals the paradox of the Christian life. On the one hand, Paul could use the word 'spiritual' (*pneumatikos*) of his readers because they had received the Spirit and, theoretically at least, all the spiritual wealth available in Christ was theirs. The later chapters of the letter reveal that many of them had received impressive gifts of the Spirit and were using them in the community. But, on the other hand, Paul finds it impossible to address them as 'spiritual' and is forced to call them 'carnal' or 'flesh-natured' (*sarkinos*: 1 Cor. 3:1). The way they are living and behaving, their lack of love and consideration, their selfishness and pride – all these, and more, indicated that they had a long way to go before the Spirit could say they were really his. But Paul does not give up on the task of reminding them of their inheritance in Christ and their proper obedience: 'Do you not know that your body is a temple of the Holy Spirit, who is in you, whom you have received from God? You are not your own; you were bought at a price' (1 Cor. 6:19–20).

It is true, of course, that the Spirit and our possession of him are not the totality of our experience but merely its 'first-fruits' and we look ahead to the fullness of the inheritance which will be ours at the end of time. Nevertheless, we should not be fobbed off by claiming a 'mess of pottage' when we could be enjoying a jolly good meal! I mean that God wants us to live victorious, whole lives. He wants healing for us; he desires changed lives which will testify to his power and love. In short, he longs for each one of us that we will take the atonement deeply into our lives, allowing its radical medicine to make us the kind of people who will sing his praise not only with our lips but also in our lives. This will happen as we allow the Spirit to channel the grace of Jesus Christ to our lives.

The Spirit in the Church and sacraments

We are pleading for a balanced doctrine of the atonement which not only looks back to the finished work of Christ on the cross but which expects the radically transforming grace of Christ to be effective in our lives. The transforming agent is, of course, the Holy Spirit of God whose first job at Pentecost was to create an environment, a nursery, a family, an army, a people which would be the physical and spiritual home of those who belong to Jesus. And we must remember that the Church – yes, this despised, tired-looking and often discouraging fellowship – is essential for God's plan of salvation. Bishop Geoffrey Paul, the former Bishop of Bradford, remarked in a memorable phrase: 'There is no way of belonging to the body of Christ, except by belonging to that glorious rag-bag of saints and fatheads who made up the one, holy, catholic and apostolic church.' Saints and fatheads, yes; but part of the Church which is God's *gift* to his people. This is borne out by the New Testament understanding of the Church. As we saw earlier, Paul found it quite difficult to distinguish between Christ and the Spirit at times when he wanted to describe the ministry of sanctification. A believer could be 'in Christ' or 'in the Spirit'. But Paul also spoke in terms of another environment in which the Christian moved and had his being – namely the 'body of Christ'. So he reminds the Corinthians that they were called 'into fellowship with his Son', that is, to that body which has its origins in him (1 Cor. 1:9). Belonging to Christ is belonging to the fellowship: 'There is one body and one Spirit – just as you were called to one hope when you were called – one Lord, one faith, one baptism . . . ' (Eph. 4:4–5).

Now I happen to believe that the Christian Church would be a more vibrant fellowship if it had a keener awareness of the importance of the sacraments which express the cardinal truth of the atonement.

Baptism – the sacrament of justification

Most Christian groups consider baptism essential for faith but to what extent is its *radical* nature expressed in our life? For the New Testament Church baptism was 'rebirth' and incorporation into Christ. It represented a sharp break from the old life which Paul describes in terms of 'death' (Rom. 6:3). Now they have been 'clothed . . . with Christ' (Gal. 3:27; cf. Col. 3:10) and walk in newness of life. Little wonder this new existence was described in terms of new creation (2 Cor. 5:17); new birth (John 3:7); new life (Rom. 6:11); regeneration (Titus 3:5, AV). Following conversion (and we must remember that the New Testament is singularly hazy about the link between the personal act of accepting Jesus as Lord and the corporate act whereby he was baptised and identified himself with the body of Christ), the believer had no doubt that he was a changed person and that the Spirit of the risen Jesus indwelt him. It is very clear from the evidence of the early Church after the New Testament period that baptism was a very precious rite to the first Christians. They guarded it jealously. It was not administered frequently – it would seem that Easter and Pentecost were the main occasions when believers were admitted to the fellowship after a time of painstaking preparation, examination and teaching. But it was no hole-and-corner affair. The church admitted them into fellowship with much rejoicing and praise and the new Christian was only too well aware of the tremendous privilege of being allowed to join the family of God.

New Testament and Patristic practices of baptism challenge both our theology and conventions. If, as I have said, baptism is the sacrament of our justification and proclaims that we are accepted and made children in the one family of God, we have to question all approaches which treat it very lightly. The sacrament of baptism is abused when ministers and priests extend it to others without proper nurture, pastoral care and sensitive concern for the spiritual welfare of the entire family. Indiscriminate baptism is wholly without theological support – it degrades the gospel and undermines the Church.

On the other hand, over-rigorous baptismal policies are equally reprehensible because they discriminate on the basis of law, ignoring the fact that grace, central to the Christian faith, is not always transparent and accessible to human enquiry. It is a regrettable fact that many young parents who are a woefully long way short of a mature faith have brought their infants for baptism and have felt rejected because they have been unable to fulfil the specific conditions of that particular church. And here is a dilemma that confronts churches, such as my own, which want to respect the nature of the sacrament and yet which do not wish to impose yet another law which supersedes grace.

I suggest that the only way in which the dilemma may be addressed is for the sacrament of baptism to be administered within a flexible and pastorally sensitive discipline of nurture which has the family, as well as the child, as its focus. Somehow, within the two commands of Christ – 'Suffer the little children to come unto me' (Matt. 19:14, AV) and 'Take up your [cross] and follow me' (Matt. 16:24), the Church must hesitatingly work out its baptismal teaching and practice. The openness of the former does not rule out the commitment expressed in the latter; but, equally, we should not expect the rigour of the call to follow Christ to deny that there will be many whose journey into faith will be cautious, slow and sometimes timid.

But there is still an even more radical implication at the heart of baptism. If it is a sacrament of our justification then it is also a sacrament of our membership of the one Church of Jesus Christ. This is so radical that few of us are prepared to face up to the uncomfortable repercussions of it. It is commonplace these days to accept that Christians baptised in the name of the Trinity are full Christians, but few of us are prepared to face the possibility that this offers a way forward ecumenically. In other words, if through the death of Christ baptised Christians are brought near to God and made members of his body, what possible reasons can there be for our separation from one another? It is very likely the case, as I firmly believe, that our traditions express deeply important truths, yet none of them are of such definitive significance that they should be allowed to affect our unity in Christ expressed in our common baptism. I find myself here in substantial agreement with Dr Paul Avis, who asks the following disturbing questions: 'Is a closed table the Lord's supper? Is a eucharist from which other baptised believers are excluded a genuine eucharist? Is it not rather both theologically indefensible and morally intolerable? If some want to raise questions of "validity" at this point, could not the validity of a segregated eucharist be equally well called into question? Can we claim to accept Christ as saviour and Lord when we do not give unconditional acceptance to all his people? Is it plausible to protest that we do indeed offer them such acceptance when we do not accept them at the Lord's table, the place of communion par excellence?

'These questions cannot be disregarded. And we cannot ignore the radical implications of the cross.'[5]

The Eucharist – the sacrament of the Lord's presence

We have already noted that the effect of the cross of Christ was that a Church was born. Not immediately, of course, because it required the life-giving work of the Spirit to bear fruit from the sin-crushing victory of Calvary. We may well describe Pentecost as the birthday of the Church as long as we hold in tension with it the cross that made it all possible. The curious thing about the early Church is that the first thing we find out about them in Acts 2 is that they have a common meal together. There appears to have been a four-fold shape to their common life: apostolic teaching, fellowship, breaking of bread and prayer (2:42). A few verses later Luke repeats this and tells us that they continued worshipping in the temple and 'broke bread in their homes' (v. 46).

We have to admit ignorance about the character of the common meal in Acts 2. Luke does not tell us how it relates the Last Supper. However, it must have taken its significance from the table fellowship the first disciples enjoyed with their Lord. This meal quickly developed into the sacrament of the Lord's Supper which is dear to all Christians today. But this meal could only have acquired its prominence in the Church because Jesus himself had invested it with meaning and purpose. The breaking of the bread, therefore, together with drinking of wine, was a vivid recalling of the Last Supper Jesus had with his friends before his death. From this developed the closest of links between the broken body of Jesus, the bread and wine of communion and the body of believers. So Paul states in 1 Corinthians 10:16f: 'Is not the cup of thanksgiving a participation in the blood of Christ? And is not the bread that we break a participation in the body of Christ? . . . we, who are many, are one body, for we all partake of the one loaf.' In the following chapter Paul attacks the divisions in the fellowship and cites the Corinthian practice of people bringing food along but eating it separately, so that the rich were satisfied and the poor went hungry. After giving a description of the Lord's institution of the Supper Paul adds these words: 'whoever eats the bread or drinks the cup of the Lord in an unworthy manner will be guilty of sinning against the body and blood of the Lord ... For anyone who eats and drinks without recognising the body of the Lord, eats and drinks judgment on himself' (1 Cor. 11:27, 29).

It is highly unlikely that Paul meant by 'without recognising the body of the Lord' that the Corinthians had failed to discern the Lord's body in the actual elements of the Eucharist. What is more probable is that Paul is bringing sacrament and fellowship together to challenge the Corinthian church about the nature of Christian unity, fellowship and common love. We must recall that he was speaking earlier about the discords and selfishness in the common meal (v. 21) and it seems self-evident that if a person fails to discern the body, that is the Church, he will see the Christian fellowship as no more than a fellowship of men and not as it really is – 'the church of God' (v. 22). So he must examine himself and his attitude to the fellowship to see if his behaviour is worthy of his standing in Christ. Only so can he safely participate in the family meal. But this argument is only possible on the basis that Paul saw the most intimate of connections between the people and the shared meal. The subtle overlapping of the bread as 'body' and the people as 'body' shows the nature of the Christian community as a people created by Calvary and Pentecost. It is but a simple step from this rebuke of failing to see the importance of the people of God to Paul's comprehensive teaching about the Spirit in the community which is worked out in chapters 12–14.

I am sure that this has a lot to teach us today. Let me suggest what we have done to the sacrament of the Lord's Supper, the Eucharist, or Holy Communion. We have lost the meal element and all we have retained are the tokens of a sip of wine and crumb of bread; we have lost the note of celebration and replaced it with a religious service which concentrates upon right reception, dignity, order and reverence; we have lost the deep note of fellowship and retained only 'The Peace' which is a very tame gesture of love compared to the original intention. As I am not an anarchist, I would plead only that we work hard to bring back into our fellowship two central ideas. First, that our Eucharists should really be thanksgivings! Let our Holy Communions be times of celebration in which we celebrate the victory of Calvary instead of our usually successful imitation of a funeral service. And because it is, scripturally, the centre of our fellowship, let us see it as embodying in a very special way our love for one another and our desire for the fellowship to grow so that others may find Christ's love for themselves. It is not without accident, therefore, that Paul could see the Lord's Supper as 'proclamatory': 'For whenever you eat this bread and drink this cup, you proclaim the Lord's death until he comes' (11:26). In my experience, and that of many other Christian leaders, our joyful celebrations of the Supper of the Lord have indeed been real proclamations and have led many to the Christ they have been seeking. Secondly, if we are the body of Christ centred upon the 'table-fellowship' of his death and indwelt by his Spirit, we owe it to him to work at our fellowship and expect to see the fruits and gifts of the Spirit expressed in our common life. The fact that often they are not, is a scandal to the gospel we purport to proclaim.

THE CROSS, THE SPIRIT AND CHARISMATIC RENEWAL

As one influenced by the renewal movement and who is deeply appreciative of its contribution to worldwide Christianity, I have to say regretfully that some quarters of this movement are woefully deficient in their theology of the cross, even to the extent of ignoring it altogether. Such is the concentration upon the gifts of the Spirit, the ecstatic, the miraculous, the signs and wonders, that the cross appears to be left out of it.

It is abundantly clear that no one wishing to be faithful to New Testament faith can leave the cross behind. It is for ever our contemporary and colours all we do. Let us try to relate the cross to the charismatic dimension in the Church today.

First, a consequence of the link between the cross and Pentecost as argued in this chapter is that spiritual gifts are as much gifts of Calvary as they are of Pentecost. True, they come from the Spirit but he himself is a gift which comes to us from the victorious, ascended Lord. I mean by this that all gifts when 'unpacked' have a 'Calvary shape' about them. Gifts, such as administration, healing, teaching, wisdom, hospitality or whatever, are all marked with the sign of the cross. Paul hints as much when he introduces the theme of love in his discussion on spiritual gifts. In that marvellous chapter, 1 Corinthians 13, it is as if he is saying: 'You Corinthian Christians are always talking about spiritual gifts and boasting about how you excel in them. But without love you are nothing. Love forgets itself. The triumph of love is complete when it is totally self-giving. So let your gifts take on the same character of sacrifice, love, surrender – and death.' Perhaps spiritual gifts today might lose their somewhat 'froth and bubble' character and gain a great deal in credibility if the nature of the cross were to fill them. It is only a conjecture, but I wonder if one of the reasons why the quality of New Testament Christianity is so markedly absent from contemporary church-life (at least in the West) is owing to our failure to live cross-centred lives?

Secondly, it is a natural temptation in charismatic circles to emphasise the immediate experience of the Spirit and to see blessing, renewal and success in terms of immediately discernible results. This sometimes leads to an over-glorification of Pentecostal gifts and advances to the mischievous suggestion that if you are totally yielded to God's Spirit and have 'this' experience you too can have a successful ministry with hundreds at your evening service!

For the sake of clarity I must repeat that I am certainly not denying the reality of blessing, answered prayer and the like. But I would want to insist that the Spirit-filled servant cannot be denied a ministry different from that which his Spirit-filled master passed through. The 'cross-less' Pentecost experience can lead us into thinking that failure, difficulties, disappointments, apathy, 'resultlessness' and so on, are owing to spiritual negligence on our part. Sometimes, of course, this is so. But often it is not. Often following Christ will take us into suffering and hardship, and his Spirit is as much there as he is in the smooth and pleasant places. At the heart of this issue is a failure to take seriously the provisional character of the Christian life and ministry which is lived *in between* Christ's return to his Father and Christ's return to his people. In between is the time of ministry when the Church is incarnate in the world. Here below, the Church lives with pain and bears in her body and members the scars of living in the shadow of the cross. Living a full Christian existence may take us to barren pastures and it may mean that our roles in Christ's service may not result in great blessing, and it would be a cruel deceit on many a godly person to suggest otherwise.

The Cross – the Only Way?

The cross is a very challenging and disturbing fact. It shakes comfortable attitudes to religion because of its implication that human destiny depends upon our response to the definitive message of Jesus Christ. One simple New Testament phrase goes to the heart of this conviction: 'Jesus Christ is Lord.' It ruled out any other form of allegiance; it denoted that only Christ was worthy of worship.

Collision was at once inevitable with the religious systems which seemed more tolerant and accommodating. Judaism excepted, the religious life of the Roman world was a marketplace of faiths in which pluralism was an accepted norm. Roman authorities, it would seem, were quite prepared to affirm the deity of Christ and give him a place alongside other 'saviours', but they were not prepared to tolerate an exclusive claim that he was the only way. So the first persecutions began because such was the impact of their faith on their lives that Christians were not prepared to compromise.

This background is important for inter-faith issues that we now have to face. It is certainly not the case that the early Church knew nothing of the challenge of other religions. They knew it and took it seriously, so seriously, in fact, that they paid other faiths the greatest compliment of all – they were willing to die in opposition to them. They were called *atheoi* – people who did not believe in other gods. Later in the life of the Church, this clear affirmation was codified in Cyprian's formula that 'outside the church there is no salvation'.

Whatever the issues raised by such an uncompromising stand, the virtually unanimous opinion of the Church until present times has been that what Jesus Christ did and repre-- sents is the only basis for salvation.

This clear view is now being challenged vigorously and two major arguments are behind it.

First, we are told, the religious map of the world has changed because the world has changed. We are now a global village. Christianity is no longer a colonial faith riding on the back of commercialism but one among many ways of reaching the divine. It is no longer faced by subservient and quiescent faiths that know their place, but by confi- dent and militant movements that are expanding greatly. Furthermore, Buddhism, Islam, Hinduism, and so on, are no longer 'out there' beyond our shores but are now here in our communities, and their children are now in our schools. The reality of the situation is, so the argument goes, that we have to recognise other faiths, not as inferior religions but as equal contributors to human fulfilment and partners in the search for God's fullness.

That argument from experience is reinforced by an opinion by some Christian theologians who feel the time has come for the Church to abandon its exclusive claims because we are now much more aware of the inextricable relationship of religion and culture. For the theologian Ernst Troeltsch each religion is relative, indissolubly bound up with the distinctive elements and needs of its own culture. Therefore, Christianity is the religion of European culture, just as Buddhism is inseparable from the culture of South Asia or Shintoism from that of Japan. Troeltsch asserts: 'A truth which is a truth for us does not cease because of this to be very truth and life . . . Each religion is God's countenance as revealed to us; it is the way in which, being what we are, we receive, we react to, the revelation of God.'

The same point is made, though differently, by Professor John Hick, for whom the conviction is self-evident that God is savingly present in all great religious traditions. He suggests that human thought is undergoing a major revolution similar to the Ptolemaic/Copernican revolution, which changed the way sixteenth-century civilisation saw the world. The traditional way of seeing Jesus as the centre of faith is, according to Hick, tantamount to the Ptolemaic view of the universe, in which the planets of our solar system revolved around the earth. But the Copernican view is to see the shift from the dogma that Christ is centre to the view that God is central, and that all religions, including Christianity, revolve around him. In another book Hick finds the idea of the death of Jesus as the door to eternal life to be excessively parochial because it appears to present God as the tribal God of the Christian West who is being imposed on the rest of the world.

It is very clear that such views have the most momentous consequences for the gospel, the Church and its work and witness. Is it the case, in fact, that 'all roads lead to God' and that Christianity is but one way of perceiving truth?

THE VALUE OF OTHER FAITHS

Before I deal with the crucial question of the uniqueness of the Christian revelation, it is important to make the point that a person can at one and the same time affirm the uniqueness of Christ as the definitive and full focus of God's revelation and yet appreciate and value the contribution of other faiths. It is the worst kind of imperialism which asserts that 'my' religion is in every respect more valuable, more enlightened, than 'yours'. Students of other cultures are well aware that non-Christian religions can show, just as well as Christianity, an impressive record of values, human achievements, distinctive and admirable social service, as well as theological scholarship of a high order. I am quite prepared to accept the intrinsic value and noteworthy commitment of the spirituality of another faith – its devotion and prayer life. I, too, am prepared to go even further and accept that God is not absent from other faiths and that they can echo truths to be found in the Christian faith. I think of Judaism's sense of community and family; Islam's understanding of the transcendence of the majestic One God; Buddhism's emphasis on the importance of meditation and its relationship to transience and suffering. We cannot easily dismiss these aspects as superficial and non-essential – they represent important truths about God and about us.

And neither do I dismiss the possibility that God reveals himself savingly through another faith. I can fully accept that there can be, and often are, 'grace-filled' moments in the lives of non-Christians through which the one God speaks authentically and really. We might well take as an example a form of Buddhism in medieval Japan which anticipates the doctrine of justification by faith as expressed by Martin Luther. Shinran (AD 1173–1262) experienced a conversion experience which revealed to him that all human merit was useless and without profit in the eyes of Buddha: 'However good a man may be, he is incapable, with all his deeds of goodness, of effecting his rebirth in Amida [Amida is thought to be the Buddha of Infinite Light who dwells in the western paradise, the Pure Land]. Even the rebirth of good men is impossible without being helped by Amida's specific vow, issuing from his great love and compassion which are not at all of this world.' For Shinran, all spiritual merit proceeds from the Buddha – including the gift of faith itself. As Shinran meditated on this he experienced the grace of 'acceptance' and he writes: 'O how happy I am. My mind is established on the Buddha . . . I have experienced Amida's compassion deeply and I sincerely cherish the kindness of my teacher. Happiness abounds, reverence grows deeper. I am only mindful of the depth of Buddha's grace, and I am not ashamed of the ridicule of men.'

We have only to replace 'Buddha' with 'Christ' and we find a remarkable affinity of experience and theology: who can doubt that that was a grace-filled moment?

PARTICULARISM AND UNIVERSALISM

Nevertheless, even though I and many Christians are prepared to accept the value and contribution of other faiths, and even to recognise that they can be, and often are, carriers of divine grace, we cannot accept that the claims and the contribution of Christ are negotiable. The fact has to be faced squarely that the scandal of Christianity – indeed, 'scandal' is not too strong a word, it has always been the case since the writing of the New Testament – is this: Christians say that through a particular man, at a particular time, in a particular nation, God made himself known. And, furthermore, through this particular man he saved humanity. This is the scandal of particularism. I don't think we can avoid this fact. But let's not apologise for it, for it seems to be at the centre of what it means to be a Christian. Particularism, I suggest, will not go away but is required by three important considerations.

It is the teaching of the New Testament

Highly damaging to theologies and ideas which attempt to bind Christianity to western culture is that it just did not seem to have occurred to the writers of our foundational documents that Jesus was but a contribution to the religious quest of humanity. They see him as quite *definitive* for humanity; his coming has transformed the human situation and because of him our future has changed completely.

A feature of this is the use of absolute terms to describe him. He is the *only* teacher (Matt. 23:10), the *only* Lord (Eph. 4:5), the *only* shepherd (John 10:16), the *only* mediator (1 Tim. 2:5), the *only* high priest (Heb. 9:11; 10:10–14). Peter addresses the Jewish leaders quite fearlessly on the issue of the nature of salvation offered through Christ: 'Salvation is found in no-one else, for there is no other name under heaven given to men by which we must be saved' (Acts 4:12). Although the context is that of healing, Peter is making an exclusive claim over against Judaism. Other New Testament writers are no less emphatic. This Jesus has a 'name that is above every name' and one day universal homage will be given to him (Phil. 2:9–11). This does not exhaust the New Testament witness, by any means. Paul, writing to a community which was only too conscious of the presence of other religious groups around them, states, 'For even if there are so-called gods, whether in heaven or on earth . . . yet for us there is but one God, the Father, from whom all things came and for whom we live; and there is but one Lord Jesus Christ, by whom all things came and through whom we live' (1 Cor. 8:5–6). When addressing the Colossian Christians, who were being challenged by a Jewish–Gnostic sect, as far as we can tell, Paul makes the most amazing confession of Christ as the image of the invisible God, creator of all, and head of the Church (Col. 1:15–22) and that in him 'all the fullness of the Deity lives in bodily form' (2:9).

If, then, we are going to be faithful to the New Testament we cannot avoid the implication that the problem of particularity is not an invention of the Church but it is a problem which is inextricably linked to the essence of Christianity, at least as far as the New Testament writers are concerned.

It is at the heart of the theology of the cross

It is difficult on Professor Hick's terms to see the relevance of the cross if Jesus is not the final revelation of God and humanity's only hope. Hick understands the emergence of religions as a pluriform revelation, a series of revealing experiences which occurred independently within different streams of human history. Jesus and the emergence of Christianity are but one form of the divine revelation. But why should God choose the way of the cross if he had equally satisfactory ways of making atonement through other religions? This vitiates the power of the cross and makes it more mysterious, and ultimately purposeless. The New Testament, however, vibrates with the conviction that Christ's redemption is total and finished and any suggestion that it is deficient in any sense, or that some can be restored to God without him, or that we can bypass the cross in any way, is vigorously denied by the unanimous testimony of Scripture.

It is required by our missionary commitment

Adoption of the so-called 'Copernican' revolution in theology would, in my opinion, take the heart and nerve out of missionary incentive and purpose. It is scarcely credible that anyone would want to serve as a missionary unless he or she believed in some final way that Christ is 'The Way, the Truth and the Life'.

I am confident that thousands of missionaries, whatever their church allegiance or tradition, would be instantly united in their rejection of this apologetic and anaemic version of Christian witnessing. I think of pioneer missionaries such as Carey and Ward of India, Hudson Taylor of China, Temple Gairdner of Egypt, Judson of Burma, and wonder what they would have made of this 'Copernican' revolution. Perhaps they would say to us: 'A missionary does not risk suffering, disappointment, the possibility of an early death, separation from your loved ones for many years, surrender of a good career – unless you are convinced that upon Christ's death hangs the eternal salvation of others and that "Christ's love compels us, because we are convinced that one died for all, and therefore all died".' In Stephen Neill's book *A History of Christian Missions*[1] attention is drawn to the work of Carey, Marshman and Ward in India. Neill emphasises their labour over many years in understanding the culture of India before their important translation work began. Neill makes two important points. That the motive of such awesome and dedicated service and sacrifice was the innermost conviction that Jesus Christ is matchless and that knowing him was the whole point of human existence. Integral to this point is another: missionaries such as Ward and Carey did not spend years trying to understand another culture unless they first respected the beliefs and ideas of another people. Believing that Christ is the only way doesn't mean that we treat other faiths with disdain or disrespect, and their culture as though it were worthless.

But we should not be defensive about the nature of Christian particularism because we have to balance it with the universalism which is at its heart. Although Hick accuses Christianity of being 'parochial', nothing could be more parochial than his vision of world faiths, because Christianity on his terms cannot but become the religion of the West. We have to assert against this that the gospel is universal in its scope. Christ died for all. In one way we already live in a redeemed world. There is no need for Christ to die again. Calvary stands for ever as a symbol of God's universal love and forgiveness. In Paul's verse quoted above, 'Christ . . . died for all' (2 Cor. 5:14), we have the simple statement that through this one man (particularism) *all* may find salvation (universalism). I certainly do not want to suggest that all have found salvation, because that is not what Paul is saying. Indeed, he goes on to say in an impassioned appeal to the Corinthians that the work of reconciliation goes on. The basis of it is that Christ has died and a new age has begun. The task of the Church, says Paul, is to preach the message of reconciliation and to proclaim Christ to a needy world.

Perhaps we can now see Hick's basic mistake in his statement quoted earlier that the 'Copernican' revolution 'involves a shift from the dogma that Christianity is at the centre to the realisation that it is *God* who is at the centre'.[2] Apart from the pejorative use of 'dogma' to describe the traditional understanding of salvation, we observe that God and Christ are put in two distinct camps. But in point of fact we must insist that at the centre of a faith which is true to the gospel is the understanding that Christ, on his own, is not and should not be the ultimate point of reference. And neither should God be, at least, not the kind of God as understood by Hick. What the New Testament encourages us to believe is that 'God in Christ' is the heart of our teaching and preaching and is the basis of Christian mission.

EXCLUSIVISM AND INCLUSIVISM

We have already seen the dangers of a pluralism which starts from the assumption that Jesus Christ came to make 'a contribution to the religious storehouse of mankind' to use Visser't Hooft's description of this kind of pluralism.[3] There is, however, another argument that is used of the relationship between Christianity and other faiths, namely that Christianity does not exclude other faiths but includes or completes them. Whereas the 'exclusivist', it is said, sees Christ as the definitive, complete and only way, the 'inclusivist will affirm the value of other faiths and acknowledge the activity of God in the world, in other cultures and other religions. The inclusivists will probably not deny the supremacy of Christ or the finality of his revelation, but they will want to insist that although God's saving presence is defined by Jesus it is not confined to him. Through his Spirit God is operative beyond the Christian context, bringing salvation to those who may not have ever heard of the name of Jesus.

There are in fact many different versions of 'inclusivism' and we must commend the desire which is at the heart of these theories to treat the different major religions with respect, acknowledging quite properly their contribution to human culture and civilisation. One inclusivist position is that other religions are a preparation for the gospel, just as Old Testament Judaism prepared the way for Christ. The problem with this idea is that whereas Hebrew faith was a true preparation for the gospel, with its prophetic and legalistic background, in some faiths it is difficult to say what the preparation is. For example, there is such a huge difference between the Christian concept of God and the view of the divine in Theravada Buddhism that it is scarcely possible to compare their truth claims, let alone state how this particular Buddhist view serves as a preparation for the gospel. Our respect for another faith deters simplistic solutions.

Another variation on an inclusivist theme is that each religion contributes something distinctive to the human quest. The sense of the transcendence of God (Islam); a sense of the world's anguish and sorrow (Buddhism); belief in a moral universe (Confucianism) – these and others are reckoned to be part of the whole truth about God and the world. But in Christ, it is said, all these values are found in their proper balance and fullness. The problem with this approach is that it separates the values from the religions which convey them and does not do justice to their essential nature.

Two other versions of inclusivism may be mentioned briefly. There is the view popularised by Karl Rahner that sincere followers of other religions may be regarded as 'anonymous Christians'.[4] Rahner establishes this opinion on the basis that because God wills the salvation of all people, and because his grace is active in all cultures, it cannot be that other world faiths are outside his divine purposes. While his objective may be well-meaning, it must seem to non-Christians very offensive to be told that really all along they are anonymous Christians. Another view, which we may call the 'last chance' theory, says that all who are saved must come through Jesus Christ, but those who have not had the opportunity to meet him in this life will have another opportunity in the life beyond. This seems to keep intact the exclusivism of the gospel, while getting around the disturbing fact that so many die without knowing him. This theory has tenuous New Testament support, the general witness of which suggests otherwise – that this life is the time of decision, not beyond.[5]

The problem with this exclusive–inclusive alternative is that the positions are too rigid and we must not separate what the Bible holds together. In Romans 9–11, for example, we are made aware of Paul's great sorrow that Israel is cut off from God's promises. He struggles to make sense of it and finds it not only in God's electing love (11:25–6) but also in our response to the universal claims of God. 'For there is no difference between Jew and Gentile – the same Lord is Lord over all and richly blesses all who call him, for, "Everyone who calls on the name of the Lord will be saved" ' (10:12–13). We have to hold in tension the fact that while Christ is the only way of salvation, he does not exclude anybody. The Christian faith has potential to include anyone who comes to God through Christ.

In my opinion, then, the integrity of Christian theology compels us to hold firm to the uniqueness of Christ and the revelation which proceeds from and through him. I am as fully convinced that we must denounce the idea that nothing but evil is found other faiths and that we should have nothing to do with them. We must respect the genuine values to be found within other religions and only a most bigoted obscurantist will deny that good, honourable and godly men and women are to be found among people of other faiths. If God's grace is at work in human life through the Holy Spirit – in Reformed theology this is known as 'common grace' – we should expect his grace to be experienced beyond the Christian faith. Charles Davis used to distinguish between 'implicit' and 'explicit' grace. Implicit grace, he remarked, may be found in the world and in other faiths, whereas explicit grace is only known in Christ.[6] I think there is a lot to commend this observation. I have been struck by examples given by missionaries of converts who first began to search for Christ through insights given through their first faith. They speak appreciatively of the link between their former faith and their new life in Christ.

This is not, of course, to reintroduce the argument that other faiths merely prepare the way for Christ. What I am asserting is the familiar theology that if God by his grace is working in his world, this surely includes non-Christian religions. We fully accept this of secular society – why do we not recognise that this is the case in societies steeped in the ways of another faith? It is incumbent on Christians, then, to take very seriously the nature of other religions; to respect their inheritance and to admire values which are genuine expressions of goodness, love and charity. We will be willing to accept that other faiths may enshrine truths to which we have been blind: truths about God; truths about the world and human relationships; truths about prayer and spiritual values. We will want to express the attitude of 'open, congenial understanding' of which Hendrik Kraemer speaks.[7] And, rubbing shoulders with other faiths, in whatever culture we are placed, we will be anxious to strive to build harmonious communities based upon tolerance, compassion and respect. We do not go to them with arrogance and superiority because this is not the way of Christ. We go to them as we do to those born within the Christian framework, with news of a Saviour who can transform their lives as he has done ours, and we extend to them the offer which he has given to us.

PROCLAMATION AND DIALOGUE

However, it is often said that it is disingenuous to believe that proclamation of Christ and dialogue with representatives of other faiths can be done with integrity. Some will say: 'Real dialogue is when one of the parties is intent on converting the other,' and others will say: 'True mission is vitiated if the aim of the exercise is just to engage in courteous understanding.'

Both views are desperately flawed. Creative and honest dialogue is not ruled out because one of the parties believes passionately that it has been given a gospel mandate to share faith with all. Dialogue does not have to mean either the collision of porcupines or the slither of jellyfish – it can actually be the meeting of courteous, civilised people who are divided by their interpretation of the meaning of life, yet united in their desire to understand, to discover points of contact and to face each other with the issues that hurt and anger.

The importance of this is all too evident. Religion is far from peripheral to the world community; indeed, it is arguably the case that religion is a more potent force for good and evil than it has ever been. Why is this so? Civilisations in the past either ignored each other or fought each other. Today, in our 'global village', cultures and civilisations not only meet but also interpenetrate: in Calcutta and Karachi, in Leicester, Brixton, New York, Los Angeles and Frankfurt. Not without cause, then, did Wilfred Cantwell Smith, that great historian of religions, remark, 'Religious diversity poses a general human problem because it disrupts community.' Sadly, that comment is easily verifiable: in Northern Ireland, in Lebanon, in India, in Israel, in the Ukraine – to name but a few of the trouble spots. For the sake of the unity of the world community, sincere believers are challenged to face up to what is sometimes called 'the shock of diversity', especially when the inner dynamics of the shock waves are unquestionably religious.

But how do we hold in tension, and with integrity, proclamation and dialogue? Alongside the scriptural admonitions to preach Christ – to proclaim (1 Cor. 2:1); announce (Eph. 3:8); make known (Rom. 16:26); make manifest (Col. 4:3); tell (Col. 4:4); enlighten (Eph. 3:9); teach (Col. 1:28), there are other pictures and metaphors which convey a different mood and approach, and these are often forgotten when it comes to sharing faith. We can think of seed that is sown (Matt. 13:3ff); leaven that is part of the lump (1 Cor. 5:6); branches that are grafted on to the stems of a plant (Rom. 11:22); the unction (1 John 2:20, AV) of oil which is given as a blessing to others. And when we consider the picture of Jesus Christ in his ministry, we note the emphasis falls as much on being with others, as on preaching to them. His gentleness is palpably evident as he ministers to people where they are. The Greeks' evocative statement to Philip: 'Sir, we would like to see Jesus,' has a surprising response from Jesus. 'Except a grain of wheat falls to the ground and dies, it remains only a single seed. But if it dies, it produces many seeds.'

The two portraits are not set in opposition but in tension, because both belong to the ministry of Christ and his Church. Followers of such a Lord do find themselves in the uncomfortable position of being disciples as well as heralds; pilgrims as well as witnesses; learners as well as teachers; people with others as well as for others; seekers for God as well as those who have found him.

There is another reality Christians have to face. People of other religions, and even of other Christian traditions, have suffered, not from loving and genuine proclamation of the Lordship of Christ, but from what Fr Tom Stransky calls 'the transference of human pathologies to God'[8] as zealous Christians import their own agendas under sweeping statements such as 'Scripture says' and exclusive claims which may be a form of spiritual violence to cow people into submission. Honesty compels us to admit that the claims of Christ have sometimes been hi-jacked by evangelistic attitudes, insensitive God-squads, and motivations based more on results than genuine care for people.

Dialogue, then, is not an optional extra which we can leave to the specialist, the curious or the ecumenical enthusiast. It is an integral part of our encounter with people who differ from us. Dialogue will reveal very important parallels and points of similarity in theology and practice and such are to be valued. Equally, dialogue will reveal significant differences, and even major elements of direct conflict and inalienable offence. No matter: as members of God's human family we are called to listen, but as members of Christ's family, his body in the world, we will be able to share our story of what our faith means to us – and we have to learn to leave the future of that dialogue open to God.

CHRIST – THE CENTRE OF HUMAN HISTORY

We come to the conclusion, then, that we must hold in tension the particularism of the Christian faith, with its universal application, and the exclusive claim that Jesus is the way who includes everybody. As P. T. Forsyth said long ago: 'A gospel deep enough has all the breadth of the world in its heart . . . A Christianity which would exclude none has no power to include the world.'⁹ This, indeed, is at the root of the great commission in Matthew 28:19, 'Therefore go and make disciples of all nations'. It is there in John's famous words: 'For God so loved the world that he gave his one and only Son, that whoever believes in him shall not perish but have eternal life.' Christ, we have to say lovingly to our non-Christian neighbours, is absolute and non-negotiable. He is more than the 'man of universal destiny', to quote Hick's phrase again, he is Saviour and Lord; he is the way, truth and life; he is Alpha and Omega; he is the morning star; he is the lily of the valley; he is . . . everything.

And part of this 'everything' is the teaching of the New Testament that the whole of creation is moving towards him. The universe in its many facets and features is awaiting its redemption and fruition in Christ. Paul in Romans 8 looks ahead eagerly to the fulfilment of all things when disease, decay, corruption and death – present within the whole of life – will be no more. Now, within this majestic compass of God's purposes in Christ there are two aspects we have to hold in tension. First, as a Christian attempting to be faithful to Scripture, I must acknowledge that with my limited vision of what God can do in Christ I cannot be sure of those who will be saved. Whenever I have taken funeral services of those who, I am fairly certain, have never given God a thought all their lives, I have had to arrest such judgmental thoughts because who am I to condemn – and on what basis do I write them off? What do I know of the activity of God in their lives? I cannot tell what forces led them away from the Christian family – perhaps it was a judging Christian like me who made them reject the love of Christ! Furthermore, no one knows what happens in the last days and hours of another person and we are wrong to judge by our own limited perspectives. It is God's work to forgive – it is ours to be a heralding, witnessing body. I think we have to extend this to other faiths. Paul in Romans 2:14ff suggests that people who have never known God's revelation may be judged according to the light they have received. This implies, I think, that God's infinite wisdom and love take into account more than we realise and that his burning love desires to encompass everyone in Christ.

But, with that aspect, we must hold the fact that the New Testament teaches the sober and sad truth that exclusion from God is the end of all those who reject Christ and his salvation. Of course, we don't like to be reminded of such an element in Scripture and the fact that this is so rarely preached today is witness to the discomfort it gives us. But, I repeat, the cross only makes sense against the stark blackness of human sin and wickedness on the one hand, and eternal separation from God on the other. We ignore this element at our peril. To do so will vitiate our preaching and teaching and, possibly, reduce Christianity to a tired and timid western faith trying to find reasons to exist.

We come to the conclusion, therefore, that the cross of Jesus spells out God's final answer to the religious quest for God. There may be a great deal of good in other faiths, but the fact remains that the cross is the hinge of world history. All swings on what Jesus did there. That unique deed is splendidly summed up in Christopher Fry's verse:

> And sacrifice has so been made, by God
> To God in the body of God with Man
> On a tree set up at the four crossing-roads
> Of earth, heaven, time and eternity
> Which meet upon that Cross.[10]

That decisive event does indeed threaten religion and we have to remember that Jesus' death called into question the religion of those who crucified him, as it does any religion which tries to bypass the cross. Christianity itself is not immune from the criticism the cross brings, because the cloak of ecclesiasticism can obscure – indeed, often has obscured – the gospel of redemption by its rules, its religion and its humanity-centred ways. We in the comfortable West are not immune from the judgment of the cross. The further we wander from its shadow, the further away we retreat from God's will and our mission.

Lesslie Newbigin, in his splendid book *The Open Secret*, makes the point that, in his experience as a missionary and as one who has spent years sympathetically studying other faiths, he has been struck by the testimony of many converts from other faiths that, when they first considered Christianity, Jesus appeared as one who threatened all they regarded as precious, but following their conversion they could look back and see that all that they considered important was fulfilled in him.[11] This is well expressed by Dr Kali Charan Chatterjee, who wrote long ago:

> It has often been asked of me why I renounced Hinduism and became a disciple of Christ. My answer is, that I was drawn almost unconsciously to Christ by his holy and blameless life, his devotion to the will of God and his works of mercy and benevolence towards suffering humanity. The excellency of his precepts as given in the Sermon on the Mount and his love for sinners won my admiration and my heart. The incarnations I have been taught to worship, Rama, Krishna, Mahadeo and Kali were all incarnations of power – they were heroes, sinful men of like passion with ourselves. Christ only appeared to me as holy and worthy to be adored as God. But the doctrine which decided me to embrace the Christian religion and make a public profession of my faith was the doctrine of the vicarious death and sufferings of Christ. I felt myself a sinner and found in Christ one who had died for my sins – paid the penalty due to my sins . . . This was the burden of the thought of my heart, Christ has died, and in doing so, paid a debt which men could never pay.[12]

14

The Cross at the Centre

Our study of the cross is nearly over. I have viewed it as a priceless jewel which cannot exhaust the gazes of its admirers as they see ever-new wonders in its mysterious depths. But the analogy I began with was to compare our task of understanding the cross as being like that of a mountain which few have ever been able to climb. Perhaps we haven't got all that far in our struggle to reach the top. We still see the summit ahead, beckoning, and we labour on, knowing that the climb is eminently worthwhile. But one thing I am confident about, the cross puts everything else into perspective. We have all noticed, when we have climbed high into the hills on holiday, that everything else seem so small and insignificant. The houses, cars and roads seem so tiny. And the cares and worries we had a few hours ago are not as important or as pressing now as they seemed then. Somehow, our walk above has given us a clearer vision of it all and new perspectives have emerged. The cross, likewise, brings everything else together and reduces them to their proper proportions. From its perspective we can evaluate the true tasks of the Church. As we look down on the seemingly endless business of Church organisations, committee meetings and services, we can begin to see their relative unimportance as compared with the task of proclaiming the riches of the cross. As we look down on the many problems of the world we are reminded that Christ has redeemed humanity and he has accomplished what he set out to do.

My plea, then, is for the Church to put the cross back into the centre of our work and witness – where it properly belongs, pre-eminent in both our lives and in the Church's preaching.

LIVING UNDER THE CROSS

Just as Jesus himself lived under the shadow of the cross, so must his disciples. The Church has watered down a radical 'Cross-tianity' and replaced it with an insipid 'Churchianity' which is scarcely different from the world around. How we need to discover radical lifestyles which are a real embracing of the humiliated and scorned Jesus.

The Church, I believe, must live both sides of the cross. On the death side of the cross we must enter, as an incarnational body, into the darkness of people's lives as Christ did and show them his love and acceptance. There must be a real working out of the cost of being Christians today and living as disciples who want to walk with their Lord. This will cost us a great deal as we consider our lifestyles and ambitions. But as churches, also, we must begin to work out the implications of living incarnationally. We see the life and death of Jesus as a real 'letting go'. Paul reminds us in Philippians 2 that Christ 'being in very nature God . . . made himself nothing, taking the very nature of a servant'. That willing and deliberate surrender is, of course, the pattern for Christian living today. Failure to work this out in church life results in disobedient Christians who want to live from the benefits of Christ but are unwilling to follow his example. Letting go is, as far as I am aware, the necessary condition for successful witnessing. The call to live incarnationally will bring the Church, from time to time, on to a collision course with forces which alienate and imprison others. Many a church has slid into disobedience because of the fear of losing its wealth, membership and status in society. The irony is that the church which tries to cling on to what it has got and to where it stands will, of course, fossilise and die. A church which remembers that it has an existence on the death side of the cross will not be afraid to let go of all it holds dear for the sake of its Lord. This is of special importance to us who live in the rich and privileged western world. We are beginning to realise that though we value, as we should, the long history of our churches in the culture and customs of our lands, it has not been without its adverse side. We have become comfortable, rooted and settled in our lands. Our liturgies have reflected, perhaps more closely than we have realised, the mores and expectations of our times, with the result that our faith has become domesticated, tamed and confined. I repeat, this is not wholly bad: it is right that the Church should adjust itself, challenging and being challenged by the culture in which it exists. But the western Church, especially in its European manifestation, is finding that its increasingly secularised culture is steadily distancing itself from a committed faith. The challenge, then, is very clear. Now is the time for the Church to renew itself in a faith lived out in incarnation, cross and resurrection. Such living on the edge of security is the most authentic witness the Church can give.

But the Church lives on the resurrection and Pentecost side of the cross, as well. On this side it stands to proclaim the finished work of Christ; that Christ's death was God's victory over sin and death. I shared earlier my concern that we Christians are not living the cross and I am just as concerned that we are not preaching it. One rarely hears a full-blooded proclamation of the death of Christ. It gets a mention, of course, from time to time. Preachers may drop gnomic comments about the 'sufficiency of the cross', 'redemption by the cross' and so on. But even the most ardent supporter of the modern Church has to admit that the work of Christ has been replaced by the immediacy of God's action in the Church. All right: we are aware of some of the reasons for this shift of emphasis and this book has considered a number of them, but now we need to press the question: how may we over-arch the centuries to show the freshness and excitement of the cross? How may we preach it so that it really comes across as 'Good News'?

PREACHING THE CROSS TODAY

The message of Christianity is a story with immense appeal. That has been well demonstrated down the ages. Our problem is that it is so well known. Just as a good joke told over and over again can become irritatingly boring, so the gospel can pall when it is told in the same way repeatedly. But the idea of 'story' gives us a clue. We have to recount it in our own terms and according to our own culture and times. We have many examples of this in Church history. Justin Martyr, Athanasius, Anselm, Abelard, Luther, McCleod Campbell, R. C. Moberley – all these and many others have attempted to express the truth of the cross in contemporary forms. This, of course, is vital. Culture changes, and theology which fails to express its faith contemporaneously will be washed up as the flotsam of history and placed on display as a historical curiosity.

There are many different ways of telling the story. First let us see the cross in the widest possible setting. Many sociologists tell us that central to the most fundamental urges of the human spirit lie three deep-seated human needs; all of us want to be delivered from loss of meaning, from moral guilt and from finitude. In other words, all of us long to experience the joy and fulfilment of living in a spiritual world of moral meaning, where our lostness is dealt with and where life leads to life and not disintegration and nothingness.

If this analysis is correct we shall discover in our newspapers, television, films, books, plays, sport, and so on, all the necessary connections with these themes. Let me offer some suggestions from my experience.

The theme of meaninglessness is played out again and again in movies made by Woody Allen. In *Crimes and Misdemeanors* he describes a well-off, cynical ophthalmologist, Martin Landau, whose comfortable existence is threatened by his hysterical mistress, who threatens to inform his wife, Miriam. This man, who happens to be a secular and unbelieving Jew, consults his Rabbi, who advises him to confess his guilt and affairs to his wife. 'Who knows: she may or may not have the capacity to forgive you. You will probably be surprised at her understanding and forgiveness.' The film shows him wrestling with his guilt. It portrays an imaginary incident in which he visualises a Friday evening meal when he was a young boy and the subject turns to the existence of God and the plight of the Jews during the war. Now an adult, he imagines himself involved in that conversation and finding himself agreeing that the world is ultimately purposeless, random, and therefore if you can get away with a crime then do so. He consults his brother, who arranges a contract killing. The rich man is initially shocked, horrified and guilty. The film portrays him, however, getting over his guilt so that at the end he says: 'I woke up one morning and the birds were singing, the sun was shining and the torment was over. I realised then that you could live with such a terrible deed.'

While the film appears to be showing that in a purposeless world there is no meaning except that which we invest in family, friends and work, it also shows that living in such a way as that is selfish, cynical and capricious.

Such a film does not appear to be a tool that a Christian teacher or preacher can use. But that idea would be a mistake. Woody Allen's films are always profound, always exploring questions of purpose, choice and meaning, and are a rich quarry for the intelligent thinker.

But let us take the second theme, of freedom from moral guilt. The issue is that of expiation: how can I be forgiven? How may I be restored? How can I live with myself when I have betrayed all I hold dear? Having one eye on our culture and the other on the gospel, it should not take us too long before we begin to see the exciting links. The cross will quickly appear as our contemporary as, instead of moving from the past to the present, we endeavour to move from the present back to the cross. The themes are there all around us; our papers are often rich in their portrayal of substitution, of self-offering, of sacrifice, of people dying for noble, and sometimes ignoble, ideals. With alert minds keen to make the most of the connections between our culture and the meaning of salvation, we can draw upon stories which present vivid illustrations of sacrifice. Let me offer one.

In Chaim Potok's *My Name is Asher Lev* the story is told of a Jewish boy born into an ultra-orthodox home who has been given by God a wonderful gift: he can draw. Almost from birth he draws and paints, and paints and draws. It is more than an obsession; it is his life. His parents become very uneasy as this gift takes over in a community which frowns on such expressive art. As Asher grows into a teenager the gift leads to estrangement between father and son, with his mother a suffering and often inadequate reconciler of the two. Asher's devout father cannot understand such a waste of time and energy. He abhors his son's apparent idleness, while his mother simply tries to be alongside. Asher departs to Europe to develop his talent, and there in Paris he prepares for a major exhibition and a wonderful picture is created which expresses the agony, the awful sense of estrangement, bitterness and love which has tormented him. Unable to find a symbol to express his emotional feelings and longings within his own culture and religion, Asher goes to Christianity and portrays a crucifixion scene in which his mother is on the cross and his father and himself stand on either side of it. The exhibition begins and Asher's reluctant father and mother are there seeking to understand their son's success. And there to their uncomprehending and horrified eyes is exhibited Asher's crucifixion scene – not only the hated symbol of another faith, but with the unmistakably recognisable figures of father and son. The gift leads to Asher's departure from his community of faith. The cross, the only symbol adequate enough to translate his agony, becomes the reason why his estrangement from his family is complete.

This breathtaking account of the power of the Christian symbol is not an isolated incident in human culture. A recent reading of Victor Hugo's novel *Ninety-three* works out themes of identification and substitution. It is my conviction that Hugo, not a practising Christian by any means, must have been exploring the Christian faith as he wrote this masterpiece. The story explores events in the year 1793. A new and terrible phase of the French Revolution is underway. 'Madame' Guillotine has become a sinister and efficient agent of the Terror. But in the Vendée region of France counter-revolutionaries gather under the leadership of an equally ruthless man, Marquis de Lantenac. Opposing him on the side of the Republic is his cousin, Viscount Gauvain, a young, brave and merciful leader. The opposition is crushed and Lantenac is captured. He is sentenced to death. But Gauvain now finds himself trapped between two convictions: Lantenac deserves death because he had tried to overthrow the Republic, but Gauvain has seen that ruthless though Lantenac is, his cause is the only just one. Therefore, he must be freed and he, Gauvain, must take his cousin's place before Madame Guillotine. Hugo works out the themes in a masterful manner: justice and love, atonement and sacrifice, even a 'last supper' appears. But readers of Victor Hugo are not surprised; his *Les Misérables* is rich in similar themes.

And so we could go on. Thomas Hardy's *Tess of the D'Urbervilles* and A. J. Cronin's *The Stars Look Down* carry stories evocative of redemption themes. And many, many other books, films, plays and the rest will spring to mind to illustrate the truths of incarnation and salvation. And why not? Where on earth did Paul and the other New Testament writers get their themes of redemption, justification and reconciliation, if it were not from the real world they lived in?

All this is pertinent to a fact which many of us have been aware of for some time. For many of our contemporaries the medium of preaching is not the most obvious way in which they are going to be challenged by the message of the cross. Somehow the Church must consider other ways of conveying Christian truth: by way of drama itself, or by imaginative use of film and television. For example, I was greatly impressed some years ago by a slide-tape sequence prepared by laypeople of a church in Spennymoor, County Durham. Entitled *Peter Thinks about the Cross*, it represented Peter considering his life and encountering Christ as he hangs on a cross in Rome. Some might have criticised it for its free use of Scripture but I was moved by its vivid portrayal of the death of Jesus as seen by Peter and expressed in rich Geordie accents. There's a lot to be said for sometimes not allowing the theologically literate loose on such productions – we can make them seem so bland, predictable and safe. That Spennymoor production was nothing like that – it challenged, disturbed and made many draw near.

So, let's tell the story, a story which may still be Good News as long as we tell it with imagination and sensitivity, remembering that our contemporaries need help in under-standing the point of it. It may seem very obvious to add this point, but the Good News must be preached by those to whom it is good news! We cannot preach what we do not know and it cannot be a convincing message if we are not ourselves convinced of its life-giving force. Those who preach and live the cross with the greatest effect are those who are deeply in love with the Saviour. Such love will compensate for a thousand defects in style, presentation and knowledge.

Take salvation themes

We must remember that in telling the story we don't have to tell it all in one go. Jesus was often elusive in his teaching. He weaved mystery into his parables, which beckoned people on into a deeper exploration of truth. A great deal can be said for developing themes which draw out the teaching of the cross. For example, the theme of reconciliation, which is at the heart of the gospel, is still a very relevant theme in our own day. Our newspapers are often full of illustrations of this theme and it is one we can usefully employ to show that when there is breakdown of relationships both sides in a dispute must meet to achieve reconciliation and harmony. Let me develop a few more possible approaches which might be of service in our teaching and preaching.

Show the attractiveness of love

Apparently the old reredos in St Paul's Cathedral below a carving of Christ on the cross simply said: *Sic Deus delexit mundum* – this is how God loved the world. The cross, as Abelard pointed out years ago, expresses the power of love. Love itself is a powerful tool for interpreting salvation. We have all known situations when something has been given out of keeping with the nature of the needy person. Perhaps we have had the experience of receiving a gift which was so generous and surprising that we were shaken to the very core of our being. A very dear friend of mine who has been an alcoholic for thirty years was led on the pathway to sobriety (as members of Alcoholics Anonymous term it) through the generosity of a few friends who bought him his first suit. Their love restored his self-respect and gave him a dignity he had never discovered before. Love like that approximates to grace and we can draw on illustrations taken from human life which give us clues as to the wonder of God's love and grace.

Speak of the nature of law

We remarked in the opening chapters that the common criticism of the New Testament teaching about the cross is that the categories in which it comes are now foreign to the modern mind. We hear it said that concepts such as law and sacrifice no longer 'bite' in the same way. While this is partly true, it is not wholly true. The relativism and subjectivism of our time do make it difficult for people to understand the gospel, there is no doubt about that. Nevertheless it is a mistake to assume too quickly that we should dismiss these categories as out of date. I have no doubt, having had experience of penal establishments as well as ordinary parish ministry, that the nature of God as a holy being who wants humanity to walk according to his moral laws is an idea readily understood and acknowledged by modern people. I have been struck by the fact that guilty people who have done crimes of which they are deeply ashamed often feel uncleansed if their punishment does not match up with their estimate of the misdeed. I recall a lady on an arson charge who felt the full measure of her guilt. The soft sentence, instead of helping her, made her feel worse and even more of an evil-doer who deserved to be greatly punished. The gospel, when it came to her through caring Christians, led her to see that Jesus Christ accepted her as a sinner who was guilty of that and much else besides, and yet offered her a full pardon.

Without the concept of law, indeed, it is very difficult to understand the cross of Christ. The gospel needs the law to be intelligible to us and the law needs the gospel if it is truly to be law for us. As P. T. Forsyth long ago exhorted preachers of his day: 'Do preach a gospel where salvation is in real rapport with deep guilt, and redemption with holy judgement. For God's sake, do not tell poor prodigals and black scoundrels they are better than they think, that they have more of Christ than they know and so on.'[1] The Church often fails in its preaching at this very point. We are so keen to be relevant that we avoid law, judgment and sin and wrest Jesus from his context. So we preach a 'social worker' Jesus, who comes to sort out society, if we will only let him take control; or the 'therapist' Jesus, who can solve our personal problems if we ask him into our hearts; or the 'political' Jesus, who wants the Church to be a spearhead of change. What we find in the New Testament concerning his mission, however, is nothing remotely like that. He comes to restore humanity to God, to forgive our sins, to heal our wounds and to set us on the right road to God. If there is, then, a genuine understanding of law and our status before God as guilty men and women, the preaching of forgiveness will have a chance of becoming again a powerful message which will bring hope and healing to alienated people.

Preach Jesus

No, I don't mean in a mawkish, sentimental way but as the man who has changed the course of civilisation and who is the one whom millions of people down the ages have considered to be worth living and dying for. We need to keep continually before us the question that many of our contemporaries think, even if few of them will ever ask outright: 'Why this man Jesus? Haven't there been many other great freedom fighters in human history? Why should I regard him as the redeemer of humanity?' Against these probing questions we must present Jesus as seen in the Scriptures as one who does not stand before us as an object of enquiry but as the one who searches us out. Jesus in his ministry was elusive in his claims and ambiguous about his self-identity. This was deliberate, in order for those who were drawn to him to be led into an even deeper discovery of his 'otherness' and greatness. He allowed his words and works to speak for him. I sometimes feel when

I hear preachers – indeed, when I hear myself preaching – that we say too much for Jesus and not enough about him. We make post-resurrection claims as if they are self-evident; which they are not to people who do not yet share faith with us. We must allow the attractiveness of the Nazarene to break forth from our preaching so that the truly astonishing fact that God actually came among us in this man from Galilee can dawn upon the minds of our contemporaries.

THE CROSS – OUR CONTEMPORARY

It is all too easy to think of the cross as a theological conundrum which happened back there and which requires constant updating and correction, like a vintage motor-car which appears rarely on the road – and that with difficulty – and whose real home now is in the museum. The cross, before it can become a theory, has to be an experience and this has been an element we have mentioned on more than one occasion. The gospel is Good News of a Saviour who has delivered us from the bondage of the past and who has restored us to God. As such, it is our contemporary and moves down time with us, meeting our needs and bringing us home to God. It is a finished work which the Church and Christians can proclaim with conviction and power. Indeed, Christianity has no power which is not generated by the cross.

Because of what Christ has done for us, we are called to share with him in his mission of reconciliation. There is for each of us a cross to be borne and a discipline to be accepted, all in glad obedience to him who came not to be served but to serve, and to give his life as ransom for many. Well did Max Warren observe:

> Jesus Christ lived the Cross before he died upon it. His living was the teaching upon which the Cross itself threw the light of a vast illumination. Unless we can see this and understand that all Christ's living was a dying, we shall not plumb the depths of what is involved in our ministry of teaching. For if the Cross stands at

the centre of history, as Christians believe, if it is the central key to understanding the nature of God, the dilemma of man, the mystery of life and death: then we have to expound its meaning as the way in which all men are meant to live and die.[2]

NOTES

Chapter 1, The Offence of the Cross

1 Justin Martyr, *Apology* 1.13.4.
2 Origen, *Contra Celsum* 6.10.
3 Origen, *Contra Celsum* 6.78. See also 4.36.
4 Cicero, *Pro Rabirio* 16.
5 Origen, *Contra Celsum* 6.50.
6 For further reading on the cross in the ancient world, see Martin Hengel, *Crucifixion*, London: SCM and Philadelphia: Fortress Press, 1977.
7 Colin Wilson, *The Outsider*, London: Pan, 1978.

Chapter 2, The Enemy Within

1 G. L. Carey, *I Believe in Man*, London: Hodder and Stoughton, 1977; Edmund Hill, *Being Human*, London: Geoffrey Chapman, 1984; Ray S. Anderson, *On Being Human*, Grand Rapids: William B. Eerdmann, 1982.
2 A. G. Smith, *The Western Dilemma*, London, 1954.
3 See H. Darling, *Man in His Right Mind*, Exeter: Paternoster Press, 1969.
4 Rollo May, *The Meaning of Anxiety*, New York: The Ronald Press, 1950.
5 C. S. Lewis, *The Screwtape Letters*, London: Fount, 1970.

Chapter 3, Holy Fire

1 Robert Daly S.J., *The Origins of the Christian Doctrine of Sacrifice*, London: Darton, Longman and Todd and Philadelphia: Fortress Press, 1978, p. 32.
2 P. T. Forsyth, *The Work of Christ*, London: Independent Press, 1938, p. 90.
3 C. H. Dodd, *The Epistle of St Paul to the Romans* (Moffatt Commentary), London: Fontana, 1960, pp. 49–50.
4 Quoted by Max Warren, *Interpreting the Cross*, London: SCM, 1966, p. 21.

Chapter 4, Jesus and His Cross

1 For an interesting treatment of the significance of Jesus, see Norman Anderson, *The Teaching of Jesus*, London: Hodder and Stoughton, 1983.
2 Quoted by A. M. Hunter, *Bible and Gospel*, London: SCM, 1969, p. 54.
3 J. Jeremias, *The Central Meaning of the New Testament*, London: SCM, 1965, ch. 1.
4 A. Schweitzer, *The Quest of the Historical Jesus*, London: A & C Black, 1936, p. 369.
5 P. T. Forsyth, *The Work of Christ*, London: Independent Press, 1938, p. 108.
6 Morna Hooker, *Jesus and The Servant*, London: SPCK, 1959.
7 P. Toynbee, *Part of a Journey*, London: Fount Books, 1981, p. 282.
8 W. Pannenberg, *The Apostles' Creed*, London: SCM, 1972, p. 72.
9 A. Richardson, *A Dictionary of Christian Theology*, London: SCM, 1969, p. 357.
10 A. Richardson, *An Introduction to the Theology of the New Testament*, London: SCM, 1958, p. 171.

Chapter 5, The Cross in the Earliest Preaching

1 C. H. Dodd, *The Apostolic Preaching and its Development*, London: Hodder and Stoughton, 1936, p. 16.
2 A. M. Hunter, *Interpreting Paul's Gospel*, London: SCM, 1954, p. 19.
3 C. H. Dodd, *The Bible and the Greeks*, London: Hodder and Stoughton, 1935.
4 T. W. Manson, quoted by D. E. H. Whiteley, *The Theology of St Paul*, Oxford: Blackwells, 1964, p. 146; D. Daube, *The New Testament and Rabbinic Judaism*, London: The Athlone Press, 1956.
5 Leon Morris, *The Atonement*, Leicester and Illinois: IVP, 1983, p. 151.
6 Ibid., pp. 163–76.
7 A. Deissmann, *Light From Ancient East*, London: Hodder and Stoughton, 1911, pp. 326–7.
8 James Denney, *The Death of Christ*, London: The Tyndale Press, 1951, p. 43.
9 For an examination of this theme from an ecumenical angle: G. L. Carey, 'Justification by Faith in Recent Roman Catholic Theology' in Gavin Reid (ed.), *The Great Acquittal*, London: Fount Books, 1980; J. Reumann, *Righteousness in the New Testament*, Philadelphia: Fortress Press, 1982.

Chapter 6, Glory and Sacrifice

1 Charles and Wilson McMoran, *Winston Churchill: The Struggle for Survival* (taken from the diaries of Lord Moran), London: Constable, 1966.
2 See G. L. Carey, 'The Lamb of God and Atonement Theories', Tyndale Biblical Theology Lecture 1980, in *Tyndale Bulletin* 32 (1981), pp. 97–122.
3 For further reading of this theme in Hebrews, consider: F. F. Bruce, *The Epistle to the Hebrews*, London: Marshall, Morgan and Scott, 1964.

Chapter 7, Can a Death Atone?

1 T. F. Torrance, *The Mediation of Christ*, Exeter: Paternoster Press, 1983, p. 69.
2 R. Bultmann, *Essays*, London: SCM Press, 1955, p. 280.
3 This is well expressed by T. Torrance in *The Mediation of Christ*, ch. 3.
4 M. Warren, *Interpreting the Cross*, p. 13.

Chapter 8, Ways of Understanding the Cross

1 Gregory of Nyssa, 'Oratio Catechetica', ch. xxiv, in *The Christology of the Later Christian Fathers*, Library of Christian Classics, vol. III, Philadelphia: Westminster Press, 1954.
2 Gregory of Nazianzus, 'Theological Orations', ch. xiv in *The Christology of the Later Christian Fathers*.
3 G. Aulen, *Christus Victor*, trans. A. G. Hebert, London: SPCK, 1931.
4 H. Waddell, *Peter Abelard*, London: Fontana Books, 1958.
5 *A Scholastic Miscellany*, in Library of Christian Classics, vol. X, Philadelphia: Westminster, 1953, p. 283.
6 Abelard's 'Commentary on the Epistle to the Romans' in *A Scholastic Miscellany*.
7 Hastings Rashdall, *The Idea of Atonement in Christian Theology*, London: Macmillan, 1920.
8 Ibid., p. 26.
9 R. S. Franks, *The Atonement*, Oxford University Press, 1934, p. 172.
10 Quoted in R. S. Paul, *The Atonement and the Sacraments*, Hodder and Stoughton, 1961, p. 189.
11 John McLeod Campbell, *The Nature of the Atonement*, London: Macmillan, 1906.
12 R. C. Moberley, *Atonement and Personality*, London: John Murray, 1911.
13 Ibid, p. 42.
14 P. T. Forsyth, *The Work of Christ*, p. 131.

15 Vincent Taylor, *Jesus and His Sacrifice*, London: Macmillan, 1937; *The Atonement in New Testament Teaching*, London: Epworth Press, 1940; *Forgiveness and Reconciliation*, London: Macmillan, 1960.
16 *Jesus and His Sacrifice*, p. 302.
17 *Forgiveness and Reconciliation*, p. 290.
18 *The Atonement in New Testament Teaching*, p. 197.

Chapter 9, Jesus our Substitute?

1 G. W. H. Lampe, 'The Atonement: Law and Love', in A. Vidler (ed.), *Soundings*, CUP, 1962, p. 187.
2 H. Bushnell, *The Vicarious Sacrifice*, Sampson Low, 1862, p. 241.
3 D. Edwards, *God's Cross in Our World*, London: SCM, 1963, p. 91.
4 P. T. Forsyth, *The Work of Christ*, p. 147.
5 V. Taylor, *Jesus and His Sacrifice*, pp. 307–8.
6 A. M. Hunter, *Interpreting Paul's Gospel*, p. 91.
7 J. Denney, *The Death of Christ*, p. 103.
8 Ibid., p. 195.
9 D. Edwards, *God's Cross in Our World*, p. 90.
10 See, for example, A. Bottoms and R. H. Preston (eds.), *The Coming Penal Crisis*, Edinburgh: Scottish Academic Press, 1980. Read also Elizabeth Moberly's fine book, *Suffering, Innocent and Guilty*, London: SPCK, 1978.
11 W. Pannenberg, *Jesus – God and Man*, London: SCM, 1968, pp. 258–69.
12 W. Pannenberg, *The Apostles' Creed*, p. 87.
13 Ibid., p. 88.
14 V. Taylor, *The Atonement in New Testament Teaching*, p. 197.
15 E. Brunner, *The Mediator*, London: Lutterworth Press, 1934, p. 496.
16 K. Barth, *Church Dogmatics* IV/I, Edinburgh: T & T Clark, 1956, p. 75. See also IV/I, 14.2, 'The Judge Judged in our Place'.
17 A. M. Hunter, *Interpreting Paul's Gospel*, p. 92.

18 E. Brunner, *The Mediator*, p. 503.
19 J. I. Packer, 'What did the Cross Achieve? The Logic of Penal Substitution', Tyndale Biblical Theology Lecture 1973 in *Tyndale Bulletin* 25 (1974), p. 34.
20 Robert Paul, *The Atonement and the Sacraments*, London: Hodder and Stoughton 1961, p. 250.
21 F. Young, *Sacrifice and the Death of Christ*, London: SCM, 1975, p. 122.
22 V. Taylor, *Forgiveness and Reconciliation*, p. 205.

Chapter 10, The Glory of the Cross

1 D. Edwards, *God's Cross in Our World*, p. 92.
2 See, for example, R. Daly, *The Origins of the Christian Doctrine of Sacrifice*, pp. 54ff.
3 Protestantism is often criticised by Catholics for stressing the cross at the expense of the incarnation. See the essay on John Newman in Stephen Sykes, *The Identity of Christianity*, London: SPCK, 1984. Also Hans Urs von Balthasar, *The Glory of the Lord*, vol. I, Edinburgh: T & T Clark, 1982, p. 39.
4 V. Taylor, *Forgiveness and Reconciliation*, p. 195.
5 Ibid., p. 195.
6 T. Mozley, *The Heart of the Gospel*, London: SPCK, 1925, p. 31.
7 Paul Zahl, *Who Will Deliver Us?* London: Fount, 1984.
8 Augustine, *De Catachizandis rudibus* 4.7, London: Methuen and Co, 1912.
9 F. W. Dillistone, *The Christian Understanding of Atonement*, James Nisbet & Co, 1967, p. 330.
10 Quoted from the German edition, *Weimarer Ausgabe*, vol. XXV, p. 330.
11 Quoted by H. E. W. Turner, *The Meaning of the Cross*, London: A. R. Mowbray & Co, 1959, p. 19.

Chapter 11, The Cross and the Kingdom

1 S. N. Gundry and A. S. Johnson (eds.), *Tensions in Contemporary Theology*, Grand Rapids: Baker Book House, 2nd edition, 1983, p. 334.
2 Ibid., p. 407.
3 Gustavo Gutierrez, *A Theology of Liberation*, London: SCM, 1974, p. 153.
4 Ibid., p. 175.
5 Ibid., p. 178.
6 Ibid., p. 157.
7 Ibid., p. 176.
8 Ibid., p. 159.
9 Ibid., p. 159.
10 A very perceptive comment by the Rev. Dr Mike Moynagh, researching Gutierrez's understanding of salvation.
11 Gutierrez, *Theology of Liberation*, p. 268.
12 Ibid., p. 151.
13 *Tensions*, p. 419.

Chapter 12, The Cross and the Spirit

1 R. C. Moberley, *Atonement and Personality*, London: John Murray, 1907, (1901), especially chapters 8 & 9.
2 Ibid., p. 151.
3 James Dunn, *Baptism in the Holy Spirit*, London: SCM, 1970, p. 40.
4 Moberley, *Atonement and Personality*, p. 297.
5 Paul Avis, *Christians in Communion*, London: Mowbray, 1990, p. 58.

Chapter 13, The Cross – the Only Way?

1 S. Neill, *A History of Christian Missions*, Penguin History of the Church, vol. VI, London: Penguin, 1964, p. 264.
2 John Hick, *God and the Universe of Faiths*, London: Macmillan, 1973, p. 131.

3 W. A. Visser't Hooft, *No Other Name*, London: SCM, 1963, p. 95.

4 Karl Rahner, *Theological Investigations*, vol. v, London: Darton, Longman and Todd, 1966, pp. 115–34.

5 Read Lesslie Newbigin's helpful chapter, 'The Gospel among the Religions' in *The Open Secret*, Grand Rapids: W. B. Eerdman, 1978.

6 Charles Davis, *God's Grace in History*, London: Fontana, 1966, p. 76.

7 Hendrik Kraemer, *Religion and the Christian Faith*, London: Lutterworth Press, 1956, p. 338.

8 Gerald H. Anderson and Tom F. Stransky (eds.), *Christ's Lordship and Religious Pluralism*, Orbis Books, 1981, p. 86.

9 P. T. Forsyth, *The Work of Christ*, p. 62.

10 From Christopher Fry's play *Thor with Angels*, p. 78.

11 Lesslie Newbigin, *The Open Secret*, p. 200.

12 Quoted by Samuel Zwemer, *The Glory of the Cross*, Oliphants Ltd, 1954, p. 103. For further reading on this subject of the challenge of other religions, see S. Neill, *Crises of Belief*, London: Hodder and Stoughton, 1984.

Chapter 14, The Cross at the Centre

1 P. T. Forsyth, *Positive Preaching and the Modern Mind*, London: Independent Press, 1949, p. 105.

2 F. W. Dillistone, *Into All the World – a Biography of Max Warren*, London: Hodder and Stoughton, 1980, pp. 163–4.

GLOSSARY

Aetiological (or aitiological): Derived from the Greek, *aitia* (reason), an aetiological story is one which is invented for a theological purpose.

Anthropology: The study of humankind. When used in theology it also conveys the idea of man as a spiritual being as well as his physical and social expressions.

Anthropomorphic: From *anthropos* (man) and *morphe* (like), the term means reducing God, or a supernatural reality, to human ways of talking or understanding.

Christology: The study, or doctrine, or Christ's life and person. It reached its climax in the doctrine of the two natures in Christ as defined by the Council of Chalcedon (AD 451).

Deification: A doctrine popular in the early Church, especially with the Greek Fathers, that Christ's role was to make us more like him. 'He became what we are to make us what he is.'

Docetic: Greek *dokein* (to seem, to be like). Docetism was a doctrine in the early days of Christianity which insisted that Christ only 'seemed' to be human, and that he was not really human.

Exclusivism: Has become a pejorative term meaning that the gospel excludes all except those who believe in Christ. (See *Inclusivism*.)

Exemplar: The theory that Christ is our moral example – associated with Peter Abelard and Hastings Rasdall. See Chapter Eight.

Existentialism: A recent philosophy, most probably started by the Danish philosopher S. Kierkegaard, which asserts that meaning is found in a 'leap of faith' or commitment.

Expiation: This teaching emphasises the putting away of sin through Christ's death. (See *Propitiation*.)

Gnosticism: A popular religious philosophy which developed in the New Testament period and after. Gnostics claimed to possess special knowledge (*gnosis*) which revealed that Jesus was one of many divine manifestations.

Grace: The Greek word *charis* is a rich word meaning God's unmerited goodness. Someone once defined it as: God's Riches At Christ's Expense.

Imputation: The doctrine that God's righteousness is 'imputed' to us (that is, given freely as a gift and, therefore, not dependent upon human righteousness). In the Reformation period this theory opposed the accepted idea that righteousness is 'imparted' through the Church and sacraments.

Incarnation: (Latin *Incarnatus; incarnare*, to make flesh.) The doctrine that Jesus Christ was God's Son who became a human being.

Inclusivism: A modern theological term meaning that God's salvation includes all of humankind, irrespective of race and creed. (See *Exclusivism*.)

Justification: A metaphor meaning to 'acquit' or 'declare righteous'. In Reformation times the Reformers contradicted the accepted notion that it means 'to make righteous'.

Kerygma: From the Greek word meaning proclamation, it normally signifies the basic Christian preaching as outlined in Acts. See Chapter Five.

Mediator: In Scripture God mediates his salvation in many different ways: through the prophets, priests and law. It reaches its climax in the appearance of Christ (Heb. 1:1).

Moral Influence Theory: See *Exemplar*.

Objective: An objective theory of the atonement accepts that Christ's death changed humanity's position before God, affecting both God and humanity.

Ontological: From the Greek verb 'to be', *ontology* when used of Christ means Jesus is by nature God.

Orthopraxis: (*Ortho* – right: *praxis* – action or deed). A term characteristic of liberation theology (see Chapter Eleven), it denotes the importance of *doing* the Christian faith usually over orthodoxy (*believing* the Christian faith).

Paradigmatic: From 'paradigm' – example or pattern.

Particularism: A term which some say sums up the scandal of Christianity – God's salvation comes through a particular Messiah, Jesus.

Passover: A Jewish Festival commemorating the time God rescued his people from Egypt by sending his avenging angel, who 'passed over' the homes of the Israelites because the blood of the lamb was on the lintels of the doors: Exod. 12.

Pelagius: A fifth-century British monk who gave his name to the doctrine that it is possible to live a perfect moral life unaided.

Penal: See *Substitute*.

Praxis: From the verb 'to do', praxis has become a favourite term, especially in liberation theology, to mean the gospel in action, particularly political action.

Propitiation: From Rom. 3.23, the doctrine that Christ's death appeased God's holy law. See *Expiation*, where the emphasis falls on the removal of sin.

Recapitulation: An idea popular with the Greek Fathers that Christ's work brought Adam's destiny to a glorious consummation.

Repentance: Greek *metanoia*, means 'to think again', therefore 'to turn'.

Representation: An element within atonement theology which stresses Christ as humanity's advocate and spokesman before God. So, for example, President Bush may be said to represent the American people at Summit Meetings with other political leaders. Whereas a 'substitute' stands *in the place of*, a representative *stands for* others.

Subjective: The idea that Christ's passion affects us rather than God. That is, no *objective* change in relationship with God is brought about. God's love finds us out on the cross and we reciprocate by loving him in return. See Chapter Eight.

Substitute: That Jesus took 'my' place on the cross, dying a death that should have been 'mine'.

Penal substitution, however, stresses the notion of punishment in connection with the Atonement. So Jesus takes upon himself a penalty for sin that is mine; he dies as a condemned man to set humanity free.

The difference may be set out as follows: Fr Kolbe, referred to earlier, took the place of a man sentenced to the starvation bunker. He was a substitute but not a penal substitute. But if I take the place of a person sentenced for breaking the law, his penalty is now mine and I am a 'penal substitute'. Thus penal substitutionary theories have a heightened awareness of the justice of God and his holy wrath against sin and wickedness.

Supererogation: The performance of work in excess of that required.

Theologia crucis: A term meaning a theology of the cross. As used by Luther it meant that the cross should determine the whole of the Christian life and thought.

Theologia gloriae: A theology which bypasses suffering and death – attempting to live on the resurrection side of the Christian faith.

Vaticinia ex eventu: A theological term meaning that some events are 'read back' into the time of Jesus by later Christians.

Vicarious: 'To stand in place of someone.' Strictly speaking, it means 'substitute' but theologians differentiate these terms, believing that a *representative* may suffer 'vicariously' without necessarily being a substitute for the victim.